*"What can y[...]
on the other side?"*

"Even though we seem to be living in other dimensions, that connection of love still binds us, and will live forever. They know that we need them, and they need us to realize that they are still alive, that they are here with us, that they care about us. We should keep them alive in our hearts, go on with our lives, and try to be as happy as we possibly can. They want us to be happy, they want us to know—and to take comfort in believing—that we will all be together again. They never, ever forget us, and I think they like too know that we will never forget them."

Other Books by the Authors

WE DON'T DIE: GEORGE ANDERSON'S CONVERSATIONS WITH THE
OTHER SIDE

WE ARE NOT FORGOTTEN: GEORGE ANDERSON'S MESSAGES OF
HOPE FROM THE OTHER SIDE

OUR CHILDREN FOREVER

GEORGE ANDERSON'S
MESSAGES FROM CHILDREN ON THE OTHER SIDE

**Joel Martin and
Patricia Romanowski**

BERKLEY BOOKS, NEW YORK

OUR CHILDREN FOREVER

A Berkley Book / published by
arrangement with Joel Martin and PAR Bookworks, Ltd.

PRINTING HISTORY
Berkley trade paperback edition / April 1994
Berkley mass-market edition / June 1996

The Penguin Putnam Inc. World Wide Web site address is
http://www.penguinputnam.com

ISBN: 0-425-15343-6

BERKLEY®
Berkley Books are published by The Berkley Publishing Group,
a division of Penguin Putnam Inc.,
375 Hudson Street, New York, New York 10014.
BERKLEY and the "B" design are trademarks
belonging to Penguin Putnam Inc.

PRINTED IN THE UNITED STATES OF AMERICA

10 9 8 7 6

OUR CHILDREN FOREVER

ACKNOWLEDGMENTS

In addition to all the parents and family members whose stories they so generously shared, I would like to thank the following for their help in making this book possible: the spirit of Father John Papallo, Sri Chinmoy, the Compassionate Friends of Rockville Centre, New York, Daryl Delaney, John and Nancy Elliott and their family, Muriel Horenstein, Patricia Ippolito, Roxanne Salch Kaplan, John and Barabara Licata and the spirit of David Licata, Dennis and Suzie Martinek and the spirit of Molly Martinek, Mary O'Shaughnessy, the Reitmeyer family, Arlene and Michael Rosich, Kristina Rus, John Smith, Joseph A. Stassi, Elaine and Joe Stillwell, Max Toth, Neil Vineberg, Anna Preston and the spirit of Jessie, Dr. Greg Lux, the Tooze family, the Pell family, the Bertrand family, the late Dave and Rita Weiner, the late Bob Wayne, and the late John G. Fuller.

As always, special thanks to Stephen Kaplan of the Parapsychology Institute of America for his continued and generous sharing of his vast knowledge of parapsychology and his valued friendship.

Our most sincere appreciation to our dedicated literary agent, Sarah Lazin, and her assistant, Laura Nolan. And to everyone at G. P. Putnam's Sons and Berkley Books for their tireless efforts on our behalf: Faith Sale, Roger Cooper, Marilyn Ducksworth, and David Groff. But most especially our editor, George Coleman. Many times through the years we have welcomed George's personal interest and his ideas. We thank him for sharing our enthusiasm for this work.

I'd like to express my special appreciation to my family: Sadie Cohen, the late Charles Cohen, Evelyn Moleta, and the late Mary Moleta.

A special thank-you to my coauthor, Patricia Romanowski, for her dedication, sensitivity, and intelligence. Without her, this journey would not be possible.

My eternal thanks to Elise LeVaillant for her untiring support of my work. Her encyclopedic knowledge, spiritual strength, and love continue to guide and inspire me and everyone whose life she touches.

And, of course, Christina Martin, without whom I could not have completed the enormous task of researching, documenting, and transcribing this work. Thank you for your loyalty, patience, and belief in me.

—Joel Martin

All in all, Joel's acknowledgments speak for me as well, but I'd like to add the following: My thanks first to Joel Martin, for making me part of the team and being such a great friend. I look forward to working with you many times again. To Elise and Christina, for their support and interest in the myriad personal travails that so often get in the way of work, particularly a certain Barney-ite. To George, for sharing his gift and helping to create a readership beyond what Joel or I ever imagined possible.

Eve Yedziniak gave me the gift of time and peace of mind, without which work would have been impossible. Thank you.

Without my sister Mary's friendship and love, her great sense of humor, and her inspiring example of faith, perseverance, and common sense, I would have been lost many times. I thank her and her late husband, Rick Vitro, for the wonderfulness that is their son, Douglas. I also wish to acknowledge Douglas's grandmother, Margaret Vitro. I thought of her often during the writing of this book, always with fondness, respect, and thanks.

As always, my husband, Philip Bashe, makes everything worthwhile in my life possible, easier, and better. His keen insights and thoughtful suggestions are reflected everywhere. Finally, to my son Justin Eric Romanowski Bashe. The whole time I worked on this book, I never once got up from my desk without stopping to hug you. Thank you, again, for picking us.

—*Patricia Romanowski*

I would first like to thank my "brother" and special friend, James MacMillan, who is the best. Also my friends Neal Sims and Daryl McNicholas, and my lovely aunt Theresa Runyon.

I would like to honor the loving memory of my aunt Doris MacMillan Barbour, who no doubt brings charm and grace to the hereafter.

Special thanks to my good neighbors, the Charles Decker family—Charles, Marge, Charlie, Tom, and Chris.

—*George Anderson*

To all the parents who have helped us make this book possible, to all bereaved parents and families everywhere, and to the children here and hereafter who are our children forever.

CONTENTS

"How many hopes and fears, how many ardent wishes and anxious apprehensions are twisted together in the threads that connect the parent with the child!"

—*Samuel Griswold Goodrich*

"The joys of parents are secret, and so are their griefs and fears."

—*Francis Bacon*

"Would you know my name, if I saw you in heaven?"

—*Eric Clapton*

A NOTE ABOUT
THE READINGS

Shortly after George Anderson and Joel Martin first met in 1980, the two began a journey to learn all that they could about the psychic phenomena George experiences. As readers already familiar with George's amazing psychic abilities know, there is no one more skeptical or more inquisitive about the source, nature, and limitations of those abilities than George himself. First as an investigative reporter and then as a fellow explorer into the mysteries of discarnate communications, Joel has, over these past thirteen years, amassed detailed records and notes, as well as videotapes and audiotapes of readings. The international success of *We Don't Die* and *We Are Not Forgotten* brought to our attention thousands of cases, each unique and important not only for what the resulting readings communicated to the loved ones who sought them, but for what they taught us about the nature of life after death.

The readings presented here have been culled from the thousands George has given those grieving parents. In some cases, the subjects have requested that we either use pseudonyms for some or all names and/or that we significantly alter other biographical information about the persons discussed in their stories. The use of pseudonyms and other alterations are denoted by an asterisk and the presence of an explanatory footnote at the bottom of each page on which they first appear. For the most part, these changes have been requested to spare the families involved the hurt and embarrassment of revealing publicly the circumstances of a death or other personal facts about their lives. Only rarely do subjects request their identities be protected simply because they are ashamed or uncomfortable with the prospect of friends and family knowing they sought a psychic medium's help. Given these concerns, we are more than happy to honor such requests for privacy and we especially appreciate those families who have permitted us to use their real names.

That said, it is important to note that even when names and details have been altered and protected, the psychic readings contained here are real. No complete reading appears without the consent and knowledge of the subject. The names of such professionals as therapists are real.

In every single instance the readings themselves—the words spoken by George, the subjects, and the spirits—are real and documented, on videotape, on audiotape, or in notes Joel took while witnessing the reading. For the most part, the subjects kindly volunteered to lend us their audiotapes or videotapes as well as annotated written transcripts of their readings. Only two readings contained here were not recorded on videotape, Joel's notes, or audiotape. In these cases, the subjects carefully reconstructed the reading from memory, and because the unique nature of these particular cases stayed with George, he was able to confirm the subjects' accounts.

The transcripts have been edited for brevity and clarity, and where possible reviewed by the subject for accuracy. We have deleted pauses, repetitions, irrelevant asides, and portions of the reading that do not deal directly with the deceased child. The narrative that precedes and/or follows each reading is derived from interviews with the subjects conducted *after* the reading. In almost all cases those interviews were conducted by Joel and took place weeks, sometimes years after the actual reading. We have also relied on letters written by the subjects that described the circumstances of their coming to George, their lives with the deceased child, and other background material.

As always, we will differ with many other writers in this field and admit that not every communication from the other side is earth-shattering. Like each of us here on earth, even those who have transversed the realms can be discrete, reticent, even boring. For the first book our criteria for readings was simply how well each illuminated the mediumistic process. For the second, how each helped the subject cope with grief. We did not necessarily use those readings in which George was most accurate, because a high level of accuracy does not guarantee an interesting reading. Over the years we have also noticed that we and George learn from his mistakes.

Because this volume deals specifically with children and was inspired by the thousands of parents and other loved ones who have been touched by a child's death, our approach is quite different. Having established George's abilities and explained as much of the process as we can now, we've written a book not about George, not about psychic mediumship, not about life after death, but about children and families. With each reading in *Our Children Forever*, we sought a greater understanding of what it means when a child dies and, most important, how these children on the other side and the loved ones they leave behind here can help one another along their separate yet eternally intertwining paths.

FOREWORD

Ask any parent who has lost a child, and he or she will tell you that it is the ultimate pain. Dealing with the numbness and shock, followed by the anger and guilt, the loneliness, the loss of future plans and dreams, overwhelming sadness and heartache torment the bereaved parent.

Coping and surviving after the death of a child is a never-ending struggle. You're always missing their smiles, their voice, their laughter, their hugs, and their special ways; the little idiosyncrasies that make each child uniquely your own. Unfortunately the road through the Valley of the Shadow is a long one with no shortcuts.

After losing my two oldest children, twenty-one-year-old Denis and nineteen-year-old Peggy, in a freak car accident, I faced the heartbreaking chore of sorting through their possessions. I realized then how easily they might become "erased" from the memories of friends and loved ones. I vowed that would never happen. I wanted the world to know my Peggy and my Denis and to remember them with fondness and smiles. I wanted thoughts of them to tug at heartstrings; I wanted no one to ever be afraid to mention their names to me. I guess you could say I started a crusade. The more I talked about them, the more people came to know them, and the more people shared them with me. Miraculously, everybody began to realize that Peggy and Denis still live on in my heart; they are my children forever.

That one thought—"my children forever"—makes my heart sing. When the boyfriend of my third child, Annie, who had never met Denis or Peggy, remarked, "I feel like I know them," it was the nicest thing he could have said. He recognized that they were still part of our family and part of our lives.

When I met George Anderson three years after my children died, he told me that my children were famous. "Not celebrities," he said, but they told him that I'd hung their pictures up and that everyone I met knew who they were. Then I knew I'd done what I'd set out to do: make sure my children would never be forgotten.

That focus gave me strength, the will to survive, and a special meaning to my life. It inspired me not only to tell the world about my children but to share my experience since their deaths with others who have suffered this loss. Reinvesting that special love I had just for them comes back to me a hundredfold. The most important thing for bereaved parents to know is that their children will always be theirs, that they will never be forgotten.

—Elaine E. Stillwell
New York State Regional Coordinator
Chapter Leader, The Compassionate
Friends of Rockville Centre, New York

Introduction

As we write this, it is 1993, over five years since our first book about George Anderson, Jr., was published, and nearly thirteen years since George first went public with his remarkable psychic ability. In that time, much has changed for George, both professionally and personally. While he is now recognized as the world's most publicly tested psychic medium, he has remained true to what he believes is his calling: helping the bereaved.

The reaction to *We Don't Die: George Anderson's Conversations with the Other Side* and its sequel, *We Are Not Forgotten: George Anderson's Messages of Hope from the Other Side*, has been overwhelming. We have received thousands of letters and phone calls from all over the United States, Canada, and from as far away as Japan, Kenya, Greece, Switzerland, New Zealand, India, Venezuela, and Russia. The books have been translated into French, Dutch, Japanese, and Italian, and George has continued to appear on national television, including NBC-TV's *Unsolved Mysteries*, speaking about life after death and demonstrating the psychic-mediumistic process.

As always, we thank you for your letters and calls and apologize for not being able to answer everyone personally.

We hope to have included in this book answers to questions readers commonly ask. Both George and the authors sincerely regret that George cannot share his gift with each person in need. We can only hope that from what you are about to read, the truth of George's message—that we do not die, that death is merely a transition from this life to the next—comes through and provides comfort.

The purpose of our first book, *We Don't Die*, was to introduce George and, through readings and accounts of scientific tests, document his ability as a psychic medium. We have accepted, as has George, the limits of science to understand or explain the process by which he receives messages from people who have passed from this life. Unlike some writers in this field, we do not and simply cannot pretend to know the how and why of George's psychic abilities.

Following the many public appearances George made after *We Don't Die*, he took time off to reexamine the purpose of his gift and how he might best use it. George had been making himself available to people for psychic readings for years before he came to national attention. He had always known there was a tremendous need for what he did. But after touring the country and reading some of the thousands of letters we received, George decided that sparring with skeptics, convincing reporters and talk-show hosts that he is for real, and seeking out the next scientist with the next theory about what makes him tick stole time from helping the bereaved. That led us to focus *We Are Not Forgotten* on how the psychic process can serve as a catalyst and a comfort in grief.

With this book we address the most tormented of the bereaved, those who have lost their children.

Just a decade or so ago, such a book would have been out of the question, but attitudes toward death, dying, and psychic phenomena have evolved. No longer automatically dismissed as crazy are people who claim to have been abducted by aliens, lived past lives, traveled outside their bodies at will, or become channels for disembodied spirits. Why this is so, anyone can guess. There are, however, very clear and definite milestones in the changing attitudes toward death and dying.

The work of Dr. Elisabeth Kübler-Ross, particularly the groundbreaking 1969 book *On Death and Dying*, blazed a trail for serious scientific study of what happens to people not only physically but emotionally and spiritually at the moment of death. Dr. Raymond Moody's studies of the near-death experience were initially regarded as a fringe phenomenon. Today it would be rare not to know someone who has had such an experience. Dr. Melvin Morse's bestselling critical study of children's near-death experiences, *Closer to the Light*, added yet another dimension to our understanding of life and death.

Slowly, almost imperceptibly, death came out of the closet. This is not to say that it has fully shed its taboo. What has changed, however, is a more open acceptance of death and, most important, a deeper understanding of its impact on the bereaved.

Death takes each of us in our time. Before then, however, we will be visited by it in its many guises: the grandparent who passes after a rich, full life; the spouse who leaves too soon; the child torn away. Death finds us all, almost always without warning and never with an explanation or at least never with an explanation that answers the eternal *Why*? No matter what we may know about death and the meaning of human existence, that may be one question we all must wait to learn the answer to.

Ever since George first began doing psychic readings for neighbors and friends, he noticed that people who had lost children had the hardest time coping with their loss. That parents of deceased children do have a more difficult time dealing with grief is well known among professionals and has been proven through scientific studies.

There are many reasons for this, the most basic of which is our culture's underlying taboo against speaking of, even recognizing death. But when the deceased is a child, the social and psychological ramifications are far-reaching and in some ways permanent. To say that the parents and other survivors of deceased children come to George in desperation is not overstating the case. More than the survivors in any other kind of relationship, parents suffer severe, prolonged depressions, marital and family stress, and are prone to thoughts of suicide.

At work are two very important and compelling forces. One is the unique nature of the parent-child relationship; the second is society's inability to publicly recognize and address the death of a child. The parent whose child dies, then, is often left grieving the loss of what most of us would consider the most profound, wondrous person in our lives in the face of a culture that considers a child's death literally unspeakable. Bereaved parents talk of their isolation, loneliness, depression, and they recount stories of the well-intentioned but hurtful remarks offered to them as condolences. They quietly seethe at the memory of being told to "Get over it," or to remember, "You're young, you'll have others." They cry themselves to sleep night after night, sometimes for years.

Just how uncomfortable people are with this subject became clearer to us as we worked on. Practically every person we mentioned it to seemed compelled to ask if it wasn't a "depressing" topic, if it didn't upset us to write about it. Especially parents of young children, who often made it clear that this was something they did not want to hear about. For both the earlier books, we interviewed, wrote about, and talked to subjects who had lost loved ones young and old from a range of causes. We noticed that stories of children who died touched us most deeply of all. We would be less than honest if we didn't admit that researching and writing this book has been difficult for us.

Sadly, we had far too many cases to choose from. We based our selection on several factors. We were guided first by our belief that this is not a book about psychic phenomena so much as it is about helping bereaved parents and other survivors of deceased children cope with that loss. However, we also felt it important to include readings and stories that, through what they could and could not reveal, illuminated something about George's ability—its limitations, its range, its flaws, its power.

Each parent's story recounted here is unique. The hundreds of hours of interviews Joel Martin conducted cover the gamut of human emotions, from serene acceptance to vehement denial. There is no single textbook reaction to a child's death. Some parents draw strength from support groups; others avoid them, fearing they cannot handle anyone else's pain. While some marriages grow deeper and stronger, others splinter. While some parents discover a renewed, deeper relationship with their surviving children, others experience the additional loss of the family as they knew it before the tragedy. While some were delivered through prayer, others felt forgotten by their Lord. It seems as though the only sure thing we can say about any bereaved parent is that his or her world will never be the same.

For these reasons, we have devoted substantially more space to these parents, their stories, and, especially, their words. We were very often struck by their eloquence and willingness to give so freely of their time and emotions. They shared with us some of their most painful memories simply because they believed that through doing so, other parents might find comfort.

George brings comfort to bereaved parents through psychic mediumship. There are dozens of words for what George does and what he is. However, we have always preferred the term *psychic medium*. As an adjective, *psychic* means simply "lying outside the realm of physical processes and physical science." *Medium* is the most neutral word we know to describe the nature of George's role in the psychic process. He is truly a medium: a passive conduit through which the messages flow from the other side.

Here on the brink of the twenty-first century, you would be hardpressed to find anyone without an opinion about psychic phenomenon. In some parts of the country people go to psychics as regularly as they go to the hairdresser. In most cases it's interesting, innocent fun. This is not to say that other psychics are not genuine; there are probably thousands who are. In fact, most experts in the field of paranormal study believe we each have a degree of psychic ability, although for most of us awareness of its presence is fleeting. Virtually everyone can recount a "weird" or inexplicable experience, or foreknowledge of some event. But most of us are content to leave it at that. Relatively few of us care to develop what ability we might have.

Who knows how many other people there are in the world who can do what George does? We know for sure that he is not the only person who has such abilities. But within the realm of the psychically gifted, George is unique in several important ways. First, he has a deep spiritual faith and views his gift as being spiritual in origin and purpose. Because of this, he refuses to assume any other role in the psychic exchange other than that of passive receiver. He will not call up or conjure spirits. You could not ask George, "What does my mother say about my going back to school?" or "Can Aunt Sarah tell me how she really died?"

The word George prefers for describing what he does is *discern* spirits. Through his psychic experiences, George has learned that we do survive physical death in some form, perhaps one similar to what we understand as energy, capable of deliberately sending information. Previously we have attempted to explain what George does in terms of his being a radio or a television, a true receiver, and the spirits' messages coming through to him as if via radio waves. That analogy, however, does not fully describe the process, particularly when you take into account the phenomenon we call direct communication.

Direct communication occurs when the spirit appears, either while the subject is awake or asleep, either visibly or in a way that is emotionally discerned. A direct contact might involve a subject smelling a scent, hearing a song or a word, or seeing an object or event associated with the deceased. We were astounded to learn that virtually every parent we interviewed recounted at least one and sometimes several direct communications with their deceased child.

Why, then, can George Anderson—a total stranger to these children—sustain prolonged contact? To refine our earlier analogies, we might say that while we all have cable, George has access to a "premium" channel that most of us do not. It seems quite apparent from the thousands of readings we have analyzed that the spirits send messages constantly. As far as we are concerned, the only true mystery is why George gets relatively clear reception while for most of us, most of the time, it comes in scrambled.

George is different in other ways. During readings he remains fully conscious; he never enters a trance state and never speaks in any voice but his own. No one spirit speaks through George. Spirits close to those for whom George is doing a reading communicate their messages to him, and he then relays them to the subjects. In the course of any reading, George invariably receives information that he could not possibly have obtained through any other means but discarnate communications. These messages can concern events in the past, the present, and the future. They can explain away mysteries and reveal the heart's deepest secrets.

George may receive these messages in any number of forms, often in some combination of two or more. There are dozens of activities grouped under the heading of psychic phenomena, ranging from *extrasensory perception* (ESP) to *psychokinesis*, or the ability to move objects without physical contact. We are concerned only with the five abilities through which George receives messages and information: *clairvoyance, clairaudience, clairsentience, sympathetic pain and sensation, and, less commonly, psychometry*.

More often than not, spirits will use a combination of clues, the interpretation of which can be extremely simple or bafflingly complex. Even when the meaning is not instantly clear to George, we have found that information from the other side sometimes has its own peculiar but understandable logic. The appearance of a lightning bolt, suggesting a sudden change, or the word *AIDS* speaks for itself and would be obvious to anyone. Less clear but consistent in meaning are such symbols as a towel tied in knots, indicating a bad temper. Others, such as a drink with ice, which suggests a relationship "on the rocks," have an almost childlike literalness. In addition, George has received and accurately interpreted millions of other clues unique to individuals, among them ones concerning nicknames, special occasions, secrets, and other details.

Through clairvoyance George "sees" faces, symbols, objects, figures, places, events, and letters and numbers in his mind's eye. Clairaudience is the psychic sense through which he psychically hears voices and noises, which may include the spirit speaking in a voice as if she were still on this plane, the sounds of gunshots, cats howling, or thunder.

Sympathetic pain and sensation occur when the spirit, through means unknown, triggers a very real physical sensation that George feels as pain or pressure. He has momentarily experienced the sympathetic pain of a heart attack, the pressure of being crushed in a car accident, the shock of being stabbed. In our first book we recounted a series of thermographic imaging tests George underwent, which showed that at the moment he claimed to feel the sensation the correlating part of his body "warmed up." The exact mechanism behind this unusual phenomenon remains an intriguing mystery.

Clairsentience is perhaps the most interesting of George's extrasensory abilities because it is the hardest to describe. It has no parallel with any of the five normal physical senses, and George describes it as more the product of feeling, intuition, or a hunch. George will simply say, "I have the feeling that he passed over recently," or "It feels like he was worried before your mother passed." He cannot articulate what either of these things feels like, but something occurs in the process of discarnate communications, with this accurate feeling as the result. This is the most elusive of the five psychic senses and the one that seems the most "untestable," for who can chart where in the mind feelings arise?

The fifth sense, and the rarest, is psychometry. This sense allows George to gather information about someone or something by simply holding and touching an object associated with them. In a case recounted in our last book,

George learned information about a suicide by holding a sealed envelope that contained newspaper articles about his death. Interestingly, George knew facts about the dead boy, his family, and the circumstances of both that were *not* covered in the articles. Even more remarkably, George obtained this information without the physical presence of anyone related to the boy. Psychometric readings are most commonly associated with missing persons and murder cases, and then almost only when the police request the reading to help them solve a crime. Although George has participated in such cases, in the last several years he has found police work too stressful and no longer does it.

People who have had readings with George or who have seen him demonstrate his ability on television often ask what he appears to be scribbling on the legal pad he holds in his lap. In our first book we made the mistake of describing this activity as "automatic writing," but in fact it is nothing of the sort. We wish to emphasize that there is no time during the reading that George is not in full control of his faculties. What he is often doing with that pen and pad is simply "scribbling" (usually with the pen capped to save paper) as a form of concentration. There are cases where clues emerged from the doodles: names, initials, important symbols. But most often these pieces of information came to George in a glimpse while he was engrossed in another part of the reading—perhaps a second spirit speaking, or the subjects acknowledging a question—so he simply took a note.

Whether George is giving a private reading for one person, a small number of related persons, or a group reading of up to twenty-five, most of them strangers to one another, he always begins by cautioning everyone to answer him with only a yes or a no. He wants only the absolute minimum information to let him know whether or not he is correctly interpreting the spirits' message. When George used to do live telephone readings for broadcast on radio and television, it took only a "hello" from the anonymous subject to get the communication going. George could not see his subjects; he did not even know where they were calling from or why. Evidence from these readings proved that the information George received came only from the spirits on the other side, not visual "clues" about the subjects, since George could not see them.

In the case of private readings, George knows nothing about the subjects. Appointments are made over the phone on a first-name basis only and taken by an assistant. Often the person making the appointment is not even one of the people who will attend the reading. Because of the difficulty in getting through to George, people try every tactic imaginable, including asking friends to call on their behalf on appointment night. The more skeptical subjects make appointments under assumed names just to rule out any possibility of George "researching" them. How he might accomplish this feat with only a first name is a question hardcore debunkers have yet to answer.

Although each reading is, strictly speaking, a discernment, group readings are also called discernments to distinguish them from private readings. In a group discernment George will pick up a spirit's communication without knowing to whom in the roomful of strangers it is intended. He may ask such questions as "Did anyone lose a son named Tony?" or he may simply walk up to or gesture toward the subject. As you will see in one reading here, discernments sometimes result in crossed or overlapping messages when a second spirit seeks to make contact before the first one is finished.

While George's abilities remain the same, there is a significant difference in the content and tone between private readings and public, group discernments. The rule seems to be that spirits do not communicate anything through George when the subject is among strangers that they would not have said in the presence of strangers were they still here on earth. Whereas spirits speak freely of abortions, miscarriages, incest, and other private matters in a private reading, George senses a reticence on the spirit's part if these same topics are broached in a group setting. The spirit may tell George of these matters but caution him not to relay them. Or the spirit may ask George to perhaps couch the message in more polite terms so that, for example, a passionate sexual relationship sounds more like a close friendship.

In this and many other ways, readings are very much like the conversations we have with our loved ones every day: alternately trivial and profound, predictable and astounding. While much about life on the other side is incredibly different from our existence here, some so much so as to be almost unimaginable, certain attitudes and feelings remain the same. Further, there is virtually always a consistency of personality from this life to the next. The son who was quiet and accommodating in this world will express himself that way from the next; the daughter who was rebellious and energetic will come through to George in the same high spirits.

The more skeptical may note that in almost every reading, the child passed tells his parents that he loves them. One common criticism we hear of George's work is that parts of each reading seem similar to parts of others. But when you look at our day-to-day interactions, much of what we do in all of our relationships is pretty similar to what billions of other people do, too. Most parents kiss their children before sending them off to school. So does every other parent on their block. Does that mean that they don't mean it? What could be more natural, a more certain proof of love than the words *I love you*? George could easily eliminate this criticism by simply not repeating these "redundant" messages, but in George's opinion that would be wrong.

The world has grown much more complex, violent, and uncertain than it was even two decades ago. Children of all ages face challenges and risks that before were undreamed of. In the course of his readings, George has learned much about children on the other side and about how they view life here on earth. Due to the nature of his work, however, the information we present here is necessarily incomplete. One can't help but wonder what the child who lived only days, his body damaged by his mother's drug habit, or the little girl who was physically abused throughout her short life would have to say to us about our culture's often shabby treatment of children. However, drug addicts, child beaters, and pedophiles are not likely to seek out George. And so, for now at least, their side of that story cannot be told.

Another constant we have noted through years of studying readings is that those who cross over continue to grow and mature spiritually. They often come through and talk about their changes in attitude or their ability to see in retrospect how something they did in this life was wrong or hurtful. However, contrary to most portrayals of the afterlife, the dead are not transformed into omniscient fortune-tellers. While they can at times see the logical consequences of a given course of action and may issue warnings about particular matters, such as health, for the most part they are more rather than less like us in their wisdom and abilities.

As George works through each reading, the pieces of the puzzle begin to merge into a cohesive picture, and the story the deceased wishes to tell comes clear. Without the subjects' acknowledgments of the information he receives the process would be incomplete. There are times when every part of the message, every symbol, every allusion, every word is crystal clear. However, more often than not, the spirits desire to tell their loved ones something more. There seems to be a distinct pattern most readings follow, from the general to the specific, often ending at some point with an allusion to a fact, name, event, or thing known only to the spirit and the subjects. We believe that those on the other side want us to know that their lives there are real; that what George does is genuine.

As you will see in many of the readings that follow, the subjects prayed or spoke silently to their deceased child and gave him or her a code word or allusion by which they would judge their experience with George. Inevitably these come through in the readings.

Given all this, then, what can the surviving parent of a deceased child expect from a reading with George? That is hard to say, especially since grieving mothers' and fathers' needs are so different from those of other survivors. Often what parents seek beyond knowing that their child is safe and alive on the other side depends on the child's age at death and the circumstances of his or her passing.

Parents of stillborn babies, for example, wonder if the baby knows that they were her parents and that they loved her. Those who have lost an older baby, perhaps a toddler, need help understanding that the baby is continuing to develop on the other side and that he is in the care of other loved ones. For the mother or father of the teenager who died as a result of violence, perhaps they might hope to learn the murderer's identity, while the parents of a suicide want only to know why that tragedy occurred.

For most parents who come to George, these questions are answered as far as they can be. Sometimes there are no answers. But even if a mother walks out of George's door with all her questions answered and feeling at peace knowing that her child is safe and happy, the grief does not magically disappear. For some it is a shock and a letdown to realize hours or days after the euphoria and calm wear off that their grief remains as intense as ever.

This is not to say that the readings have no value; they certainly do. But George will be the first to point out that a reading does not replace the work of grief; it is no short-cut. A mother whose baby dies of crib death may mourn for months or years and truly believe that her pain will end if only her child would let her know that he didn't cry out in the night, or he didn't die because of some precaution his mother forgot to take. But that mother will never stop wanting to hold her baby again, will never stop thinking of him on each birthday and at every milestone her friends' children pass. There is nothing that could occur in the course of a reading to address those aspects of the loss, and certainly nothing that could make those go away.

"I cannot remove your pain," George freely but sadly acknowledges. "All I can do is ease it for a while."

For some people, however, even the small consolations readings can bring are important steps toward learning to cope with a number of problems. Children on the other side often encourage their parents to move on with their lives, caution them not to be overprotective of surviving siblings or overly worshipful of them simply because they are dead.

"Your child wants you to heal and to go on with your life here," George explained, "just as they must continue in the next stage of life. Know that no matter where they are—here or hereafter—they are your children. Forever."

1

Children and Death

A fter a reading with George, bereaved parents often say, "I feel better now knowing that my child is not alone"; "Now I know that I can talk to my daughter whenever I want, and she will hear me"; "The times I felt that my son was in his room with me, he told me through George that he really was"; "It's a great comfort to know that my baby will not forget me and that someday we will all be together again."

For some the reading reinforces or makes concrete religious concepts and beliefs. For the majority, however, these realizations strike them as new, even unfamiliar. Many subjects have told us in interviews that they are still reluctant to share with others their experience with the child after his or her death, or the results of their readings.

It seems that through George many bereaved people have rediscovered an understanding of death that their grandparents and great-grandparents probably believed without question. Of course, this is not to say that these same beliefs were held everywhere by everyone; they weren't. But many aspects of death that today we either shun (viewing or touching the dead body) or dismiss as psychic phenomena (deathbed visions and direct contact) were routinely accepted.

No other experience common to all of humankind is as intricately recorded throughout history as death. The response to and meaning of death is there to be read on every child's gravestone, in countless journals and letters, and in paintings and photographs of the dead and dying. Our general response to such things as memorial photographs—which, in the nineteenth century often provided grieving families with the only visual likeness of their deceased child—is one of shock and repulsion.

This is the "normal" response of someone living in twentieth-century America. According to *Funeral Customs the World Over*, Robert W. Haberstein and William Lamers's history of funeral customs and practices: "High development in the health arts and rapid advances in medicine place such an emphasis on health and well-being that death appears as the failure of man to insure and prolong life. Consequently, for an American the shock of death. . . is accompanied by a sense of frustration."

In many ways, what we consider a normal response to the death of a loved one is, historically, quite abnormal. We are surrounded by death, or at least its possibility, every day. Yet few of us ever have much real contact with it at all. Even as recently as 1960, half of all Americans died at home, surrounded by loved ones. In the chronology to his fascinating book *Sleeping Beauty: Memorial Photography in America*, Stanley B. Burns, M.D., writes:

1825: The time of dying continues to be a time of completion of relationships. The family and the dying say their goodbyes, give a retrospective of their lives, and pronounce their wishes. . . . Dying is an event that helps bind families together, easing guilt and any hard feelings among family members.

Today only a tiny fraction pass outside a hospital or hospice. And until the 1920s families handled almost all the funerary arrangements for their dead. Preparing the body for the customary preburial rituals were activities of the home, not the funeral parlor. In fact, the household parlor room was renamed the *living* room solely to dissociate it from its earlier primary function as a place to wake the family's dead. Around the same period these more naturalistic funeral preparations gave way to an idealized, beautified death.

In numerous ways, great and small, American culture has removed death from its midst. It's often been said that the strong taboo against sex has now been replaced by a similar taboo against anything related to death. While it might be argued that it is one's prerogative to view aspects of death as distasteful and unpleasant, the sad truth is that we carry that aversion over to the bereaved.

This is especially true when a child has died. It wasn't always this way. For one thing, the death of a child used to be commonplace. Throughout most of the nineteenth century, parents could expect anywhere from one third to half of their children to die. Now-treatable or -preventable diseases such as diarrhea, chicken pox, influenza, diphtheria, cholera, tuberculosis, scarlet fever, and measles were often fatal, with epidemics quite common.

One result was that people experienced the death of a friend or loved one usually as early as childhood. The lessons of mortality were reinforced through church teachings and school readers. Though frequently maudlin, melodramatic, and highly moralistic, these writings presented death as a force to be reckoned with. From an elementary-school reader published in 1846 comes this excerpt from a poem entitled ''The Stream of Death'':

> There is a stream whose narrow tide
> The known and unknown worlds divide,
> Where all must go:
> Its waveless waters, dark and deep,
> Mid sullen silence, downward sweep
> With moanless flow.
> I saw where at that dreary flood,
> A smiling infant prattling stood,

Whose hour has come
Untaught of ill, it neared the tide,
Sunk, as to cradled rest, and died,
Like going home.

In another a mother advises her inquisitive child:

My dear, the solemn sleep of death,
Is not like nature's rest;
The coming spring will not bring back,
Those whom our God has blest.
Only the body's in the ground,
Of those we dearly love;
The spirit hath its dwelling found,
And lives with God above.

The moral, religious messages are obvious. But rather than present merely a fatalistic view of death—which at the time was actually quite realistic—there is also a sense of hope. The deceased are depicted returning to the home from which they came. Clearly, physical death is viewed not as a termination but a transition to another, perhaps better, life beyond. In those days a child's death was something to be feared, dreaded, and mourned, but it was not the rare, isolating experience it has become today.

The only place a bereaved parent today might meet another is through a support group, whereas in our grandparents' time half if not more of their neighbors and friends would have known that pain. Today many bereaved parents are surprised by what they view as the inadequacy of physicians and clergy to respond sympathetically to their grief. Decades ago, this was not the case.

Abraham Lincoln and his wife, Mary, were perhaps the most famous bereaved parents of the nineteenth century. Of their four sons, only one lived to adulthood: Eddie died at age four of diphtheria, Willie passed at eleven of an unidentified infection, and then a few years after Lincoln was assassinated, Tad succumbed to "dropsy of the chest" at eighteen.

Mrs. Lincoln's correspondence, some of it written to other bereaved mothers, reveals that commonness and familiarity did not dull death's sting. Clearly, she never fully recovered from the death of her second son; indeed, at one point her husband warned that she might end up in an insane asylum if she did not "control [her] grief." To one correspondent, Mary Lincoln wrote, " . . . when I bring myself to realize that he has indeed passed away, my question to myself is, 'Can life be endured.' " Despite her deep and intractable sorrow, she reached out to other grieving parents in their time of need. To a friend who had lost a son, she wrote:

"Since we were so heavily visited by affliction [Willie's death] . . . I have shrank from all communication with those who would most forcibly recall my sorrows to my mind. Now, in this, the hour of your deep grief, with all my own wounds bleeding afresh, I find myself writing to you to express my deepest sympathy, well knowing how availing words are when we are brokenhearted."

Not only were friends and relatives more likely to understand the parents' grief, it was also customary to remember the child through the years. Shortly after the first anniversary of Willie's passing, Mrs. Lincoln wrote a friend, "Let me thank you for your sympathies and kindly remembrance of yesterday, when I felt so brokenhearted. Only those who have passed through such bereavements can realize how the heart bleeds at the return of these anniversaries." It's difficult not to envy our forebears the compassion and support they generally received.

Virtually all the parents interviewed for this book spoke of the disappointment and pain they felt from the realization that their child seemed to have been forgotten as if he or she never existed.

As one mother observed, "When I was little, growing up in the rural South, we used to have funerals in the home. The body was laid out in the parlor or the living room, and the neighbors came in and sat with the family."

Another source of comfort to bereaved parents of earlier generations was the belief in an afterlife. The popular imagination fully understood and accepted deathbed visions, what we now recognize as the near-death experience, and the possibility of communication and emotional exchange across death's threshold.

As we moved into the twentieth century such things were recast as superstition and psychic phenomena. As Melvin Morse, M.D., puts it in *Transformed by the Light*, "What many people don't realize is that the *denial* [italics ours] of such experiences is the newer phenomenon."

Parents we interviewed often said they were raised to believe in an afterlife, but just could not truly accept that their child was still alive. It wasn't "real" to them. Even among the teachings of organized religions, the view of a life after death is static and unreal. Whether teaching that there's a world beyond filled with harp-playing angels or that there is no world beyond at all, religion often places such a distance between the bereaved and the dead that the dead seem beyond our reach, afterlife or no.

Yet there are allusions to the near-death experience throughout literature, including the Bible. The concept of the dead moving toward a source of or a being of light recurs in a number of religious texts throughout the world. The idea that the dead are reunited with loved ones who have passed on before them is a tenet of Christianity, among other religions. If near-death experiences have always been so common, why then does it seem it's been only in the past two decades that we read and hear so much about them?

One reason may be that medical technology makes it possible to resuscitate the clinically dead. Another is that until the 1975 publication of Dr. Raymond Moody's pioneering *Life After Life*, the near-death experience did not have a name. Less than a decade later a Gallup poll found that 8 million Americans claimed to have had a near-death experience, or NDE.

An NDE occurs between the time a person's physical body enters a state of clinical death (i.e., cessation of heart function) and the time he is physically brought back to life. Each NDE is unique, but interviews with those who have experienced them (NDEers) generally reveal one or more of nine common phenomena.

The first is a sudden *sense of being dead*, accompanied by a *sudden cessation of pain and anxiety*, replaced by a feeling of peacefulness and bliss. This may occur concurrently with an *out-of-body experience*, during which the NDEer feels himself floating above his body, able to see—and later recall—such details of the scene as what others said and did.

Next comes the hallmark of the NDE, the *tunnel experience*. The NDEer travels through a tunnel which ends in a place of light where he is greeted by *people of light*—some of whom he may know—and/or a *being of light*, which some have identified as God or Jesus. Many NDEers report evaluating or *reviewing their lives*, feeling *reluctant to return to their bodies*, and either being told they must return or being given a choice. Some report feeling angry upon first realizing that they are indeed back in their physical bodies.

The ninth component of the NDE is a *personality transformation* that often includes a ready acceptance of death, and in some cases a sudden awareness of such psychic abilities as clairvoyance, telepathy, and precognition.

Skeptics might argue that adults reporting NDEs have been influenced by media depictions of the phenomenon. They might also suggest that in the physical process of dying, or because of various psychoactive drugs a seriously ill patient may take, the mind creates this fantasy. But Dr. Melvin Morse's revolutionary studies into NDEs proved that only people who actually died had them. In other words, the only cause of an NDE is death.

For argument's sake, let's say that adult NDEers are experiencing something else besides death. Call it a hallucination, or perhaps a wish-fulfilling fantasy based on religious conceptions of death and the afterlife. That still would not explain why someone who was considered clinically dead would be able to describe the color of a doctor's jacket or report verbatim words spoken by family members as they waited in a room floors away.

Nor does it explain the near-death experiences of children. Here again Dr. Morse's work is of critical importance, for he showed conclusively that children—including infants—do experience NDEs, which then transform their personalities. Rather than digress in detail on the results and findings of Dr. Morse's critical Seattle Study, we recommend his book *Closer to the Light: Learning from the Near-Death Experiences of Children.*

Dr. Morse's findings are of particular interest to us. Upon reading his work in 1990, it was clear that the child NDEers he studied were describing the other side in terms that George had been familiar with from his readings for years. An analysis of Dr. Morse's and Dr. Moody's writings and George's readings involving children reveals many striking similarities.

Not only is the near-death experience exactly like the real-death experience—except, obviously, in its outcome—but much of what child NDEers recall of life on the other side is corroborated by the accounts George has received from children who completed the transition: for instance, the sense that one is communicating with others purely through thought. Or the sadness over witnessing loved ones grieving.

As noted in the Introduction, we chose to write about children because of the extraordinary needs of bereaved parents and family. But as subjects of paranormal study, children are unique. First, until the age of ten, most do not have what we would consider a realistic conception of death and its permanence. Second, their knowledge of religious and cultural attitudes about, and especially fears of, death are less rigidly formed, if, as in the case of the very young, they exist at all. Third, children approach everything in the world differently than we do. They often lack sufficient knowledge or experience to view the unknown with fear and suspicion. Even teenagers understand the implications of death but, unlike most adults, truly cannot conceive of it ever befalling them.

"As a result," George said, "most pass on with a sense of purity of heart. By this I mean they are more likely to simply accept the experience as it happens. One of the greatest lessons, as the other side says, 'here and hereafter,' is in understanding the self. Even though children, overall, seem less intellectually or emotionally developed in this stage, they adapt and come to understand themselves pretty quickly over there. The preconceptions, the conditioning, the habits of thought, simply are not as deeply ingrained in a child as they would be in an adult.

"When we die, we withdraw from the physical body into a dimension of the nonphysical," he continued. "There the essence of self—the personality, if you want to call it that—survives and develops. When someone says, 'I miss my child,' they mean that they miss his presence, his essence, his self. That's what seems to survive physical death.

"There's never any question that children know when they have passed on. Some may experience what would seem to us to be a few moments—there is no conception of time on the other side—of darkness," George explained. "Then they will see what seems to be in the distance a light maybe the size of a pinhead, which they are attracted to. As they start going toward it, the light becomes larger and brighter. Some children have reported that a grandparent, a friend, or a pet will come up to them. It seems that this occurs to comfort the child and give him a sense of security."

We asked George how those on the other side would know that a child was about to come over. "Let me give you an example," he answered. "If your child is ill, and your mother has passed on, she would be extremely concerned about him, regardless of where she was. She would know because your and your child's needs for her would be especially great at that time. Those on the other side seem to hover around us during the times we need their support more than at others. I think you see this in the deathbed visions, where a child who is about to pass will report seeing his deceased grandparent or a deceased pet in the room with him.

"I try to help people understand that if your friends and loved ones are here for you when you're having a crisis in this life, it seems only logical that they would try to help you however they could from the next one. Of course, they can't work miracles—they cannot save someone whose time it is to go—but they can be there to comfort them and help them with the transition.''

Even for those of us who believe in an afterlife, it's difficult to conceive of what exactly that life would be like. Where does it occur? What is it like there? What do children do there?

"The other side is not someplace a million miles up in space," George said. "I know I've used this example a hundred times, but it still seems to be the one most people can relate to. In *The Wizard of Oz* Auntie Em appears in the witch's crystal ball calling to Dorothy, and Dorothy cries back, 'Auntie Em, I'm right here in Oz!' But Dorothy is confused because Auntie Em doesn't hear her.

"Many of the children come through and refer to that scene to explain what it's like for them after they've crossed over. They understand that their parents think they're not here anymore, because they don't see or feel them physically. Yet those children are reaching out, saying, 'I'm here, I'm here. Why do you think I'm dead, that I'm not here?' They often say that it's very frustrating for them to feel still a part of their loved ones' lives, yet most of the time their loved ones have no idea how close these children really are.

"Through the years I've heard countless descriptions of what it's like on the other side. It seems that to a certain extent we can create our own reality there. For example, one little girl came through, and I saw her playing on a very beautiful, very vivid, very tranquil beach.

"When I see things like scenes of gardens or this beach, they look very much like they would here," he elaborated, "but the colors are more vivid, and everything that is positive or pleasurable about that place or situation on earth is a million times more like that over there. I know it's really hard to grasp, but it's just like a tranquil beach more tranquil than you can imagine; the flowers smell sweeter than we can imagine, and so on. Some of the children interviewed in Dr. Morse's study also commented on how bright and colorful it was over there.

"The obvious question would be, Is that little girl really playing on a beach? Is there a beach on the other side? That I really don't know. Except spirits do often appear to be doing things in settings they had enjoyed here. That's why I sometimes think that when I see these things I'm either seeing that spirit's created reality, or that they are communicating to me some identifying information along with the sense that they are okay there.

"One thing I do know about how the other side is different from here is that there is no struggle," George continued. "I've used that phrase before, and what I mean is that there is no fear, no threat, no worry. Yet those on the other side have a mission to progress spiritually. There are special situations there where children are helped and encouraged, gently led rather than taught, to progress through thoughts, self-examination, and good works.

"One thing that children do over there is help older loved ones on the other side. It's very interesting when I hear someone who passed over say, 'My granddaughter is here with me, and I'm learning so much from her about patience,' and things of that nature. We function there according to where we are in our spiritual progression. Sometimes a child will come through who gives me the sense that she is unusually progressed or, if you believe in reincarnation—and it seems to be one option there—has been around many times. That's when I'll say someone feels like 'an old soul.'

"But I think parents would be comforted to know that on the other side each child is treated as a precious and unique individual. I think of it in terms of a rose as it grows from a tiny bud to a full flower. You appreciate that rose for its individual beauty, even though it may outwardly appear to be very much the same as millions of other roses. However, in that moment of appreciation, you see that rose as if it were the only rose that exists. It seems that on the other side, they treat the child as a blooming rose, and they patiently wait for each petal to unfurl, never rushing, never pushing that rose to be anything but exactly what it was meant to be.''

Virtually all parents wonder if their child suffered during death and if he was frightened to suddenly find himself on the other side. "Death itself is not painful," George stressed. "For some reason we all believe that it is, and I think that's why most of us fear death. I've often thought that if we all knew that once we got very old we would simply fall asleep one night and never wake up, our ideas about death would be very different. What we seem to fear most are the possible circumstances of our deaths: a car crash or other bad accident, a long illness, violence, and so on.

"Of course, you can be in situations that lead up to death, such as having a terminal illness, where the person will come through and say, 'I had a rough time prior to my passing.' But at death all physical suffering ends, because our physical existence ends. And the child who here was blind, crippled, mentally impaired, or had other health problems is freed of them. In a fascinating reading for a man whose profoundly mentally retarded daughter died at age eight, she told me not only that she was fine on the other side, but she indicated that, contrary to what her doctors thought, she'd actually understood a great deal of what her father had said to and done for her here on earth.

"Yet, while death itself is not painful, it's understandable that parents would worry about their child during the transition. Yes, I have had children come through to say that they were frightened at first, not quite certain what was happening. But that's why someone or a pet they know and trust approaches them to help. Often someone who passed from similar circumstances—say a boy who knows firsthand the suffering of another child with AIDS or cancer—will 'volunteer' to work with children as they come over in that condition.''

Many parents are baffled when in the course of a reading a child comes through and says that he or she was greeted by a grandparent or relative they never knew on earth. They wonder how a child would recognize a grandfather who died thirty years before she was born.

"It seems that we instinctively know who is who and what they mean to us," George said. "After all, her grandfather may have died, but he died only in the physical sense. She may not have known him here, but he has remained a part of your life and hers even though he has crossed over to the other side.

"Parents often ask me, 'If my child is very young when he passed, will he remember me thirty or sixty years later when I pass over? What if the baby is a stillborn, for example, who never "knew" me?' I always tell those people not to worry, that love is timeless. And, from what the other side has told me, we tend to be linked to certain people over and over again eternally, and for a reason.

"Your children may have grown and developed spiritually since you last saw them on this plane, but they will come to you in a form that you will recognize. Besides, we don't see each other physically as we do here. Instead, it seems that we recognize each other emotionally."

Yet as George has learned, while we remain connected forever, we change and evolve on the other side as we progress spiritually. This often creates confusion for George. "Most of the time a two-year-old comes through to me as a two-year-old, and a teenager as a teenager, and while I can't describe exactly how I know the difference, it's clear to me. But say someone loses a child at five years of age twenty years ago. That child may come to me as a five-year-old. But she may have developed spiritually and may communicate things to me that suggest she is older than that. I may also get a little confused because she may choose to manifest to me as a young woman the age she would have been had she stayed on this side. It can be very confusing. But usually the clues form a consistent pattern. At any rate, they seem to be very careful to make sure that whatever they are trying to communicate to me is expressed in terms that I and the subjects can understand.

"To give another example," George continued, "I had one case where the little girl who had passed appeared to me in a lilac-colored dress. It seems a small detail but it was actually a key fact that helped the mother feel sure that she was indeed hearing from her daughter. During the course of the reading I learned that not only was purple her favorite color but that she had been wearing a purple dress the day she was fatally injured and on the day she was buried. It always seems very important to them to be sure that their loved ones know that the communication they're receiving is genuine.''

Perhaps the universal question in all of this, and the one no one can answer, is, Why did God take my child? Why did my baby die? ''I always feel compelled to tell parents God did not take their child,'' George said emotionally. ''God, or the Infinite Light, or whatever you choose to call it, has nothing to do with it. That is an old organized-religion type of belief, that if something good happens in your life, it's because God smiled upon you. But where does that leave you when something bad happens? I'd like people to think of it this way: What could you have possibly done that was so bad that God would decide to take your child's life in retribution? It doesn't make sense when you think of it that way.

''Sometimes I think people choose to say that it's God's will because then there's nothing they can really do about it. After all, it's not very comfortable to be mad at God. And is it God's will that parents and children suffer? I cannot conceive of that God.''

We are reminded of a wonderful quotation from the Reverend William Sloane Coffin, Jr., who said of his son's death, ''My consolation lies in knowing that it was *not* the will of God that Alex died; that when the waves closed over [his] sinking car, God's was the first of all hearts to break.''

2

"Who Is Holding My Baby Now?"

What occasion could possibly be more joyful, more symbolic of renewal and love, than the birth of a child? The blissful mother, the proud father, the beaming grandparents and siblings—these are images that define birth today. Despite the movement toward more natural childbirth and advanced ultrasonic imaging that permits parents to see the unborn baby as he really appears, the bright-eyed, chubby bundle drifting down from heaven on a blanket of clouds holds sway in the popular imagination.

Fortunately, for most parents a child's birth is a happy day filled with awe, laughter, and tears of thanks. So many healthy babies are born every day that it's easy to take for granted the miraculous journey from conception to birth and through infancy. Most of us have difficulty even imagining a time when one out of ten infants died, which shows just how far we've come since the turn of this century. Generally speaking, parents are right to assume that death awaits somewhere far off in the future. That death's cold hand might reach into the womb or the nursery is literally unthinkable. Even the idea of it strikes us numb with terror.

But death is a reality of life, even for the youngest of the young. Every year about 3.3 million babies are born in the United States. Of those, about one in every hundred, or 33,000, will be stillborn; another 30,000 will die in their first month from a range of causes, including congenital defects and disease. Between their first month and age one, 6,000 to 7,000 babies succumb annually to SIDS, sudden infant death syndrome. And then there are the hundreds of thousands of unborn children whose lives end through miscarriage or abortion.

Despite our cultural belief that the loss of a child is the most traumatic anyone can endure, in word and deed our society seems ambivalent when the deceased child is either very young or passed before birth. Bereavement experts offer several theories as to why this might be so, but all agree that the deaths of the very young are often, in the words of bereavement expert Dr. Therese Rando, "discounted." As you will read in this chapter, too many parents are urged to "get on" with their lives and "move ahead." The reasoning behind such misguided advice is that a youngster who lived only a short time or not at all outside the womb wasn't really a part of his parents' lives. To tell a parent that he or she shouldn't miss a baby they never really "knew" is to lose sight of the most important thing that parents do know about their children: that they love them, that they are theirs.

What these well-meaning people fail to appreciate is that in the process of becoming parents we often establish a relationship of love and caring for a child even before she is conceived. Just as a child evolves during the nine months after conception, so does a parent. Women are mothers, men are fathers long before the baby is born.

Mary O'Shaughnessy, a bereavement counselor in private practice, observed, "As little support as we give people who have lost children, there is even less support from society and family for women who have had miscarriages, lost children from SIDS, or have stillbirths or abortions.

"Relatives and friends will make comments such as, 'Oh, you can get pregnant again,' or 'You're young,' or 'You really didn't know this child.' The women don't get as much support as they need although they actually are grieving parents.

"What bereaved parents want from George is the reassurance of hearing from a departed child one more time."

A parent's grief over the death of the very young, born and unborn, reflects a multitude of losses, not the least is a faith in the natural order of life. What could possibly be more unjust than losing one's life before it had really begun? That the majority of these losses occur without warning only adds to a parent's feelings of impotence and abandonment. Why, many wonder, did God take my baby?

Most bereaved parents who come to George seek the peace of mind that comes from the child assuring them that he or she is safe and happy on the other side. For almost all parents, it's hearing this "said" through George in the child's own words, using that child's unique expressions and manner. But what of the child who never learned to speak while here on earth? Or the child who never even breathed air while on this plane? How do they communicate from the other side?

In many cases, examples of which you will see in the readings that follow, what the baby seeks to communicate through George is conveyed by other loved ones who were chronologically older and verbal before they passed over. In one reading it is the mother's stepfather who speaks for the baby; in another from Chapter 8, siblings who crossed over as adults tell George what the brother who died in infancy wants to say. Very often when George repeats a message given him from an infant on the other side, it is "spoken" by another spirit. It's important to remember, though, that the emotion George feels accompanying it is clearly the child's. Other times he feels the emotional message as it comes directly through the young child.

"Bereaved parents are sometimes upset if they think the baby they've lost here isn't speaking," he explained. "They will mistakenly think their child has forgotten them or doesn't love them. But that's an error. Parents who feel that way are looking at this from an earthly point of view.

For example, just because the grandfather speaks for the baby doesn't mean the child doesn't love Mommy or Daddy or has forgotten them. The baby is still sending his love."

This is understandably a difficult concept to grasp, but since there is no verbal communication on the other side, it makes sense.

"I feel what they say. That's what I mean by emotional communication." Even though George does hear the spirits speaking at times during readings, they are not literally speaking to him. George has been told by the spirits countless times that their communication is done through what we would best understand as emotion. "I can *feel* what the children look like," George says, struggling to explain a phenomenon for which there simply are no words.

Just because a child cannot speak does not mean that he or she cannot communicate. The tiniest baby, from its first breath, is in constant communication with its new world. Cries, gurgles, coos, smiles, even a quiet stare, tell those around him what he feels, wants, and needs. Another fairly new area of research deals with what babies communicate to us nonverbally. As it turns out, even the simplest gestures—like clenching a fist or turning the head—in combination with other movements and facial expressions have specific meanings.

It has become increasingly clear that many of the baby's sounds and gestures are not, as was previously believed, the random outward manifestations of a developing nervous system. Whether the baby cognitively "knows" what he's doing in the same sense that you know you are reading this book, or whether part of his communication is simply pre-programmed for survival, like his cries for food and warmth, is still open to debate. What is indisputable is that through each "message" the baby communicates some emotion. How well a baby communicates is often judged by how well his parents pick up on and respond to his signals. A baby whose signals go unread or misread may be perceived by those around him as difficult, fussy, or not really "saying" much, while for those parents who patiently study their child, each day brings fulfilling and thoroughly understood and reciprocated conversations, no matter how young the child.

In observing the verbal limitations of deceased youngsters, it becomes clear that the verbal skills we develop while here on earth are, while not essential, certainly a factor in our future discarnate communications. Interestingly, as very young children mature spiritually on the other side, they apparently can and do learn language as they would have had they remained on this plane.

"In readings there are times when I've felt a youngster of one or two years of age speaking," George said. "There's a sense you're hearing from a soul that is innocent yet mature. I admit, I sometimes wonder how that's possible. I'm curious how they can talk if they're very young. In fact, because I can't conceive logically that a year-old child or an infant is talking to me, I may even block out the baby who's speaking."

As it seems to be with everything else on the other side, there are no fixed rules, and each person is as unique in the hereafter as he or she was while among us. "I've had souls who've come through in readings as they would be today, and yet they passed on in infancy," George said. "Other times, the soul comes through even years after he's passed, and I sense psychically that it is an infant or a very young child.

"I think in some cases these infant spirits still fathom themselves as children or babies in the afterlife. It is in the afterlife that they have to learn to grow and be nurtured."

But whatever a young child's means of communication, it is clear from George's readings that the babies who have passed on remain strongly bonded with their parents, siblings, and other family here on earth.

When parents learn of the strength of this eternal bond, it only adds urgency to their questions about the reason for their child's short existence. Why would a baby be born only to die? Why was his time on earth so brief? Why was I denied getting to even know her? What is the purpose of that baby's life? And his death?

"There is definitely a purpose to a child's life, even if it's for a short time," George said. "Sometimes the children will say from the other side, 'Wouldn't you much rather have had me for the short time you did than not at all?' Some say they come for a short time to give love and affection. Others say they come for a short time to *get* those things. And some say they were lucky and had the opportunity to do both.

"Others perhaps decided that they just wanted to come back to earth for a brief while to see how much they could accomplish in a limited amount of time," George said. But he acknowledged that these concepts were difficult for him to understand and probably even harder for parents to accept.

"Some might have come back to earth and concluded that perhaps things here would not work out as they hoped, and they just withdraw. Regardless, it is ultimately the choice of the soul to come here in the first place, and there seems to be a period of time during which that soul can also choose to withdraw.

"In some cases," he went on, "the soul enters a physical body that has what we would consider the equivalent of a mechanical problem or malfunction. In situations like that, the soul cannot survive here. Does the soul know that it has chosen an imperfect physical body before it enters? I don't know. I'll be the first to admit that I don't have all the answers. Sometimes I even think that those on the other side don't tell us things like this because we are not meant to know. I sometimes think that—and this may be another hard thing to accept—our not knowing is part of our struggle here. We need not know all the answers; otherwise what will we have to strive for?

"It may seem that the loss occurs for 'no reason,' that it has no purpose or meaning, but those on the other side have told me many, many times that is never true. What that purpose is, however, may be something we never learn while on this plane. In other cases, though, the children's spirits do reveal it in the readings, but I don't always understand or comprehend it. I think it's important for parents to understand that just because the purpose is not communicated or I cannot understand it doesn't mean that there is no purpose. There is. It's just that in most cases, for whatever reason, it is literally beyond us.''

Parents who lose a child through miscarriage find themselves particularly isolated in their grief for several reasons. In the case of miscarriage, which occurs in up to 25 percent of all pregnancies, a woman may not even know she was expecting until the miscarriage occurs. Or she and her mate may have decided to keep their news private for several months. Even when miscarriage occurs in the later months, it still is not generally viewed by others as a "real" baby.

A child lost between the seventh and fourteenth weeks, as occurs in 15 percent to 20 percent of all pregnancies, is not, in most people's minds, a child at all. Many parents, who have suffered such a loss, know the well-worn comments: "It wasn't really a baby." "You didn't even know the baby." "Something must have been wrong with the baby." "This is nature's way of getting rid of problems." And so on. But in most cases, even after medical examination of the miscarried fetus, no one can say for sure why that baby died. And even if they could—and if, let's just suppose, it was "better" this way—that does not erase a parent's grief.

As my coauthor Patricia once reflected, "When I lost my first pregnancy to miscarriage and people said things like that, I thought to myself, 'Better? Wouldn't it just be better if I had my baby?' Everyone thought it should be easy to just go on, but I felt very strongly that I had lost a child; my child. Even today, though I've since had a healthy, beautiful son, Justin, I wonder about that baby: Was it a boy or a girl? Would it have looked like Justin? Would he or she have looked different? And if I'd had the first baby, would I now have Justin, too? Sometimes I even wonder if my son *is* that baby; in other words, if that baby's soul returned to wherever it came from and then came back to me in Justin's body. I'll probably never know, but I'll never stop wondering."

Souls of babies who have been miscarried often come through in readings. However, George recently had an unusual personal experience that, coupled with what he's learned of miscarriages from his readings, further illuminated life for the smallest children on the other side.

George, his neighbor Charles, and Charles's teenage sons Tommy and Chris vacationed together at Disney World. To save money on accommodations, they decided to share a three-bedroom hotel suite.

George, always a light sleeper, awoke in the middle of the night to find his room sweltering. The suite's air-conditioning was too cold at night, so before turning in he'd shut it off and left on only the ceiling fans. He thought he heard Tommy exclaim in the other room, "This room is really hot!"

George got up in the dark and quietly walked down a long hallway to the kitchen for a drink. He was about to go back to his room when he saw Tommy standing near the closed drapes to his right. George recalled thinking, Why does he look like he's in a daze? Just then the boy turned toward George and glanced down the hallway, where the light switches and thermostat were located. George was sure that Tommy, still half-asleep, must have gotten up to turn on the air conditioner, then forgot what he was doing.

"Tommy," George said, "why don't you go put the air-conditioning on? Just hit the switch down."

But Tommy said nothing and stared back at George, then started to put on some clothes the boys had left lying on the couch. Why is he getting dressed just to turn on the air conditioner? George was wondering when the light suddenly came on. George looked down the hallway and saw Tommy turn on the air conditioner, turn off the light, and return to his room. But Tommy was standing at the window on the opposite side of the suite. Or was he?

When George spun around, he saw no one near the drapes. How could Tommy have been in two places at once? There was no way Tommy could have walked from the window and crossed the living room area to the hallway without George seeing him. And besides, less than a second elapsed between when George last saw the boy by the drapes and Tommy in the hallway.

George was startled and confused. He felt a chill as he realized the boy he had spoken to, the one standing near the drapes, was not Tommy. But who was he? He looked almost exactly like Tommy: same height, same build, same coloring, same face. It made no sense, and George tossed in his bed for the next couple of hours trying to figure it out.

Could he have seen the spirit of Chris and Tommy's grandfather? No, too young. Was there a friend of theirs who had died? Perhaps, but then what about the uncanny resemblance to Tommy? A coincidence?

George strained to recall a reading he had done for Chris and Tommy's parents and their eldest son, Charles III, but he was certain no child had come through. Suddenly, as if someone were eavesdropping on George's thoughts, a voice said, "I'm Tommy's older brother."

"That's impossible," George responded psychically to the spirit. "You can't be. There hasn't been a loss of a child in that family. I know that for a fact."

"No, you're wrong," the spirit replied. "Margie, my mother, had a miscarriage. It was after Charles III, her first-born, but before Tommy. I would have been Tommy's older brother. I would be seventeen going on eighteen right now. And I am Tommy's guardian angel."

Is this all in my imagination? George wondered. I read this family, and none of this came up. He started to rebut the spirit again but thought better of it. At breakfast George explained to the boys what had happened and asked if there had been a miscarriage in the family. Neither boy was certain, but both doubted it, since their parents never mentioned it. Unfortunately, Charles, Jr., had left very early that morning to visit relatives in Tampa and wouldn't be back until very late.

"There's only one way to be sure," George said. "We'll call your mother in New York and tell her what happened."

Marge was slightly unnerved to hear about George's experience, but she revealed that she had in fact lost a baby between Charles III and Tommy. That fetus, a boy, was only about six and half months along when the miscarriage occurred.

"If my baby would have been born," she told George, "today he would be seventeen going on eighteen. He would have been Thomas the first."

"That's exactly what the spirit told me," George said. "I saw him clearly in the living room standing near the drapes. He was right in front of me. He said he was younger than Charles III but older than Tommy, who's sixteen. The spirit said that if he were here on earth today, he'd be seventeen going on eighteen. And he told me he's Tommy's guardian angel."

Interestingly, both Chris and Tommy took the whole incident in stride. In fact, they spent the rest of the vacation asking George repeatedly if he had seen their brother again. He did not, and found himself wondering why a spirit would make such a brief, unexpected appearance? And why hadn't he come through during the reading?

George now speculates that he saw the spirit because, being half-asleep, his conscious defenses were down. Perhaps if he had been more alert, he might have dismissed it. He also wonders whether Tommy and Chris might have seen their brother's spirit, too, had he warned Tommy not to turn on the light.

George's experience with the spirit of Marge and Charles Jr.'s miscarried son suggests several conclusions about life on the other side. First, a spirit or soul can materialize and appear to those of us here on earth in a form that we recognize. In this case, the boy appeared as being the chronological age he would have attained had he been born. Most important, he so closely resembled Tommy that George believed he *was* Tommy. Second, the soul of a miscarriage matures and develops spiritually in the hereafter. Third, the spirit of a miscarried child knows and continues to maintain some kind of relationship with parents, siblings, other family members, and friends, even though he or she never really knew them here on earth.

Finally, even years after physical death, the miscarried child has a function and serves a purpose in our lives. For Tommy, the spirit of the child who would have been an older brother was a guardian angel.

For Elizabeth Anne Dunn,* an attractive middle-age woman with long brown hair, life had been a bittersweet adventure. In her late twenties she had been married to James less than a year when she discovered she was pregnant. Her excitement and joy were tempered by the fact that James,* a military man, was stationed in Europe while she remained stateside. Uncomfortable with traveling while pregnant, Anne, as everyone knew her, opted to stay near her parents. From the very beginning, though, she never felt totally alone. She and James wrote each other every day. Months before the baby was due, Anne felt that she somehow knew her, a girl she named Elizabeth.

Like many newlyweds the Dunns lived on a tight budget, but Anne didn't mind. She delighted in planning and decorating the room in their small apartment that would be Elizabeth's nursery. As the months passed she filled the time collecting baby furniture, clothing, toys, and other paraphernalia. She missed her husband terribly but took comfort knowing he would be home for her delivery. Each day was bringing them closer together, closer to becoming a family.

Anne was eight months into what had been a healthy, comfortable pregnancy when her friends surprised her with a baby shower. Gazing over the beautiful gifts, Anne could imagine holding her baby in her arms. After all this time of feeling Elizabeth kick and flutter, she was certain that she could also "feel" her daughter's personality. She imagined her delivery as a time of being reunited with the baby she already knew.

And then, just days before Anne's due date, she noticed

*At the request of these subjects, their names have been altered to protect their identities. Everything else in this story, however, is true.

she didn't feel Elizabeth moving. She rushed to the doctor's office, where he tried, without success, to find the baby's heartbeat. Somehow the baby had turned in the womb so that the umbilical cord wrapped around her neck and cut off her oxygen. Quietly, imperceptibly, a perfect and healthy Baby Elizabeth had died.

Anne's shock and disbelief overwhelmed her. Alone, with James still thousands of miles away and out of contact, she listened numbly as the doctor explained that it would be more dangerous for her to undergo a Caesarian section to remove the fetus immediately than to wait until the baby was full term and could be delivered naturally.

Anne simply could not absorb it all. "How could I carry a little baby for nine months with the expectation that I'd be giving life and then find I had a dead baby?" she said, describing the surreal days that followed. "You feel you know that little person inside of you. You feel a bond as a mother because the baby is part of you. I was very, very depressed."

As she waited for the onset of her labor or the doctor's decision to induce labor, she felt "like a walking tomb." Ten days later labor was induced, and she delivered her child alone. Anne had not been able to reach her husband overseas since shortly before she'd learned of the baby's death. As she lay in the hospital bed alone, her arms achingly empty, James was en route to her. He arrived at Anne's bedside bearing gifts for a baby he would never see. Mourning darkened the next days and weeks, a time they had dreamed would be filled with the trials and triumphs of parenthood.

Until quite recently, it was considered "better" for bereaved parents not to see their dead child. Doctors and other professionals were of the opinion that the sight would be too shocking. But more enlightened attitudes and research have since proved otherwise. In fact, parents who do not see and hold their baby often spend years imagining that the baby is grossly deformed or otherwise repulsive to look at. While in some cases there may be physical deterioration of the stillborn or miscarried baby, parents still see their baby as their child first, and any other problems seem not so important. As one certified nurse midwife we interviewed said, "Even in cases where the baby does not look like the perfect, sleeping baby, parents still look to see whose nose or chin the baby has. And they often take comfort in knowing that their child was real." In light of this, in many hospitals it is now standard procedure to sensitively photograph the baby and file the pictures in case the parents wish to have them later.

Very often, for parents who are denied or refuse such contact with their baby, the circumstances of the baby's life and death become unreal. Consequently, they have more difficulty focusing and resolving their grief. Bereavement counselor Mary O'Shaughnessy said, "It's really important for parents to be able to see and touch their baby so they can identify what they lost. You have to know what it is you've lost before you can get to the grief."

Unfortunately, Anne delivered Elizabeth at a time when the older attitudes prevailed. Shortly after Elizabeth's birth, the doctor and the nurses told her how the baby looked. "They said she was a beautiful little girl. She was in perfect condition. They told me she looked like a sleeping doll." But they did not actively encourage her to see or hold her child. When they asked if she would like to, she impulsively declined.

"I was traumatized, but now I'm sorry I didn't see my daughter when she was delivered," Anne said. "I had no support system at the time, really. I was in shock and I wasn't thinking clearly. I was expecting to bring up that child. She was our future. In a way I felt more disappointed than if, God forbid, an older child died, because I never even got a chance to be with her, to know her.

"We mourned as you would for any child. Her age was irrelevant. I grieved terribly, and so did James."

Unfortunately for Anne and James, they never encountered any physician, clergy, or other professional who could offer more than general sympathy. They were victims of our culture's inability to accept and fully acknowledge the loss of a very young child. Not surprisingly, people's sympathetic "advice" usually boils down to: *Let's pretend this didn't happen*. Sadly, yet all too typically, Anne endured the insensitive comments of friends and family.

Perhaps most painful for Anne were her mother Frances's words: "You're still young. You can have other children. Go on with your life." Anne wondered how she could ever replace the pregnancy or overcome the shock of losing Elizabeth.

Frances hadn't meant to be hurtful. She was one of thirteen children, ten of whom had died before adulthood. While Anne's grandmother Lydia certainly grieved privately for her lost children and sometimes even spoke of them, her stoicism and denial were typical of most mothers at the turn of the century. Until only the last few decades, mothers throughout history viewed childbirth and childrearing as times fraught with risk and danger. Still, Anne thought, *this is not what I need to hear. Nothing will ever replace Elizabeth. Nothing.*

A little more than two decades passed before Anne saw George Anderson. In that time she and James became the parents of two daughters and a son. Like most bereaved parents, she never stopped questioning why such a terrible thing had happened. She didn't blame God, as many parents do, but she never felt she had the answer, either.

In a strange way, her mother was right: Anne did go on with her life and have the family she always wanted, despite suffering two miscarriages before the first live birth. Still, she wondered, *What happened to Elizabeth after she left this world? Where did she go? Was she alone? What would she have been like were she alive today? Did Elizabeth know how Anne had prayed for her all these many years? Would she even know or remember the mother who never held her?*

Anne later recounted, her reading with George was the first time in her life someone had spoken of her three deceased children as if they were as much "real" children as her other three.

• • •

"A male close to you passed," George said to Anne.

"Yes."

"He's older. A father figure. So your father's passed?"

"Oh, yes."

"Any reason he'd apologize [to you]?"

"Yes."

"Because he's saying he's sorry."

"Yes."

"He could have been a better father to you, he says."

"Yes. That's true."

"But he passed a while ago. More than five years ago?"

"Oh, yes. Actually about seven years since he's passed. Seven years ago."

"He seems at a distance from you when he was here on earth."

"A distance?"

"Either physically or emotionally."

"Oh, yes. Emotionally."

"It's like I'm forcing words out of him. It's like pulling teeth, so to speak."

"Yes, that's true. He was very quiet. He kept a lot to himself. He didn't communicate much with us."

"That's the feeling I got. Someone who keeps a lot to himself. Definitely."

"Oh, yes."

"He passes from a health problem. Something to the chest."

"Yes."

"It's in the chest, but not the heart."

"No. It's not his heart."

"Because it feels more like something fills up or goes wrong in the lungs."

"Yes. He died from pneumonia."

"He calls to you, in any event. He's fine now. Although he admits it took him a while to adjust on the other side."

"Okay."

"And—wait. Your mother. She's still alive."

"Yes."

"Because he calls to her."

"Oh. Yes, my mother's living."

"Who's Bill?"

"Should I tell you?"

"No, no," George insisted. "What just threw me is that all of a sudden another male stepped forward to say *he's* your father. And I said to myself, You can't have two fathers. But then this other man, Bill, says he is, also."

"Should I tell you, George?"

"No. Let them tell me. Let them do the work and clarify it." George paused. "Oh, I get it now. One is like your stepfather. But which one? Bill says [psychically], 'I'm like a father.' "

"Oh, yes!"

"So Bill is really your stepfather."

"Yes. But he was more of a father to me than . . ." Anne's voice trailed off. "I called him my second father."

"Because your [real] father says he definitely wasn't the father he should have been."

"True."

"Did he have a problem with depression?" George asked.

"Yes."

"That's what he says. Now another male appears. But very young. Did you lose a child?"

"No."

"But they're saying a child is with them. Did you ever have a miscarriage?"

"Oh, yes. I'm sorry," said Anne. "I didn't think—"

"More than one miscarriage?"

"Yes."

"One seems like it was fully born. Like a stillbirth."

"Yes. That's another."

"Wait: You had two miscarriages."

"Yes."

"And a stillborn."

"Yes, exactly. Two miscarriages and a stillbirth."

"Were you married at the time? Or separated?"

"Yes. I was—I am—married."

"Then, wait. Why do I feel like there was a separation?"

"You're right. My husband was in the service—the military—at the time."

"But the stillborn feels like it was a long time ago. It was a girl."

"Yes."

"And today she'd be a young adult."

"Yes."

"Oh, I see now. The baby strangled somehow on the umbilical cord," George said, placing his hands around his neck.

"Yes. That's exactly what happened."

"It's a little girl."

"Yes."

"Well, she's fine now and at peace," George reported. "She's with others in the next stage. She's not alone."

"Oh, good!" Anne blurted.

"She singularizes herself. Was she your oldest or something? You know, your firstborn?"

"Yes. She was my firstborn."

"She was named for you, she says. She has the same name as you: Elizabeth."

"Yes. That's the name I'd chosen for her."

"She shows me that she was a perfect little baby. She tells me she was in a bad position and turned the wrong way somehow in the womb and strangled."

"Yes, that's exactly what the doctors told me."

"But it seems this happens very close to when she was supposed to be born."

"Yes. It happened ten or eleven days before I was due."

"Your daughter says you memorialized her. You gave her a funeral service."

"Yes. Yes. Does she say anything or something more about it?"

"No. It's just that she's acknowledging it."

"Is she okay, George?" Anne asked wistfully. "What has she done all these years [in the hereafter]? Has she grown up?"

"Well, for one thing, there's no conception of time [on the other side]. But she's fine. She's with a lot of loved ones. They say they take care of her now. They raised her, so to speak. She grows, matures, spiritually. Of course, not physically, because there is no physical body in the next stage. So the soul is mature even though she passed on before birth.

"And the soul that entered the body returned to the other side," George continued. "In fact, she was able to meet [the souls of] the miscarriages when they made the transition [to the other side]."

"Does she remember me? That I'm her mother?"

"Oh, definitely."

"Oh, good. I'd worried about that. Thank you."

"You have other children, living."

"Yes."

"She calls to them. Another girl? Two girls?"

"Yes."

"And a boy?"

"Yes."

"So you have three children on earth."

"Yes, three."

"Now, you said before you had two miscarriages, right?"

"Yes."

"They're with this daughter—the stillbirth—also. Had the cycle of birth continued, one would have been a girl."

"Oh."

"And the other would have been a boy."

"Okay."

"Your mother, you said, is alive."

"Yes."

"Because the children are also with a mother figure. Your mother-in-law is also passed on?"

"Yes."

"Then it must be that she's with your grandmothers. And she's with your mother-in-law; *her* grandmother, also. Because they all draw close, also to say they're taking care of the children. They're all together. Who is Lydia?"

"Yes. That's my grandmother. My mother's mother."

"That's who met your daughter. Lydia says she crossed

Elizabeth over and welcomed her to the light. That's who draws close. The children are with her. Did Lydia pass young?''

"Oh, yes.''

"It's like many, many years ago. I mean, I'm going back a long time, like literally to horse-and-buggy days.''

"Yes, just about.''

"Lydia passes from a health condition. But she goes young, even for that generation.''

"I would say so.''

"It feels like her heart goes.''

"Yes, I believe so.''

"Do you take the name Helen, or Helene?''

"Yes. My other grandmother.''

At this point in the reading George gave other accurate details that applied to Anne's children, husband, career, health, and other personal matters.

"Your daughter [Elizabeth] is still around you like a guardian angel. She calls to *her* sisters and brothers here. She's around *her* siblings.''

"Are you sure she's okay?''

"Oh, definitely. Once she was out of her physical body, she was in God's light. She says, 'Don't worry.' You've been worrying about her all these years. You don't have to. She hands you roses. And Bill [the stepfather] comes forward also with roses. It's a spiritual blessing. But it's more. It also means something special.''

"Oh, yes. Shall I tell you? Bill had planted roses right outside my mother's window, and he always brought her roses, almost every week.''

"She calls to your husband; her father,'' said George. "She sends her love to him. 'Tell Daddy you've heard from me. I didn't forget him.'

"She says she's closer to you than you could imagine. The others send their love, too. So all the three children are together.''

After the two sat silently for a moment, George continued, "She [Elizabeth] says something about one of your children, like one has a health problem.''

"Yes."

"It's one of your daughters."

"Yes."

"I don't think I'm telling you something you don't know; it's fairly serious."

"Yes."

"Well, it seems she's aware of it from [the other side]. It affects her blood."

"Yes."

"Elizabeth is especially close to this sister who's ill. . . . And she says don't feel like you were singled out or that God punished you. It doesn't work that way. She knows you pray for her. That's helped her to move on; to progress on the other side."

"Oh, yes. We've always prayed for her," Anne said. "George," she asked, "will we see her again? Will we be reunited?"

"Oh, definitely. Of course you will."

"It seems so senseless that she died so soon."

"There's a purpose for everything. Even when it's for such a short time. No matter how briefly your daughter was here [on earth], there was a purpose to her life. Even if it isn't always clear to us."

Lauren and Jim Bellamy were living the American Dream, eighties style.* They were a two-career couple with a beautiful home in a New York suburb, a comfortable lifestyle, and their second baby on the way. Jim's computer-software business was a great success, making it possible for twenty-seven-year-old Lauren, a legal secretary, to take a six-month leave of absence after the baby was born. She looked forward to spending those months pampering the new arrival and their four-year-old son, Michael.

When little Melissa was born on November 10, 1990,

---

*At the request of the subjects, all names and other biographical details and facts pertaining to their case have been altered to protect their identities. Everything else in this story, however, is true.

Lauren and Jim felt blessed. With her large, dark eyes and light ivory complexion, Melissa glowed with love and happiness. As the early weeks passed, Melissa, though petite like her mother, grew bigger and stronger. She delighted everyone with her smiles, coos, and accomplishments, like sitting up. At each of the baby's regular medical checkups, her pediatrician assured Lauren of her daughter's good health.

Lauren's only question for Melissa's doctor was one he had heard a million times: "When will the baby sleep through the night?" It wasn't that Lauren minded waking once, or twice, even three times a night at Melissa's cry. She, like so many mothers, secretly welcomed those invitations to cuddle and hold her baby in the quiet of night. But the end of Lauren's leave of absence was nearing, and she knew that if Melissa didn't learn to sleep through the night, both she and Jim would be exhausted. The closest thing to an assurance her pediatrician could offer Lauren was, "She'll sleep through the night—eventually."

One Thursday evening in late March Lauren kissed Melissa and put her in her crib. It was about eight o'clock. By ten-thirty Lauren and Jim had crawled into their own bed, and Lauren drifted off to sleep half-listening, as mothers always do, for her baby's cry.

Lauren woke up—much to her surprise—to find the sun shining. What a pleasure, she thought to herself, to finally get a full night's sleep. While Jim dressed for work, Lauren quietly peeked in on Melissa, whose nursery adjoined her parents' master bedroom suite. She's still sleeping, Lauren thought, as she gazed at Melissa, bundled in her soft blankets. She closed the door.

Downstairs Lauren said goodbye to Jim, prepared Michael's breakfast, and while he ate, returned to awaken Melissa. The first thing she noticed upon entering the silent room was that the covers were still over the baby. As she gently pulled the blankets back from Melissa's face, she noticed that one of her eyes was open, unblinking. Still not comprehending that anything was amiss, Lauren carefully turned over the baby, only to discover that she was blue.

In mere seconds Lauren's life was violently wrenched into a parent's worst nightmare. Though she wouldn't know it until later, Melissa was a victim of SIDS, or sudden infant death syndrome, the baffling, silent killer of children under one year of age.

Lauren froze as the terrible realization took hold, then burst from the room screaming. Despite her shock, she had the wherewithal to call 911, then grab Michael and run next door, shouting for help. Her neighbors, a retired firefighter and his wife, raced across the lawn to Lauren's house and immediately began administering cardiopulmonary resuscitation to the baby. Within moments paramedics arrived and took over the rescue effort, while neighbors gathered around. Several tried to console Lauren, who was sobbing uncontrollably. She had called Jim's office, but he'd gone out. His sister Tricia, who lived nearby, had arrived. Still, Lauren felt alone.

As if in a dream, she watched as the paramedics placed Melissa in the ambulance. A short time later she was pronounced dead on arrival at a local hospital. The police asked her several questions as part of their mandatory on-the-scene investigation, which Lauren answered. In the meantime Jim had rushed home, but amid the confusion Lauren was losing all sense of time or place. How could Melissa, a healthy baby, safe in her own home, in her own little crib mere feet from her parents, just die like that? It just couldn't be true.

But it was. About five hours later Jim and Lauren found themselves at the hospital, standing in an examining room where Melissa's tiny, lifeless body lay on a metal table. All Lauren could think was how small and helpless her daughter looked lying there.

It seemed so bizarre that in the midst of such a tragedy, the official work of death continued. First a doctor asked them if Melissa had been sick recently? No, Lauren answered woodenly. Ever? Did either of them notice anything unusual prior to finding her? Did they hear her cry out? No. No. No.

The only comfort came from their family priest, who

joined them at the hospital. Lauren, a Roman Catholic, expressed her concern that Melissa had not yet been baptized, to which the priest replied, "Yes, she is. In God's eyes, Melissa is baptized now." Lauren took great comfort in the priest's words and, as she says today, even in her deepest grief, "I never doubted for a minute that Melissa was with God."

While SIDS was the suspected cause of death, without an autopsy there would be no way of knowing for certain what killed Baby Melissa. Nonetheless, a nurse gave Lauren the telephone number of the local chapter of a SIDS organization. Jim and Lauren agreed to the autopsy. It merely confirmed the doctor's initial diagnosis. Lauren soon contacted the SIDS group, which put her in touch with a parent contact and a home nurse, who counseled and assisted with Michael.

Neither Lauren nor Jim knew of anyone who had lost a child to SIDS. Although she vaguely recalled hearing of "crib death," as the syndrome is more commonly known, she'd never even heard the term SIDS. In the weeks that followed she listened carefully to doctors and other experts; she read everything she could find about SIDS. But no amount of medical information or reassurance could quell her obsessive guilt over two points. The first, as irrational as it might seem, was the terrible feeling that because she had so wanted Melissa to begin sleeping through the night, she had somehow tempted fate. The second thought was that Melissa had suffocated under the covers.

As the doctor took pains to explain, and as Lauren learned later, SIDS is a mysterious and largely unexplained occurrence that kills an estimated 6,000 to 7,000 babies between the ages of one month and one year. It is the leading cause of death for children under a year. We know that SIDS has stalked children throughout history, and while medicine has made tremendous strides in reducing infant mortality from almost all other causes, SIDS persists. Though countless theories on the causes of SIDS have been offered up, virtually all that is known about SIDS comes in the form of statistical patterns.

We do know, for example, that babies who are born premature, of low birth weight, into poverty, or to mothers who smoke cigarettes, drink alcohol, take illegal drugs, and/ or fail to receive adequate prenatal care while pregnant are at greater risk for SIDS. We also know that SIDS exacts a greater toll among black and Native American babies than among white and Asian babies. A baby who has experienced a previous life-threatening episode during which he stopped breathing is also at higher risk. As experts are quick to point out to alarmed parents, even a so-called high-risk baby's chances of succumbing to SIDS are quite small, as low as 1 in 100. And for babies in general, the chances are about 2 in 1,000.

Given the plethora of mysteries surrounding a baby's death from SIDS, it's no wonder that parents very often torment themselves with questions and guilt. The authors of *Sudden Infant Death: Enduring the Loss* studied nearly four hundred family members of children who died of SIDS. They found that while about 40 percent of parents accepted SIDS as the cause of their baby's death, 60 percent felt they could identify another cause; for example, the child "forgetting to breathe," having a cold, or being chosen by God to die. Others grasp at such possible causes as lack of iron in the baby's formula, air pollution, or a pet cat sucking the baby's breath away. While these parents' responses reflect their care and concern for their child, they also hint at our inability to accept the unacceptable and our insistence that there must be a reason, an explanation, for such a loss.

When a baby dies of SIDS, parents are often overwhelmed by guilt and self-recrimination. In Lauren's case, the blankets wrapped around Melissa became the focus of her thoughts. What could I have done differently? Lauren wondered dozens of times a day. What should I have noticed? What did I miss?

"I kept asking myself, Did Melissa suffocate in the blanket?" she reflected. "I knew intellectually that she had not, but it was another thing emotionally.

"I can remember those first nights after Melissa died. I

was just crying myself to sleep thinking about how I wanted to die. Not because I was suicidal, but because a baby needs her mother. And where is my baby? Who is taking care of her? As much as you may wonder these things if, for example, a parent dies, this is different: This is a helpless child. I had always believed in the afterlife, but I had all these questions.

"We had a funeral for Melissa just as we would have if an older child or loved one had passed on," she continued. "One thing that was very important to Jim and me was that we wanted a full funeral. I think our parish priest was a bit surprised at first. I don't recall there ever being a SIDS death in our parish. With other kinds of early infant deaths—stillbirths, premature babies, for example—they have always had very quiet and small ceremonies with just the immediate family. We had more than a hundred family and friends attend. It was comforting to be surrounded by so many people who cared about us."

Within a few days of her baby's death, Lauren was struck by a premonition that her baby was in the hereafter with a close friend from childhood named Robin. Bobbi, as her friends and family called her, had died in an automobile accident two years before at age twenty-six, leaving behind a husband and a two-year-old son.

"I remember even at Melissa's funeral, I remarked to Robin's husband, Mark, that I just knew Melissa was with Robin," said Lauren. "The thought of that comforted me."

Lauren moved through the next few months trying to cope with Melissa's loss. "The church was a real source of strength for us, but going to church after she died was hard. There wasn't a week that I wasn't just in tears in church. That's the way I was for months. I don't know what people thought of me. Melissa died in March, and when Easter came I could still barely stand up."

Like most couples, Lauren and Jim grieved for their daughter differently. "I tend to tune in," Lauren said. "I would read, I would talk. My husband Jim's reaction was more traditional, I think, more typical of many men. He would keep his feelings in. Jim would come home from work and watch TV; I couldn't.

"But Jim was very good about going with me to the support groups. At first he was a little reluctant, but I think he began to see the value of it. I've seen tremendous growth in him as a person. And, in a strange kind of way, I think our marriage has grown stronger."

They began attending meetings of a SIDS support group and the Compassionate Friends, where they met and shared with parents who had lost their children to SIDS and many other different causes.

"What I liked about the Compassionate Friends was that their focus was not on how the children died but on the grieving process. A couple of months after Melissa's passing, it became apparent to me that the grieving process was the more important thing than rehashing how she died.

"I think people are beginning to realize that grieving is not a two-week process," Lauren observed. "It seems there is less taboo about it today. I don't know how my mother's or grandmother's generations dealt with infant death.

"In fact, one of the hardest things for me was a comment from my grandmother, who is so dear to me. She had a premature child die many years ago. Her reaction was 'Well, you've just got to snap to and get over this.' That hurt me terribly in a way that a stranger's comments could not, because my grandmother, of all people, should understand. But I think that's what they were told years ago."

Her grandmother's words would not be the only well-meant but hurtful comments made to Lauren. "I would hear things like 'You couldn't have known this child as well because she died so young.' Probably the most insensitive comment I heard was 'It's only an infant, so get over it. You didn't know her.' I think it was the most hurtful thing, because the grieving process was no different than with any other type of passing."

At a SIDS support group Lauren met Jill, a young woman whose baby son had died of SIDS. The two became friends and shared their feelings. Jill read many books on death and near-death experiences, which she would pass on to Lauren. But where Jill found comfort in the books, Lauren closed each with more questions about Melissa than before. She had also entered a period of having what she described as "serious spiritual doubts."

"As much as I wanted terribly to believe in the hereafter—and I do—at the same time I just felt so disconnected from my daughter," Lauren explained. "Melissa's death shook my faith, in a way. I just couldn't imagine a hereafter in a way that would seem plausible to me. I mean, I'd lay in bed at night and think, How could it be? When I read Raymond Moody's books about near-death experiences, it was the first time I could understand the hereafter."

Still, Lauren had questions about Melissa. "I thought, as a mother, will my child remember me in the hereafter? Will she know me? Will she love me? What age will she be when I see her again? Will I know *her*? There isn't a day that goes by when I don't think about those things. I hope and pray she remembers me. I hope I recognize her."

One of Lauren's few comforts during this time was a dream. As she described it, "I was looking into Melissa's face, and she was looking into mine. When I woke up, it was almost with the sense that she wasn't talking but that she was communicating with me telepathically. Her message was that she was okay."

Among the books Jill gave Lauren was one about George Anderson. "After we read about George," Lauren recalled, "we knew we wanted to see him."

This excerpt from Lauren's reading, which occurred six months after Melissa's death, does not include the many other accurate names and details George gave that were not directly relevant to Melissa's death.

"A male close to you passed," George said to Lauren, a slender woman in her mid-twenties, dressed casually in a sweater and slacks.

"Yes," she acknowledged.

"He's older. He comes to you like a father," George said.

"Yes, my grandfather's passed."

"*Both* grandfathers passed."

"Yes."

"Because both embrace you," George continued.

"Okay." The woman nodded.

"But your dad is living."

"Yes."

"And so is your mom."

"Yes."

"Your grandfathers call out to them; your parents."

"Okay."

"But a grandmother *is* passed."

"Yes."

"And one's living. Because a grandfather calls to her here. She's way up in years."

"Yes, she's elderly."

"Well, the three grandparents who've passed call out to your parents here. It's your mother's mom who's still here, right?"

"Yes."

"That's what she says. Now, there's a young female who passed," George said.

"Yes," the young woman acknowledged.

"You lost a child."

"Yes."

"A girl."

"Yes."

"Like a toddler, or even less."

"Even younger. Yes."

"Well, she looks very small. She's an infant. She definitely passes very young."

"Yes."

"But you have another child."

"Yes."

"Because she calls to a brother. You have a son?"

"Yes."

"But your daughter passes tragically. She says she's an infant," George explained.

"Yes."

"She says you just find her . . . passed on."

"Yes."

"She passes on in infancy. Her heart just stopped. Like in crib death."

"Yes."

"Because they're telling me [from the other side] that is what it is; a traditional crib death. That's what they're calling it," George said softly.

"Is that what she—they—are saying?"

"Yes. They say for me to tell you, 'traditional crib death.' They use those exact words. She says you're worried that maybe you could have done something differently. You keep asking yourself, 'What did I do? What did I do?' "

"Yes."

"Well, you didn't do anything wrong. Her heart just stops."

"Is that what she says?" Lauren asked.

"That's what I'm hearing. Were you worried that maybe the baby suffocated in the crib?"

"Yes, I was," she answered.

"Well, she's telling me for you to put yourself at peace. You did nothing wrong. 'I didn't suffocate. I didn't smother.' That's what I'm hearing."

"She said that?" Lauren asked, wondering how Melissa could possibly speak.

"Well, it's more like I *feel* what she's saying than the actual words," George explained. "But again, it was nothing anyone could have prevented. There is no way you could have known in advance. They emphasize: It was a traditional crib death.

"Do you take the name Robin?"

"Yes! Yes!"

"She comes in *like* she's a sister."

"No, she's not my sister."

"Well, she comes in *like* a sister or a very close friend."

"Yes. We were very close."

"She still is. She says she passes tragically, both age and circumstances. She passes accidentally."

"Yes," Lauren acknowledged.

"She shows me a vehicle. She passes in a vehicle accident."

"Yes, it was a car crash."

"But she's a young adult. Less than thirty."

"Yes, she was about twenty-six."

"She passes before your daughter."

"Yes."

"Because she says, 'I was there to meet the baby,' " George explained. "That's what she tells me: 'I crossed the baby over.' "

Although Lauren wasn't entirely surprised by George's words, she felt a chill. He had just confirmed her premonition that Melissa was with Robin.

"George, can I ask you a question?" she asked.

"Well, just so long as you don't feed me any information."

"Who told you that my daughter's death was traditional crib death?"

"Your grandmother who passed on. She said it to me. Do you take the name Eva?"

"No."

"Are you sure? Eva?"

"I don't know anyone by that name."

"That's not your grandmother?"

"No, my grandmother's name was—"

"No! No! Don't tell me," George interrupted. "If it's going to come through, let it without telling me."

"Oh, okay. I'm sorry."

"But it sounds like *Eva* comes through." George paused briefly, listening to the communication from the other side. A moment later he said, "Oh, I get it. She's saying she's your *great*-grandmother."

"Oh, I don't know, George. My mother's grandmother, you mean?"

"Yes."

"I don't know her name. I never knew her. She died before I was born."

"Well, she says, 'I'm Great-grandma Eva.' Maybe you can check later and find out."

"Okay, I will."

"Who's Bobby?"

"I don't know."

"Bobby says, 'I'm with the baby.' "

"Bobby? I'm not sure, George."

"That's funny. It sounds like it could be your friend Robin, who came in just before."

"Oh, my God!" Lauren exclaimed. "Yes! Yes! I forgot. Of course. Bobbi is Robin's nickname! I'd forgotten that we used to call her that when we were growing up. We always called Robin Bobbi for short."

"Oh," said George. "Because I was going to say it sounds like your friend Robin kept saying, 'It's Bobby.' At first I thought it was a man she was referring to. But then she said, 'No, no, *I'm* Bobbi.' So Robin must be Bobbi."

"Yes, yes."

"Are you sure you don't know Eva? Eva is back again."

"I'm sorry, George, I don't know."

"Okay, I'll let it go for now. But Eva says she's looking out for *her* daughter. So that would be your grandmother. She's with her, she says, and Eva is waiting, she says, for when your grandmother crosses over. She'll be there to meet her."

"All right. I'll have to check on the name with my mother."

"Who's Jack? Do you take the name Jack?"

"Yes."

"A father figure. Something like that."

"Well, yes. My father-in-law."

"He's passed."

"Yes."

"Because he calls out to family on earth."

"Does he say anything else?"

"He just says to remember him. He's kind of quiet. He doesn't seem to talk much. But he definitely sends his love."

"Yes, he was quiet. He didn't have much to say when he was alive. He was a very quiet man."

"He still *is* alive," George emphasized, "only in the next stage."

Laura nodded.

"He passes from a condition in the chest. A heart attack. That's what it feels like."

"Yes."

"Your daughter—your baby—you've had dreams about her. She's come to you in dreams. This [the reading] is not the first time you've heard from her."

"Yes. Once, at least. I can only remember one time. She came to me in a dream once clearly."

This portion of the reading, Lauren felt, confirmed the vivid dream she'd had of Melissa in which she clearly saw the baby's face.

"Does my friend Robin—Bobbi—say anything else?" she asked.

"She says, 'I welcomed her over. I met the baby when she came over.' And she says also to stop putting yourself on a guilt trip. You didn't do anything wrong. It was a crib death. You *couldn't* have prevented it. Robin, or Bobbi, is saying to you what your grandmother and Great-grandmother Eva said before.

"Robin also says she's taking good care of your daughter. 'Don't worry. That baby's in good hands. She's fine now. All the relatives are with her, too. She's definitely not alone.' "

"Oh, good! I'm so glad."

"Who's Mack?" George asked.

"I don't know."

"Mack . . . or wait . . . *Mark*. That's what I'm hearing. Who's Mark?"

"Mark. Yes! That's Robin's husband."

"That's what I thought. Because Robin was calling out, 'How's Mark? Send my love to Mark.' Let him know you've heard from her if he can accept this. At first I thought I heard 'Mack.' But then I realized it was 'Mark.' "

"I'll tell him. I'll tell Mark."

"Do you take the name Frances?"

"Yes."

"A woman?"

"Yes."

"A mother figure. A grandmother."

"Yes. My father's mother."

"Well, she's with your baby, also. So she's definitely not alone."

"Oh, good. I'm glad."

"Well, she and Robin and the others, they all want you to go on with your life. Do you take the name James? Jim or Jimmy?"

"Yes. That's my husband."

"Well, one chapter of your life has ended and another begins. Your daughter says she knows you'll always love her and you'll never forget her. She says you want to have another child. But her death was a terrible letdown. It frightened you badly. It's shaken you."

"Yes," Lauren admitted.

"It left you afraid to have more children. But you needn't be, she says. You must go on with your life, just as she must with hers. She says, they say, a new baby will be fine. You need not worry.

"I think they're getting ready to go back now," said George. "Your friend says, 'Don't worry. The baby is in good hands.' The grandparents, the others, too. They all say to remember to pray for them. And there's definitely another birth in your future. Don't be afraid. She [Melissa] thanks you. Although she was a baby, she knows how much you love her. Your daughter is fine and at peace. And definitely *not* alone. She'll be there someday a long time from now to meet you. She'll be waiting. She won't forget you're her mother. Until then, go on with your life. She sends her love to Jimmy, her father. 'Tell Daddy I love him.' They all send their love. And with that, they all step aside. They go back."

Lauren's mother later confirmed for her that Eva was indeed her great-grandmother, just as George had indicated. It also eased Lauren's mind to hear from Melissa herself that she had passed from a "traditional crib death." Finally Lauren could accept that there was nothing she might have done to change the outcome.

Shortly after her reading with George, Lauren reflected, "I don't know that I'll ever be over Melissa's passing. I certainly don't feel I'm anywhere near being over it. But knowing that inevitably I'll be together with Melissa again is a help.

"One part that I admit I still haven't come completely to terms with is acceptance," Lauren continued. "I don't think I really know what acceptance means. I can't accept. I can't help it. I feel like every family photograph we take now is incomplete. I just see Melissa there—and, of course, she's not. There was no chance to say goodbye."

For Lauren, Jim, and little Michael, Melissa will never be forgotten. But like so many other families, they have found healing in the passage of time. A little more than a year after George's reading for Lauren, she and Jimmy became parents of a baby girl. Although for the first several months the baby was placed on a fetal heart monitor as a precaution, she suffered no health problems and is growing up happy and content.

Like Lauren and Jim, most parents who have experienced the loss of a young child must decide whether or not to have another. For these parents, pregnancy, birth, and child-rearing have lost some of their happy associations. Events once eagerly anticipated are viewed with quiet dread. It is often only with great difficulty that parents learn to quell their fears and not be obsessed with wondering, Will it happen again to us?

As one young mother recalled, "After our miscarriage, I knew we were going to try to have children again. But I also knew that I would never experience that same pure, blind happiness about being pregnant again. It was impossible not to be somewhat afraid."

George has learned through many readings that no one better understands a bereaved parent's reluctance to have another child than the child who has crossed over. The following is excerpted from a reading for a young couple who lost one baby to miscarriage and another to a health problem.* The son who passed as a baby assures them that his time had come and encourages them to have more children. For parents who may subconsciously fear that they will somehow "betray" their deceased child by having others, the decision to go forward is often filled with conflicting emotions. In these cases, the deceased child's blessing comes as a great comfort and relief.

"You lost a child," George said to the young couple sitting across from him.

"Yes," the woman answered. She was thin with blond hair. Her husband sat quietly. He was of average height, dark-haired, and wore glasses. They both appeared to be in their late twenties.

"But did you also lose one [a child] that was a miscarriage?"

"Yes," the young woman acknowledged.

"Because if the cycle of the birth had continued, it would have been a boy. But there's also the loss of a child who is born and was growing up."

"Yes."

"It's also a boy. It's your son who passes."

"Yes."

"You have other children living?"

"No."

"Oh, wait, I understand," said George. "You *want* to have other children."

"Yes!"

"Your son says you're afraid after losing two children already."

"Yes." At this her husband nodded in agreement.

"Now, I'm not endorsing religion," George cautioned. "I don't even know if you're Catholic. But pray with Saint

---

*The names and other biographical details and facts pertaining to this case have been altered. Everything else in this story, however, is true.

Philomena for thirteen days. It's like a protection. Because they [the other side] tell me you have difficulty in child-bearing.''

"Yes."

"And you have a fear of going through it again. It's like you want another child, but after what you've been through, you're afraid to go through it all over again."

"Yes, exactly."

"Well, you should not have any fear about childbirth. Your son says, 'Mommy, don't be afraid.' He says to me that children are life renewing itself. Your son passes as a child."

"Yes."

"He's definitely a youngster."

"Yes."

"He had a health problem. That's what he passes from."

"Yes."

"I feel a lurching in my chest. There's pain there. He passes from a condition in the chest."

"Yes."

"But it's not the heart."

"No, it's not," the husband answered for the first time.

"His lungs fill up. There's a problem in the lungs. It's as if I'm not getting enough oxygen. There's tightening around the heart," George continued.

"Yes," the young woman replied.

"Well, he tells me he's fine now. He's okay and at peace."

"Oh, good."

"He says his grandfather is with him. I think he means your dad," George said, pointing to the man.

"Yes," he answered.

"He's young, but he's mature for his age."

"Yes," the woman confirmed.

"He's precocious."

"Yes."

"And hyper! He's a bundle of energy. He doesn't stand still long."

"Right!"

"He says he knew he was going to pass on."

"We don't know," the man replied.

"Well, that's what he says. He knew somehow—maybe in the back of his mind—that he wasn't going to be here for a long time. In any event," George added, "he's a happy child."

"Yes," the woman responded.

"You'd certainly never know he was sick."

"That's right. You wouldn't know."

"He's an old soul. It's funny. You know, he's a child, but he's independent."

"Yes."

"I'm seeing FDR. It's my psychic symbol that you have nothing to fear but fear itself. So your son says again, 'Mommy, don't be afraid to have another child.' Don't fear childbirth, in other words."

The couple did not answer.

"It feels like my lungs and chest are filling up. It feels like I'm drowning. So his lungs and chest were affected," George said.

"Yes," the man confirmed.

"I see Saint Joseph, symbol of a happy death. He falls asleep. He just drifts off."

"Yes," the woman answered.

"He says we're near the anniversary of his passing."

"Yes, it just passed."

"He says he knows what a tough day it was for you both to get through," George said softly.

"Yes," the woman said.

"He shows me the number ten. He's less than that, though. Now he says to drop in age. He's very young."

"Yes, he was a baby when he passed," his mother explained.

"Well, I see another child in the future. There's another birth. It's a girl, although I wouldn't stake my life on it. Your son says that one chapter of your life has ended and another begins, although he knows that you will always love him and that you'll never forget him."

"Yes."

"He keeps dropping me in age. He's showing me that he wasn't even a year old when he passed."

"Yes, that's right."

"He asks that you always remember to pray for him and know that he is near. He's closer to you than you can imagine," he continued. "And, again, he says he's totally fine now. It was the physical body that was ill, not the spiritual body. And he says that someday you'll all be reunited—when the time comes. And he says again to try to have a family.

"Do you take the name Joseph?"

"Yes. It's his great-grandfather," the woman answered.

"Because he's with him on the other side, along with the others," George explained.

"Oh, okay."

"But the emphasis is on you having more children. He wants you to try to have a family. He says that way he'll have brothers and sisters here, too!"

"Okay," the woman said.

"He says remember to pray for him. And know that he is all right and at peace. And, I don't mean to sound like a fortune-teller, but he definitely says there's a birth in your future. But don't be afraid! It's the fear that's holding you back. But you must overcome that, he says. Go on and have a family.

"He thanks you. Although he was a baby, he knows you love him and always will. And he feels the same way. 'Until we meet again,' he says, and he and the others go back."

3

No Matter How Careful

For the child who has passed toddlerhood, the world is an exciting place to explore. We try as parents to shelter them from danger, reminding them to look before crossing the street, admonishing them not to speak to strangers, and so on. Gradually, however, a child needs to test his wings. During the preschool years children begin to move, step by step, out of the nest. They play outside or at other children's homes. Alone they venture to the end of the block or to a neighbor's house. They endure and survive a number of scrapes and falls, the gamut of contagious childhood illnesses, the occasional misadventure. We kiss the skinned knee, wipe the fevered brow, and reassure them—and ourselves—"This is all part of growing up."

These three stories involve children who, in the course of otherwise normal, uneventful lives, die suddenly. Although the circumstances of each passing are unique, all three children pass, or in one case fall violently ill, at or near home.

In none of these cases was there abuse or neglect; none fell prey to a stranger. In another odd coincidence, all three were in the care of their mothers. Two of them opted to stay at home and raise their children because they believed no one else could care for them as well. But as each parent attests, there are some things you simply cannot protect your children from, no matter how vigilant you may be.

For these parents especially, their child's death left them burdened by guilt and feelings of inadequacy. Every one believed there must have been something he or she should or could have done to bend the tragic course of fate. In each reading, however, George relays from the children perhaps the most painful message any parent can hear: "It was my time to go."

While parents may feel relieved of guilt when their child sends this message from the other side, the idea that a child's time here was limited raises other potentially troubling questions. What of fate? What of free will? If a child was meant to be here for only a short time anyway, was the fatal accident really an accident? Was there a meaning or purpose behind the chain of events that led to the passing? At what point is life simply beyond our control? Are all the precautions we take on our child's behalf in vain?

"These are important but unanswerable questions," George said. "Each situation or case is different. In most instances when a child passes, it is his or her time to pass. Sometimes, however, there are truly accidents: 'wrong place, wrong time.' The other side has said that accidents *do* happen.

"The important thing is that everything has purpose and meaning, even if we can't comprehend or understand it. Even the briefest time on earth has a purpose.

"Of course," he went on, "as a parent you just take precautions. We do have free will. It's not in vain to do that. It's being realistic. Why tempt fate? But when tragedy happens despite your having done your best, it's out of your hands."

Perhaps, like so many things about the other side, these are questions that have no answers; or they have answers we are not meant to comprehend.

The June heat hung over the Philadelphia area even as evening crept up and darkened the sky. Tim O'Connor ran frantically through the dense woods behind his home calling out to his five-year-old daughter.*

"Maureen! Maureen! Help! Maureen! Are you here?"

He paused for a moment, praying for her answer, but as the clouds merged and the woods fell dark, Tim had never felt so helpless in his life. It had been hours since his wife, Patricia, last saw their little girl. Now here he was, standing in the middle of—where? For a few moments he felt utterly lost and disoriented. It all seemed so unreal. Then the clouds parted and, catching a glimpse of the setting sun, Tim regained his bearings and continued.

Where could she be? She was so good, so obedient, so content in her little world with its clearly set boundaries and rules. She wouldn't have just wandered off on her own. But if not that, then, what? Tim couldn't stop to think. He just had to find her.

In front of the O'Connors' colonial-style house friends and neighbors had gathered, some taking off in different directions to join the search. An ambulance parked at the house reminded Tim and Patricia of what could happen. Tim had already spent hours crisscrossing the neighborhood in the family station wagon, going everywhere little Maureen could have gone. Where was she?

At about ten that evening Tim and his father, James, were standing near Tim's car. Emotionally and physically exhausted, the two were catching their breaths and getting ready to continue when James asked his son, "Did you think to check for Maureen in the station wagon?"

"What?" Tim asked, surprised. "Why would she be in there? You know we never let the kids play in the car. It never even entered my mind."

"I know, Tim," James replied calmly. "But she's only five. She's only a child. It was just a thought."

"No, Dad, you're right," Tim answered wearily.

---

*At the request of the subject, all names, and other biographical details and facts pertaining to their case have been altered to protect their identities. Everything else in this story, however, is true.

"There's nothing to lose. I'll take a look."

Tim opened a door on one side. Nothing. He walked around the station wagon and opened a door on that side. He leaned inside and pulled up the rear "third" seat. Lying there, crouched under it, lay Maureen. Tim's screams brought paramedics running to the car. As they lifted Maureen's limp body up from under the seat, Tim knew at once that she was dead.

Little Maureen O'Connor's seemingly untimely death was an accident of fate. For the O'Connors, strict but reasonable parents who were careful never to allow Maureen to stray farther than two houses away, there was painful irony in the fact that she died in her own driveway, in the family car. But as the O'Connors would learn later in their reading with George, if Maureen's death was an accident, it was an accident of circumstance only. As she would tell them later through George, it was her time to go. Through George she would indicate that her supposedly innocent heart murmur doctors had assured her parents she would outgrow may have been a factor in her death.

Maureen was a pretty, petite little girl, with large sparkling eyes, shoulder-length brown hair, and a freckled, turned-up nose. She was in many ways an ideal child: friendly, outgoing, loving, and obedient.

Most of the time Maureen played in the O'Connors' fenced-in yard or out in front of the house. Never, ever was she allowed to cross the street. Even though Maureen would be starting school that fall, Patricia and Tim, an elementary-school principal, felt she was not yet ready for that.

Two houses down from the O'Connors, on the same side of the street, lived Kelly, a twelve-year-old girl who regarded Maureen as her little sister. Earlier that day Maureen came in from playing outside alone and asked, "Mommy, can I call for Kelly? Can I go to Kelly's house, please? I want to play with her dog."

"Well, all right," Patricia replied. "But you know you can't go any farther."

"I know, Mommy."

"Be careful, Maureen."

"Okay, I will," the little girl answered, jumping up and down.

"I love you, sweetheart," Patricia called as Maureen ran out of the house. She then gave Baby Robby his lunch before taking him to play with his friends next door. Patricia continued through her usual routine, stopping to talk briefly with a neighbor over the backyard fence. The next thing she knew it was one o'clock, about an hour since Maureen went to Kelly's. She should have been back by now, Patricia thought to herself. Maybe she lost track of time.

Patricia found no one home at Kelly's, and assuming the girls had gone for a short walk, she began to search the neighborhood. After finding no trace of either girl after an hour, she began knocking on doors, but no one had seen Maureen.

Despite everything, Patricia still was not really worried. There had been no significant crime in the neighborhood. One neighbor she asked did recall seeing Maureen standing in front of the family station wagon parked in the O'Connors' driveway. Maureen had smiled and waved to him. That's all he could recall.

By the time Tim arrived home later that afternoon, however, Patricia was panicked. They called the police, who responded immediately with tracking dogs. As word of Maureen's presumed disappearance spread, hundreds of neighbors, family, and friends joined in the search. Later that evening, when Tim discovered Maureen in the car, the search ended.

How had Maureen come to get in the car in the first place? How had a child so responsible under the care of a vigilant mother come to die in front of her own home? These were questions that tormented the O'Connors. Quickly several pieces of the puzzle fell into place. They learned that when Maureen got to Kelly's house, she found no one home; Kelly and her mother were out shopping. Presumably, Maureen returned home, but finding her mother gone, waited outside. Apparently that's when the neighbor spotted her standing by the station wagon.

But then what? Why had she decided to climb inside the unlocked car? How did she become trapped under the extra fold-down seat in back? Did she panic? Did she cry for help? Or did she just fall asleep? It was a very hot day, so the car's interior was surely well over 100 degrees. But why did no one see her?

"Who knows what thought was going through Maureen's head or what possessed her to get in the car," Patricia said. "In fact, we had a rule: The children were not allowed to play in the car. Our big fear was that the emergency brake could accidentally be released. We never dreamed that just being in the car would be a hazard!"

The only comfort the O'Connors could claim in those early days was that regardless of the exact circumstances of Maureen's death, she probably did not suffer before she died. But the couple agonized over the fact that they had walked past the car, inches from their daughter's body, dozens of times during the search and never once thought to look inside. Tim is still haunted by the memory of driving around the neighborhood with Maureen lying dead behind him.

"Every time I get into a car that's hot, all I do is think about her," he said recently.

"I had a lot of guilt," Patricia added, "because I was the one watching her. I always wanted to stay home with my children because I felt nobody could watch them better than I could. Maureen's death made me feel inadequate as a mother."

"I never asked why this happened," Tim recalled. "I didn't see the point in that. My daughter was dead. She was no longer with us. I didn't ask, 'Why us?' I said, 'Why not us?' What makes me so special that something like this shouldn't happen? I didn't ask those questions because I knew I'd never find an answer. And I didn't want to get bogged down in that, because I was weighted down enough dealing with my finding Maureen in the car."

Several months after Maureen died, Patricia dreamed that she saw her daughter. "Maureen didn't speak to me. She didn't look at me. She was lying on a bed, and in the dream I knew that she had died. So I thought that when I would go to touch her, she would feel cold. But she felt warm. I leaned my head close to her and she said—actually communicated to me telepathically—'Mommy, I'm going to visit you again in a month and a half.'

"When I woke up," Patricia continued, "I wrote down the details and the date of the dream, so I wouldn't forget them. It was April twenty-sixth."

The next day when Patricia told Tim about her dream, he became upset and replied, "Why did you tell me that? It either means you're going to dream about Maureen again in a month and a half or that *you're* going to die."

Patricia was determined to see George Anderson. Tim was somewhat more skeptical, but Patricia started calling for an appointment in April. Their appointment was set: for six weeks to the day after Patricia's dream. Patricia entered George's home with one question uppermost in her mind: Had it been Maureen's time to go?

"There's a male close to you passed over," George said to the young couple seated before him.

"Yes," Patricia answered.

"One is younger. One's older. There are two. There's also a female."

"Yes."

"[She's] young. A young female."

"Yes."

"She's close to both of you."

"Yes."

"Because she has her arms around the two of you. I take it that you're husband and wife."

"Yes."

"Because as she stands between you, she links you as a married couple. Now she says that she is the daughter that passed on. Your daughter?"

"Yes."

"She keeps saying, 'I'm the daughter.' So I assume she meant you [both]. You have other children?"

"Yes."

"Because she kept saying, 'I'm their daughter.' Then she said, 'I'm the sister.' So obviously there are other children—or another child—because she keeps talking about sibling or siblings. This daughter [was] very close with you."

"Yes."

"She passes on very young. Because she seems to be a child when she passes. She's less than thirteen."

"Oh, yes."

"She tells me she's a little girl."

"Yes."

"Is she your baby?"

"No."

"Well, wait a minute. Is she the only girl or something? I don't know what she means. She's singularizing herself. Well, we'll have to drop it. I don't know what she means."

"We also had a miscarriage," Tim offered.

"Oh, I understand," George replied.

"She's not the miscarriage, if that means anything to you," he explained further.

"Did you lose a boy?"

"Yes," Patricia confirmed.

"Oh, you did. Now I know why I got a young male around you. Probably her brother. She's talking about her brother, and I'm thinking she's talking to him here [on earth]. But it could be her brother in the hereafter. Now, [your daughter] is less than eight years old when she passes. She keeps dropping me in age and she's getting younger and younger. I'm definitely talking to a little girl. Unquestionably, her passing is totally devastating, and she just wants to let you both know that she is all right. She passes on quietly."

"Yes."

"Because she says she goes to sleep. I see a vision of Saint Joseph, which means a happy death; she passes quietly in her sleep or a sleeplike state. Were you afraid you did something wrong?"

"Yes," Patricia said, weeping.

"Your daughter keeps saying you didn't do anything wrong. Why do you think you did something wrong? As a mother you probably feel you should have known something was wrong, like watching out for her. She says to stop tormenting yourself. She says you didn't do anything wrong."

Neither parent said anything, and George continued. "[Your daughter] passes in a sleep state."

"Yes," her mother said.

"Like a crib death or something. Because she just passes in a sleep state in her bed or crib. I don't know if it is or is not. Is it *actually* a crib death?"

"No," Tim replied.

"Okay. That's the feeling she gives me. So I guess she's trying to tell me that she goes in a sleep state. Did she have health trouble?"

"I'm not sure," Patricia answered.

"Well, if it was, was it undetected?"

"Yes."

"Because she gives me the feeling that there's health trouble that you didn't know about. You know, like heart trouble."

"Yes."

"Like her heart fails. She passes in her sleep."

"Yes."

"It feels like she's having a heart attack."

"I would say so," Tim said.

"That's what the feeling is. Like she passes in her sleep. It's as if she's having a heart attack or heart failure. Again, she keeps bringing up the fact that you torment yourself, thinking that you did something wrong. She says just because you're a mother doesn't make you infallible. She says you did *not* do anything wrong. 'You didn't fail me,' she says. So she says to please bring peace into your heart and mind, and start thinking that. It seems there was trouble with her heart, but you didn't know about it. She just went to sleep and never woke up again, technically. In this world, anyway.

"Your dad passed on?" George asked suddenly.

"Mine is alive," Tim answered.

"Mine isn't," his wife said.

"Your dad passed before [your daughter]. Because she claims that when she wakes [on the other side], your father wakes her up. She says when she passes in her sleep into the hereafter, your daddy comes to her. I don't know if she knew him or not, but it doesn't matter. She knows it's her grandfather, and she says that she's with him. He wants you to know he never abandoned you. He's very much with you emotionally, and your daughter is with him. He says he's taking good care of her."

Patricia nodded.

"How old is [your daughter]?"

"She was five," Tim said.

"And she's very tiny," Patricia added.

"That's probably why she keeps telling me that she's a little girl. She keeps dropping in age. She said eight. Then she said six, and she kept going down. Was she having breathing troubles?"

"Most likely," Tim said.

"She said there was a shortness of breath and there was concern for [her] heart. But it was undetected. You did not know it. As far as you knew, she was a young, healthy child. She knows you would much rather have her here physically than spiritually. But she says to look at it this way: You'd much rather have had her here for the five years than not at all. She has the essence of a little child, like a toddler, and yet she's very grown up. And she tells me that, as hard as it might be for you to understand, she was only supposed to be here for a short time. And that's why she just quietly lets go. . . . She's talking about a brother."

"Yes," Patricia responded.

"She says, 'Please tell him you've heard from me.' She says she's around him like a guardian angel. It's funny. It's almost like he talks about her once in a while. He might say something about her, or he knows she's there. She's also come to you in dreams. You've dreamed about her?"

"Yes."

"So she's trying to reach out to you to let you know that everything is all right. Because she sees from the afterlife what you are going through. . . . She comes to you in dreams to let you know that she is all right. She's not alone over there. She's not lost, or anything of that nature. Do you say the rosary for her?"

"Yes."

"Because she keeps thanking you for saying the rosary, and I saw white rosary beads go around the both of you. She says, 'Please continue to pray [the rosary]' for her. It is most definitely a powerful form of grace and certainly is helping her; not that she needs to be helped. But it's a tremendous gift to her in the hereafter. . . .

"Did you find her?" George asked.

"Yes."

"What happened? Had she complained of illness?"

"Accident."

George looked up, puzzled. "But why does she say she goes in her sleep?"

"We found her in the third seat of our car," Tim explained as his wife began crying again.

"I see," George replied. "No wonder. She keeps saying it's not your fault. Oh, of course, she loses her breath. *That's* why she tells me she's having trouble breathing. But she says her heart stops. Her heart fails. And I'm thinking she has heart trouble, from the way you answered me. Then she's telling me that she keeps losing her breath. [You said] she was in a car."

"Somehow she got in the rear of the station wagon."

"Oh! That's why it looks like she's asleep. Lying down. I'm thinking she's in her bed. She tells me she's asleep. She's lying down. Now she says she's in a vehicle. This happened during the day."

"Yes," Patricia replied.

"You feel you're to blame for it because you didn't know she was there. She keeps saying that's what you think. But she says it's not your fault. You're afraid she's mad at you and that she doesn't love you anymore because you think that you didn't protect her. She keeps saying,

'No, no, I love you. It's not your fault [Mommy].' "

"Yes," Tim remarked.

"That's why it looks like you're coming into her room and she's passed on. I see her going down like she's in a room and she's passed on. . . . Was she playing in the vehicle?"

"We think so," Patricia said.

"That's what she says she was doing. She tells me she was playing in the vehicle. Was it a very hot day?"

"Yes."

"Because it feels like it's pretty warm. Very humid. But as far as you were concerned, she was out playing."

"Yes."

"Exactly. And everything was all right. So she goes into the vehicle and somehow gets trapped."

"Yes," Tim said.

"Because she admits that she gets locked in, trapped, somehow, and then I start to feel like I lose my breath. But [as that happens], I get knocked unconscious from a lack of oxygen to the brain. Obviously the heart gives out. She's having heart failure. She might have been playing in the car. I think she might also have fallen asleep.

"Now I understand why she tells me she goes to sleep. I thought she went to bed that night and didn't wake up. . . . She's telling me the right thing, but I misunderstood it."

The couple simply listened.

"Do either of you take the name Mary, or Marie?"

"It's close," Patricia answered.

"Is it [your daughter's] name?"

"It's close."

"Don't tell me, but it sounds like she's saying Mary or Meri."

"Yes."

"All right. Let's just try. We'll get it [psychically]. She still talks like a child."

"The way my daughter pronounced her name is not the way she spells it," Tim explained after George continued having difficulty understanding the message from the other side.

"Oh, maybe that's what's confusing me," George remarked. "She keeps telling me. I can hear her saying it [her name]. But I can't understand it. She's kind of laughing at me, but I can't understand what it is, especially since she keeps telling me it begins with [the letter] *M*."

After a few more moments of struggling with the child's name, George finally said, "Maureen. That's it. I just realized she said it to me. Maureen is such a pretty name. Did she pronounce it differently?"

"Yes," her mother answered.

"I hear her saying her name differently, which is probably why it sounds like a nickname. It was almost like somebody was saying 'Marine.' "

"Yes! That's the way Maureen pronounced her name. She [called herself] Marine," Patricia explained.

"Exactly. *M-A-R-I-N-E*," George said. "Marine. That's probably why I thought I was hearing Meri. She's saying Marine. I'm hearing something with that inflection in it.

"Are you traveling?" he asked the couple.

"Yes," Patricia replied.

"Because she is wishing you a happy trip and telling you to go. It's like part of you is still holding back with your lives. You still have to go on. She just doesn't want you to think that if you go on with your life, you're leaving her behind. She's always with you spiritually. And, again, she wants to let you know, as her mother, she definitely loves you. . . . She wants you to leave here with peace, knowing it's not your fault. . . .

"She hands you both white roses. Yours for Father's Day, yours for a Mother's Day greeting. She's a very family-oriented child. You were really starting to get to know her. She has a very likable personality."

"Yes."

"Do you light candles for her, also?"

"Yes."

"Because she keeps thanking you for it. . . . Your grandmother passed on."

"Yes."

"Because a grandmother seems to be with [Maureen]. There are also other people around her. Grandparents are there with her. She keeps talking about the other brother that's there, had the cycle of the birth continued. Were you planning on having more children? Because [Maureen] shows me a vision of Saint Philomena, which means a happy birth. And she says you were considering having more children. She encourages it. You want to, and yet you're afraid. She says don't be. Children are life renewing itself. Go ahead. It's all right.

"You might feel a little funny because you feel it's like replacing her," George continued. "She says, 'No, no, no. You shouldn't think that way. If you want to have another child, have one.' She knows that she's herself in her own unique soul and always will be. She knows you'll always feel like that about her, so you don't have to worry about her thinking that you're replacing her. So she says to please go ahead and do what you wish. But I do see you with [another] child. Again, Saint Philomena is a sign of a happy birth. Are you thinking of moving or changing residence or something? Do you live out of New York state?"

"Yes."

"There's talk about you changing residence, and it may be for the better because you need a fresh start. And, again, don't feel like you're leaving her behind. Because she's always your child and part of you. She goes with you spiritually.

"There's a new start. A new beginning. There's the birth of a child in front of the two of you, which represents a new beginning. Do you work around children? Because I keep seeing children. Like in a school or classroom."

"Yes, I'm an educator," Tim answered.

"Do you have authority in your job? You're in a school, but you're in charge."

"Yes. I'm a school principal."

"The moving [mentioned earlier] comes in with your career."

"We haven't been able to decide whether to move or stay," he answered.

"Well, a thing like that has to be your decision."

"We know that."

"Your daughter says you have to decide if the [job] promotion offers a better opportunity in your career. You know. Your common sense tells you, you know what to do.

"Maureen says she works with animals in the hereafter. I mean little ones like fawns, puppies, and kittens. . . . It looks like if she stayed here, she might have been a veterinarian. She seems to be very attracted to animals. There are colors all around her, which is a sign of creativity. She might have been creative here on earth."

At this point George gave the couple a number of personal details about Tim's relationship to his own father. While accurate, they were not relevant to Maureen or her passing.

"Your daughter calls out to you personally, too," he told Tim, "because she knows you're brokenhearted within. She doesn't want you to think anything went wrong [on your part]. Don't feel, Did I fail as a father? Did I do something wrong? She says, 'Don't press yourself with guilt.' She says [her death] was an accident. It was no one's fault."

Tim nodded slightly.

"Did you also lose a pet?"

"Yes," Patricia said.

"A dog?"

"Not a—"

"Wait. Wait a minute. Did you lose a cat? Because your daughter says there's more than one. She talks about the pets being there with her. But I heard a cat—and I heard a dog, too."

"Yes. It's—"

"I thought maybe somebody else lost a dog that Maureen would have known."

"She does."

"She's very pet conscious, and she says the pets are there with her. She not only works with animals, but all the pets are there. Maureen looks upon the dog as her pet. The cat, also. The cat and the dog are being linked with her. When you lost the cat, it was almost like—''

"Yes, yes," Patricia answered, crying.

"—losing a link with her. So she says the cat is with her, and she's taking good care of it. The cat's back with her again. Definitely, when the cat passed on, it was like she's really gone. Because the cat was such a link with her. It was her pet. Is your anniversary coming up?"

"Yes."

"Because your daughter extends white roses to the two of you. She wishes you a happy anniversary. Are we approaching the time of her passing?"

"Yes." As Patricia and Tim explained to George afterward, they would be celebrating a wedding anniversary the following week. "Our anniversary is the twenty-eighth. Maureen died on the twenty-ninth—the day after."

"Because she's saying that she's going to be celebrating an anniversary in heaven. She says she will be extremely close to you on that day because you're going to be a basket case. Remember to pray for her. Don't remember only the unhappiness. Know that she's with you spiritually and that she's all right."

"Okay."

"With the exception of this tragedy, your lives are pretty normal. Like any family, your lives are up and down."

"Yes."

"You're a little overprotective of your other child. You can't protect him from everything in this world. Since you lost [Maureen], it's as if you have to know where your son is every second. Maureen says *don't* live your life in fear like that. Just know that children have to find their own way. She says, 'Don't ever feel that I'm not with you. And we'll all be together again someday.' She says what happened was an unfortunate accident."

George continued to give forth names of several relatives, along with their correct relationships and details about their personalities, all of which Tim and Patricia confirmed as correct.

"Can I ask you a question, George?" Patricia asked.

"Okay."

"Was it Maureen's time to leave us?"

"I have to say yes. Because from the beginning [of the reading] she claimed she was destined to have been here for a short time. But, yes, the circumstances are a sheer accident."

"Can I ask one more [question]?"

"I know," George answered, anticipating Patricia O'Connor's question. "It bothers you that you feel Maureen died alone."

"Yes," she said.

"Maureen keeps saying, 'Mommy, you feel I died alone. I didn't die alone. They were here for me.' She says that now she and the cat are together. She says, 'Someday we will all be together again. You'll see me again. But in the meantime, live out your lives peacefully.' Be at peace about her passing and the circumstances. Please stop tormenting yourself. Maureen wants you to continue to pray for her. Again, know she's all right. With that, they all sign off."

The reading concluded, George and the O'Connors spoke for several minutes. George explained the problem he had understanding how Maureen died.

"I kept seeing her psychically lying down, and I thought, in her room; in her bed. She showed me it was like crib death. It wasn't. But seeing that she died in her sleep, it looked like she was enclosed in a room. She told me she was having [something like] a heart attack. I psychically saw a door open, and I thought that you had gone into a room and found her."

"She did have heart trouble," Tim told George.

"She was supposed to have heart catheterization [a diagnostic procedure]," his wife added, thus explaining why George kept insisting that Maureen had heart trouble.

"So the lack of oxygen probably weakened her heart," George surmised.

Patricia then talked about wondering if Maureen's death was supposed to have happened. Was it her time to pass?

"I think we decide when we are here and for how long and when we go," George replied. "I don't think God has anything to do with it. I think it's all our decision and we're here for a purpose. Whether it's for a short time, five years, or a long time, like one hundred and five years. We let go when we're ready. Maureen came here for a short duration and went back to the hereafter."

"After the reading," Patricia recalled months later, "I can say that I feel at peace knowing Maureen really is okay."

It had been a big decision to uproot their three young children, sell their home, and move from New Jersey to Milford, Pennsylvania. But Ellen and Tony Baliotis knew they were doing the right thing. Even with Ellen staying home temporarily with Jack, three, Amy, six, and Nicholas, eight, they were getting by. At last, the Baliotises thought, we're moving ahead instead of just treading water.

Situated on a small knoll, the chalet-style home the Baliotises rented suited them perfectly. On the main floor were the kitchen, living room, two bedrooms, and a large screened-in porch. Up one flight of stairs was the loft where Nicholas and Jack slept in bunk beds, and across the hall, their bathroom.

On the evening of August 21 Ellen prepared dinner while the children romped through the house. As she did most evenings, she cooked some food in the microwave oven Tony gave her on May seventh, three years before, the day Jack was born. After dinner Ellen bathed the children, spent time playing with them, then tucked each into bed. Silently an unknown fire was slowly wending its way through the walls of the house. Oblivious of the tragedy about to befall her family, Ellen sat down on the couch to watch a little television and immediately fell asleep.

At around ten or ten-thirty Nick awoke to go to the bathroom. He climbed down from the top bunk and stepped quietly across the hall. The family's puppy was whimpering. Ellen always kept the bathroom door open a crack so that the children could see the nightlight inside. Typical of his age, eight-year-old Nick feared "monsters," so his parents made sure he was never left totally in the dark. Still half-asleep, the little boy opened the door a few inches, then felt himself being hurtled back with great force. He looked up to see the bathroom engulfed in flames and long, angry arms of fire grabbing for him. Nick screamed frantically as he ran downstairs, "Fire! Mommy! Fire!"

Ellen jumped from the couch in terror. Coughing and choking, she and Nick stumbled through the living room, now totally darkened by the acrid black smoke billowing down the staircase. Within seconds of Nick's screams, Amy awoke and ran to the door, as did the puppy. Looking back on the tragedy, the Baliotises now believe that the dog smelled the smoke first and his whimpering probably awoke Nick. Ellen instinctively grabbed Amy and Nick and ran onto the porch.

"Mommy, get Jack!" Amy cried. "Mommy, get Jack!"

Jack! Ellen thought. *Oh, my God!*

She dashed back into the house, fighting through the smoke and fumes but got only halfway up the stairs before she was forced back down. She ran to the porch, gulped a huge breath of air, and tried again to save her baby. This time she barely crossed the living room before flames beat her back. By then the house was an inferno. Ellen didn't notice, but she had suffered severe burns on her hands and face from the heat of the air. In fact, her hands blistered so badly, they looked as if she were wearing white plastic gloves.

But Jack was still upstairs, and Ellen had to save her baby. She got halfway up the stairs when she felt something physically blocking her way. Of course there was no one there. All Ellen knew was that she couldn't go any farther. Groping in the darkness, she phoned a neighbor.

"Rick, this is Ellen! My house is on fire! Call the fire department!"

She threw down the phone and ran to the porch, where Amy and Nick huddled. "Get into the car!" she yelled. As the little girl turned away, she screamed in panic, "Where are you going, Mommy?"

Ellen, by now numb with shock, replied, "I'm going back to get Jack!"

Ellen hadn't stepped more than a few feet into the house when she heard the ceiling begin to fall. She barely made it out of the house alive, and Jack, poor Baby Jack, was still upstairs.

Rick arrived within minutes. Unbeknown to Ellen, he was also a firefighter, and he quickly and calmly took control of the situation, telling Ellen to get the car out of the driveway to make room for the fire engines. Soon the still night was torn by glaring red lights and piercing sirens as four fire companies responded to the call.

Tony Baliotis didn't give it too much thought at first when he turned onto his street and found himself tailing a fire truck. Even the appearance of several fire trucks in front of his house struck no alarm until he glanced up at the hellish orange sky and then realized his house was in flames.

He leapt from the car and raced to an ambulance parked with its back doors open. Inside he saw Ellen and the children. He looked at each, silently counting, and for a moment felt relieved that they were safe. Then it hit him.

"Where's Jack?"

"I tried to get him out, but I couldn't!" Ellen screamed hysterically. "I tried! I couldn't! I tried!"

Tony ran to the house. Several firefighters had to restrain him from running inside. Even with their sophisticated protective gear and oxygen, the firemen were unable to enter the house, then burning at a temperature of over 3000 degrees.

It would take nearly another hour and half before the fire could be contained sufficiently for anyone to reach Jack. The firemen found him burned beyond recognition. They surmised the little boy had been dead from smoke inhalation for some time before the flames reached him. He lay in the same position he always slept: on his back, hands clasped behind his head.

Ellen would not learn of her baby's death then. She and the two children had been rushed to a hospital, where she was treated for burns to her hands and face. Despite her excruciating physical pain, the doctors released her that morning to go home to her parents. Throughout the ride there, Ellen, still hysterical and irrational, kept insisting to Tony that they go back home and get Jack.

"Somebody must have gotten him!" she cried over and over. "This can't be happening!"

Tony tried his best to calm his wife. "Ellen, don't worry," was all he could think to say. He saw there was no way that Ellen, in her state of mind, would comprehend the truth. At least not now. When the county coroner called later, Ellen could take no more shelter in denial. Baby Jack was dead.

Tony saw to the funeral arrangements, planning a memorial service at the family's Catholic church. Because Jack was so horribly burned, an open casket was out of the question. The family decided there would be no casket at all, since Ellen could not abide the thought of her baby "lying under that cold ground." Jack was cremated and his ashes placed in an urn and interred at a local cemetery. The family chose a place atop a hill overlooking a valley. Nearby stood a statue of the Virgin Mary with her arms outstretched.

Although the day of the graveside memorial service was dark and rainy, something unusual occurred that stuck in Tony's mind. As he, Ellen, and other mourners turned to walk back down the hill, he paused to look back at where Jack was laid to rest, under the Virgin's arms. The pouring rain gradually stopped, and the sun broke through the clouds to shine a perfect beam of light directly on the ground above Jack's remains.

In most instances when a child dies, his grieving family can at least return to their familiar home and some semblance of a normal routine. Not only were the Baliotises reeling from the loss of Jack, but they had no home or possessions. The pajamas Ellen, Amy, and Nicholas fled the house in, the suit Tony had worn to work that day, were all the clothes they had left. Their family pictures, mementos of Jack—everything with the exception of an heirloom family Bible—either burned or was ruined by water. Never believing such a tragedy might befall them, Ellen and Tony had not insured their belongings. After twelve years of marriage, they suddenly found themselves grieving the loss of their youngest child and starting over from scratch economically.

The stress of those early weeks overwhelmed them. But as Ellen recalled, "People were really there when we needed them." The community rallied, and the church spearheaded a drive to raise money for the family. Slowly, surely, the four began to piece together their lives. They lived for two months with Ellen's parents, then rented a furnished home.

Ellen and Tony both sought bereavement counseling and briefly attended a local bereaved parents' support group. Ellen tried very hard to take it one day at a time. Her goal each morning was to get through to night without thinking about the tragedy. But it was impossible: their new home, the missing possessions and photos, the sadness of her surviving children, the burn mark on her thigh.

"The scar bothers me," she admitted. "It's a reminder. Everything is a reminder. Things aren't the same. My son is not here.

"We were very happy. We're a close-knit family. My husband and I are very happily married. We're good parents, and they're good kids. I know many couples who've broken up after losing a child. Tony and I were close to begin with. We've become even closer. Our relationship is even stronger.

"But I have to admit there are times when I get in the car and ask myself, Do I put on my seatbelt or not? Because I really don't care if I die. Then I'll be with my son. Sounds sick? Other bereaved parents think these things, also. Because you're not so sick when you do, you're just human. There are days when I cry because I physically want to hold Jack."

"It's been a roller-coaster ride for us," Tony explained. "Ups and downs. There isn't a day that goes by when Ellen doesn't include the fire and Jack's death in our lives.

"I lost a brother when he was very young," Tony continued. "Back then we kind of did the exact opposite. It got hushed up and nobody talked about it. I think it's better this way; that we deal with the death by talking about it. But the tragedy of losing our son was devastating."

Despite understanding intellectually that there was nothing anyone could have done differently, Ellen was consumed with guilt. An open, honest woman, she said to her husband, "Tony, if that was you who was home, I don't know if I'd forgive you for not getting that child. 'What do you mean you couldn't jump in the flames?'" she asked rhetorically. "'That was your child up there!' How can you forgive me for not going up those stairs? If this was somebody else I was listening to, I'd ask, 'What do you mean you couldn't go any farther up the stairs?'"

"Ellen, I feel God was up there doing His work, and you were not invited to watch," Tony replied. He understood his wife's feelings, but he also felt that she had to get over this crushing, irrational guilt if she was ever going to heal. "It would have been too painful for you to see it. Besides, by the time you would have gotten to Jack, he was already gone."

But nothing Tony or anyone else said changed Ellen's attitude. In her mind, she had failed and deserved no forgiveness. "I feel guilty just being here!" she cried. "I wish I had gone back!"

At one point Ellen's depression became so severe she was hospitalized. "We tried everything," Tony recalled. "Eight different doctors, therapy. Our hospital bills were up to six thousand dollars a day. I didn't care. I just wanted Ellen back."

Even after the treatment, Ellen's bad days came more frequently than the good ones. The couple's decision to see George Anderson was what Tony honestly described as "an extremely desperate move."

"We'd exhausted all the avenues, and I was a big skeptic," Tony said. He also admitted being a little frightened, not so much of what George did or how he did it, but what, he wondered, would happen to Ellen if George couldn't help her?

Over a year and a half after the fire, Ellen and Tony left their new home in Stroudsburg, Pennsylvania, and drove to Long Island for their reading.

"I just want to hear that Jack is all right," Ellen repeated often during the drive. "That's all. Tell me he's all right."

"There's a strong fatherly presence with you. Did one of you lose your dad? Has your dad passed on?" George asked Tony.

"Yes," he answered.

"He passes kind of young by today's standards."

"Yes. Quite."

"Because he says he's been over there [on the other side] for a while."

"Yes."

"He says he could certainly show us around. Did you *not* know him?" George asked Ellen.

"Right," she answered.

"Because he's introducing himself to you."

"I did not know him," she said.

"Because he keeps coming up to you, saying, 'Hello. How do you do? I know who you are, but you don't know me. But you've heard about me.' "

"Does he like me?" she asked.

"Oh, yes," George replied. "He spoke another language."

"Yes," Tony acknowledged.

"Did he speak a little Italian?"

"No."

"Well, there's another language in the background. I apparently can't make it out. He just wants you to know that he's always been around you like a guardian angel."

"Okay."

"One of your grandmothers has passed on. Did your mom pass on?" George asked Ellen.

"No," she said.

"Okay, then it's not your mother. It seems to be more

of your grandmother. I just wanted to make sure I wasn't missing something. She's there. She calls out to you. Your parents are still living.''

''Yes.''

''*Your* mom is still living,'' George said to Tony.

''Yes.''

''She's also told to watch her health. Your father tells her that.''

''Okay.''

''Did you just move?''

''Yes. We just moved,'' Ellen said.

''Because he's [Tony's father] congratulating you on a change of residence or a move. You might move again, though. Because you're not there very long, he tells me.''

''Yes.''

''You've moved. But he says congratulations with not too much enthusiasm.''

''Yes.''

''I keep seeing Saint Philomena over your head, which is the sign of a happy birth. So there could be news of a birth up ahead. But did you lose a child?''

''Yes,'' he replied.

''Because your father keeps saying, 'The child is with me.' So I assume he means your child.''

''Yes,'' Ellen said as her tears began to fall.

''Wait a minute. Did you lose twice? Did you ever miscarry?''

''No.''

''My brother passed on,'' Tony offered.

''Because your father talks about two children [who have] passed on.''

''Yes.''

''Wait a minute. Now there's another one. Did you lose a girl? Was there a loss of a daughter in the family through a miscarriage, though, not born?''

''My cousin,'' the woman replied.

''Because he tells me a female has passed. Then there are two of the same sex, which obviously are the other males. Now, you said your brother has passed.''

"Yes."

"As a youngster—"

"Well, not—"

"—A young adult," George clarified. "That's the thing I'm getting at. He's still young, because your father keeps saying, 'The child is with me.' But his child is a grown-up. Your child is obviously his grandson. *Your* son passes quietly?"

"Yes," Tony said.

"Because—I'm not trying to sound crude—but I just find him passed on."

"Exactly. Yes."

"I find him dead. He just passes on quietly. Because again I see the vision of Saint Joseph, signifying a happy death. It's very peaceful, tranquil. Did you feel you let him down?"

"Yes," Ellen said, now racked with sobs.

"Because your son keeps saying—he tells me to tell you—that you didn't let him down. It happens, surprisingly. Because he says it's an accident."

"Yes," she replied, having regained her composure.

"It suddenly happens."

"Yes."

"Now, wait a minute. This could be a symbol. Was this a crib-type death, or does this mean he passed on as a very young child?"

"He was young but not in a crib," Tony explained.

"Oh, okay. That's what I'm looking for, because the crib could [psychically] symbolize someone very young. And it could be a double symbol. It could mean crib death."

"No, not crib death."

"He passes in his sleep."

"Yes."

"Because [your son] says he's asleep and he lets go. He passes in his sleep. His heart stops."

"It could have," Ellen answered.

"Because he told me in little-boy language that his heart stopped beating."

"Okay."

"I feel like I walk in and I find him dead. I walk in and it's just the way he is. But again, don't feel that you failed him, either of you. It's almost as if you think, if there was something wrong, shouldn't we have known as parents. Maybe he wasn't capable of telling you or explaining. What happened, happened. Your father, of course, passed before your son. Your father claims—even though they didn't know each other—he helped cross over your son and the other children who passed on, like your brother."

The couple listened attentively.

"Was your son having any trouble with his ears?"

"Yes. He had a lot of infections," Ellen answered.

"Because it seems there could be congestion in his system," George continued.

"His eardrum ruptured a couple of times," she explained.

"He tells me his ears are fine now, but while he was here on the earth, he had ear trouble. At that age, most kids do. But then he told me, 'No, it was more than that.' It's almost as if you feel that you got punished in a way. Slapped in the face. There is some major congestion in his system that caused his heart to stop. He gives me the impression that it just stops. He lets go."

Tony Baliotis sat stoically as his wife wept. At this, George remarked, "It's not that your husband's not upset, but he kind of suffers more inside. Your son says that, at times, you let your imagination run away with you. Put yourself at peace. You are driving yourself crazy about [your son's passing]. You *didn't* fail him. He says don't create little demons that don't exist. You've been having trouble sleeping."

"Yes," she replied.

"He's telling you to go home and have a good night's rest." Turning to Tony, George said, "Your dad and brother talk about meeting over [on the other side], so apparently the two of them are together. Your father calls out to your mother. He says, 'Tell her you've heard from me.' Is there a Max passed on?"

"I have a relative, Max. He's not passed on," Ellen answered.

"It's funny, because somebody called out to Max. I'll leave it with you, because either it's wrong or it's somebody you can't think of right now. . . . Does the name Nick mean anything to you?"

"That's my father," Tony said. He paused, then added, "It could be my son. That's my son's name."

"Because I'm hearing 'Nick,' and I see Saint Nicholas behind you. The son that's passed on was named Nick?"

"No. We have a son [living] named Nick," Ellen said.

"Then it is your dad. Your dad is calling me to tell me what his name is. Also, there's an Anthony."

"Yes, that's me," Tony said.

"Because I keep hearing your father calling out, 'Anthony.' He's saying it in the other [foreign] language. I can't pronounce it."

"It's funny that he would say that. He would call out to me that way."

"His language is heard in the Mediterranean [area]? He keeps telling me I'm in the right part of the world but in the wrong country. The only country left is Greece. Did he speak Greek?"

"Yes."

"Your father says 'Maria.' "

"Yes."

"She's living."

"Yes."

"Your father calls out to her. I keep seeing [psychic symbol] the opera star Maria Callas in back of you. I'm sure you're not related to her, and chances are, you're not an opera singer."

"It's my mother's name," Tony explained.

"Because he's calling out to Maria, to your mom. 'Tell her you've heard from me,' he says."

"Okay."

"Your mom is devout in her own way. Spiritual."

"Yes."

"She does pray for your dad."

"Sometimes."

"He acknowledges that. He just calls to her in love. He hands you white roses [a psychic symbol of a spiritual blessing]."

"Okay."

"You have two children on earth now."

"Yes."

"Because your son who passed on would be the third. He's in a shadow. But the thing is, I still see the possibility of [you having] one more child up ahead. I mean, it's your choice. Your decision."

"Yes."

"But the thing is, your son is bringing it up. But you're afraid. Don't be afraid."

"Yes, we are," Ellen admitted.

"That's why he keeps bringing it up. Again, Saint Philomena is over your head. It's the symbol of a happy birth. Because of your son's passing, you're afraid to. His death was one incident. The birth of another child would certainly be another incident. Always continue to pray for him and know that he's all right. It's as if that's all you have to hear. That he's all right. Somebody's looking out for him. He says he's all right."

"I agree," Ellen said.

"He says if you didn't hear anything else. He just heard me say that you loved your son. He says he's all right. Somebody's taking good care of him [in the hereafter]. That's what you need to hear and you'd be happy."

"That's exactly what I said."

"So thank God I can know you'll leave here happy," said George.

"I'm happy [hearing that]," she answered. For the first time since the reading began, Ellen smiled.

"In any case, your son says that he's fine. Your father-in-law is taking good care of him. His grandparents. There are other people who come through. They're all around. He's not alone. There's family in the next stage. There are people looking out for him. You were afraid that because he's a little boy that he'd be lost over there, not knowing what happened. They certainly knew he was coming, and they came to his assistance immediately.''

"Okay," Ellen said, nodding.

"Is your mother devout with the Blessed Mother, or something? I keep seeing Our Lady of Perpetual Help over your head. The icon.''

"My son is buried at the base of her [the Blessed Mother's] statue," Tony said.

"Do you take the name Mark?''

"Yes," the woman said.

"Passed on or living?''

"Living. A close friend.''

"There's a white-lace celebration around you. News of a wedding or a birth. It could very well be your own birth. If you could put the fear aside. Of course, it's your decision. But your son says to put the fear behind you and go on. Your father-in-law kids you that you're too prepared for disaster all the time. You think about the worst before it even happens. Life is a series of lessons and cycles. Go through it. Your spiritual being is on a human journey. Don't be afraid. Just move on ahead.''

"Okay.''

"Besides what happened to your son, there's another crisis you're coming out of.''

"Yes. It seems that way.''

"You're coming out of a time of distress. Saint Philomena appears again, over your head to symbolize distress, but she pulled away from you. So you're coming out of a time of distress. It's becoming more tranquil and more balanced.''

"Yes.''

"Somebody's coming around saying, 'This is Catherine.' ''

"Possibly.''

"She keeps saying, 'Tell her Catherine is here.' She says that she knows your son is there. So, she says, you can be guaranteed that she's also looking out for him. They are doing this to give you the security they know you need from tonight's experience, because Catherine comes in like an adopted aunt.''

"Exactly."

"She calls herself 'Aunt Catherine.' She says she's your son's adopted aunt [on the other side]. So just continue to pray for him and know he's okay. Stop thinking you did something wrong the night before. Should I have paid attention? Did I do this? Did he call out? You're creating things that don't exist. It just happened. Like your son says, it happened in his sleep as it would happen to anybody who passes in their sleep. You sometimes wonder, did he call out? Did he stir? Did you not hear him? Didn't you respond? You're torturing yourself needlessly. If anything, your son wants to relieve you of the feelings of guilt.''

After a moment, George resumed. "I think with that they're going to step aside, because your dad calls out to the two of you, 'This is Nick going back.' He's calling out to your mom and family. Tell them you've heard from him. He says your son is 'in good hands over here with me.' He says he can guarantee it.''

At this, Ellen started to cry again, and the reading ended.

Jeannie and Dwight Marshall's daughter Katy was always, in her mother's words, "special." Always very affectionate, Katy was also known for being protective toward other children, thus inspiring her nickname "the little mother." Even at age eight, blond, blue-eyed Katy seemed unusually mature and independent. Still, she would always be Jeannie's baby. Jeannie had other children from a previous marriage; Katy was her and Dwight's only child.

One day Jeannie came across some of Katy's school papers, which she had signed "Maria." It was a well-known piece of family lore that Dwight chose "Maria" as their daughter's name but that Jeannie preferred "Katy." As Jeannie explained, the baby just didn't look like a Maria, so the couple compromised with Maria Kathleen. Through the years, the story of Katy's name became a running joke. Jeannie called her Katy, Dwight called her Maria, and little Katy reveled in the attention of having two first names.

When Jeannie asked Katy why she signed her name Maria, the child explained, "I didn't want to hurt your feelings, Mommy, but I'd kind of like to be called Maria. I know that's what Dad wanted but you didn't."

"Whatever name you choose," Jeannie answered, "is fine with me."

It was the first day of February 1989, and Dwight and Jeannie were en route from their home in Paducah, Kentucky, to New Orleans, where they were to visit one of Jeannie's older daughters. Without a second thought they left Katy and Jeannie's ten-year-old daughter in the care of Cindy Messer, the family's full-time baby-sitter. Though fifty-six, Cindy could be childlike and naive, yet she never failed to care for the Marshall girls as if they were her own. Cindy, who grew up in an orphanage, found in the Marshalls the family she'd never had.

Earlier that day Katy had pleaded with her mother to let her wear her new purple dress to school. Purple was Katy's favorite color, and she was thrilled when Jeannie agreed. They also discussed Katy selling Girl Scout cookies in the neighborhood after school and planned for Katy's older sister Sarah to accompany her. Everything settled, Jeannie and Dwight drove away, promising to call that night.

Katy returned from school to find that her sister wouldn't be home in time to take her out, so she and Cindy set out walking down the road. It was seasonably warm with the first hints of spring in the air as the pair walked briskly down the road that ran almost perfectly straight for a mile near the Marshalls' home. Only a few homes sat on either side of the road, so there was never much traffic. Any car that did appear gave wide berth to pedestrians on the shoulder.

At about 4:45 P.M. Katy and Cindy instinctively turned toward a loud sudden noise. No one knows what happened next, but clearly Cindy and Katy tried desperately to elude the speeding car that appeared from nowhere. They ran off the shoulder, away from the road, but the car pursued them, plowing through a ditch before hitting the two. On impact, Katy was thrown forward, and Cindy was flung onto the car's hood. Both sustained massive, fatal head injuries.

Startled by the noise, several neighbors witnessed the crash and then watched in stunned amazement as the Thunderbird jerked out of the ditch and sped off, only to return a few moments later. Finding Katy and Cindy dead at the scene, the police turned their attention to the driver, a thirty-eight-year-old local named John Ricky Clark. He was charged with driving under the influence of both alcohol and drugs, including the depressants Valium and Darvon and some amphetamine-based diet pills. In Clark's initial account of the accident, told in a drunken slur, Katy and Cindy had stepped in front of his car. And he wasn't drinking. But the cops knew better, one even testifying at Clark's trial that "he smelled drunk."

The police learned later that Clark left the scene to hide an open whiskey bottle and a quantity of pills inside his home. He was charged with two counts of murder and was later convicted and sentenced to forty years in prison.

As Cindy and Katy lay dead by the road, hundreds of miles south Jeannie and Dwight continued driving toward New Orleans. Not far from the Crescent City, they stopped overnight at a small motel in Mississippi. Jeannie dialed home and was surprised when her twenty-one-year-old son Shayne answered. Her first thought was, *Why isn't he at work? I'll bet he's goofing off.*

"What are you doing there, Shayne?" Jeannie asked sharply.

Shayne said nothing for nearly a minute. Finally he replied mournfully, "Momma. Momma. Oh, Momma . . ."

"What?" Jeannie asked, her first thought going to her elderly mother.

"Momma, oh, Momma," Shayne cried weakly.

"What is it?" Jeannie asked in alarm. "Shayne? What's wrong?"

Suddenly another voice came on the line. "Jeannie, this is Barbara Reed.*" Katy's teacher.

---

*This name has been altered. Everything else in this story, however, is true.

"What the heck are you doing at my house?" Jeannie asked.

"Sit down," Barbara answered evenly. "I have something to tell you."

Jeannie clenched the receiver as she sat down.

"Katy's dead," Barbara said. "And Cindy, too."

Barbara's words formed Jeannie's last clear memory of the day. She and Dwight immediately drove on to New Orleans, where they planned to catch a plane back to Paducah. To their shock and disappointment, they learned that because of Mardi Gras there were no available seats until the next morning. They spent the night with Jeannie's daughter, crying, trying desperately to make sense of the news. Jeannie remembers only that "it all seemed unreal, a fog, a nightmare," a state of mind from which she would not fully emerge for another year and a half.

Jeannie and Dwight arrived home the next day to find their house filled with sympathetic family and friends. While most of the events following the deaths remain unclear to Jeannie today, she fondly recalls the immediate outpouring of love and support. At the funerals mourners filled the church to overflowing. But like many bereaved parents, Jeannie awoke just days later to find no one. It was as if, she remarked, everyone who'd held and comforted them in their home, at the mortuary, in the church, and at the gravesite simply vanished.

"People go back to work, and they expect you to take off a week or two and then go on with your life. But you can't. You can't," Jeannie said.

No more than six weeks after Cindy and Katy were buried, one acquaintance lectured Jeannie, "You've got to get on with your life. It's over."

"That's where you're wrong," she replied angrily. "It's *not* over! It won't be over until the day I die.

"I cried a lot," she told us. "I wanted to cry all the time. But you have to hide that because people don't want to see your tears. They think you're cracking up. Even my husband would get impatient with me because I was still grieving and crying. He was able to shut out what happened for a long, long time.

"I had always been a very strong person, so people around me weren't quite sure how to deal with me being this way. My husband would say, 'You used to be so strong, Jeannie. Pull yourself together!' But when you don't know *how* to pull yourself together, it takes a long, long time."

The Marshalls went for bereavement counseling but received little comfort. After their first session, the counselor said bluntly, "I really don't know what you expect me to tell you."

Jeannie succumbed to depression and even contemplated suicide. "I was dying inside," she recalled.

Several months after Katy's and Cindy's deaths, Jeannie read about George Anderson. She was desperate to hear from Katy in some way. However, when she confided to close friends her decision to have a reading, she was surprised by their vehement objections.

"Because of my religious beliefs, nobody could understand why I couldn't just say, 'Katy's okay. She's with God,' and leave it at that," Jeannie explained. "Some of my friends thought I was crazy." One friend sent a lengthy letter, full of quotes from the Scriptures, admonishing her for wanting to see a psychic. Living in the Bible Belt, Jeannie certainly understood her friend, whom she answered by saying, "I know you wrote the letter because you care about me. I care about you. However, my faith is different from yours, and in *my* Bible it speaks about the gifts of the spirit."

As do many parents, Jeannie also endured a painful trial of faith. "I felt alienated from God, like He had turned His back on me. I'd go to mass and cry. I'd get on my knees in front of the Blessed Sacrament, and all I could say over and over was, 'Help me! Help me!'

"I talked to a priest once and explained to him that I couldn't pray; that all I could say was, 'God help me.' He said it was the most profound prayer he'd ever heard.

"I honestly did believe Katy and Cindy were with God

and that she was all right," Jeannie stressed. "But all at once we're not talking about someone else's child or someone else's life. We're talking about *my baby*! And my baby is gone!

"I can't hold her anymore. I can't touch her. I just wanted to see George, to talk to him, to touch Katy. And going to George was the only way I knew to really touch her. The entire trip to New York—getting on the plane, renting the car, going to George—I was thinking the entire time, I'm going to touch Katy! I'm going to touch Katy!"

That evening in May 1989 Jeannie was one of some twenty anonymous subjects participating in a group reading at George's home. She waited nervously but patiently for her turn. All the while, however, she couldn't help but notice that in a reading for another couple George gave several messages that could have applied specifically to her: The couple's daughter died from head injuries suffered in an automobile accident. George said that he psychically saw the young woman dressed in what appeared to be a lilac or purple gown. Katy, of course, had worn a purple dress the day she died. The Marshalls then buried her in another purple dress. George also received several pieces of information, presumably for the other couple, that they could not confirm; for example, the names Jean or Jeannie, and Maria.

Each time the other couple failed to acknowledge a detail, he glanced in Jeannie's direction. George then said to the man and woman, "Your daughter says she's going to fade now, so someone else can get through."

After a pause George asked, "Does the name Ginny or Jenny mean anything? I thought I heard Jennifer before, or Jeannie. Because she says somebody is 'on her back' on the other side. She tells me to let them through." George directed his attention to Jeannie.

"There's a female. Someone close to you passed?" She did not answer.

"I'm going to say yes," he continued, "because there's a female presence around you."

"Yes," Jeannie acknowledged at last.

"Your two grandmothers have passed on."

"Yes."

"There's a male close to you who's also passed on."

"Yes."

"There's a male presence. Wait a second. Who's Marie? Because Marie is the female close to you that's passed on."

"Maria," Jeannie corrected.

"Maria," George repeated.

"We didn't call her Maria," Jeannie interjected.

"It wouldn't matter. If that's her actual name, let her come in that way to me. She said, 'This is Mary or Maria. I'm the one who is close to you who passed on.' So let's just accept what she says. She is a relative."

"Maria is a relative," Jeannie acknowledged.

"She comes in as a strong motherly figure. Let's just leave it go for a moment. Did you lose a child also? Because she keeps saying the child is there."

George's momentary confusion here is interesting. You will remember that Katy/Maria was often referred to as "the little mother."

"Now wait a minute," George said. "Is Maria related to you?"

"Maria is my child," Jeannie answered, beginning to cry. "Maria's my child."

"All right. That makes sense. Thank you. . . . Now she talks about her father. He's still living."

"Yes."

"Because she calls out to him. Your daughter was called by a nickname or something."

"She was. Maria was her first name. We used her middle name."

"So her actual birth-certificate name was Maria. That's how she keeps coming to me, as Maria. Yes. That's what she wanted to be called. . . . She has a rough time prior to her passing," George noted. "She passes tragically."

"Yes."

"There are other people around her when she passes."

"Yes."

"Did anybody else pass on with her?"

"Yes."

"Because there are other people with her now. A vehicle is involved in her passing."

"Yes."

"Why do I see a big vehicle?"

"It was a big car."

"Because she emphasizes that it's a big vehicle."

"And she was little."

"She passes on as a child."

"Yes."

"Other children passed on, too? She has other children around her on the other side."

Jeannie did not acknowledge this statement. Like countless other subjects, she was concentrating so carefully on George's words that she interpreted the question as applying only to the moment Katy died. At that time, there were no other children around her. But Jeannie was not thinking about the deceased children from the family who would have been with Katy on the other side: Jeannie's miscarried son, an infant nephew, and a grandson who passed only months before Katy. Only after the reading did Jeannie realize that George was correct.

"Your daughter is thrown by the vehicle," George continued. "She's hit by the vehicle."

"Yes."

"She seems to be a little girl; under the age of ten."

"Yes."

"Your daughter is near home when this occurs."

"Yes."

"She says she's hit [close to home]. She doesn't blame anyone for it. Was she playing or something? Why does she seem to be running? Does that make sense?"

"It might. She might have run when she saw the car," Jeannie answered.

"It seems like she's running, and that's when she's hit. Now, she's less than ten years old."

"She's eight."

"She says her daddy's father is with her. So that would be her grandfather."

"Yes."

"She suffered injuries to the head?"

"Yes."

"From her being thrown. Is your husband open to this?"

"Yes."

"Oh, good. Because she's been calling out to him. She says, 'Tell him you've heard from me.' She says she's okay. She's there with both grandfathers, and they're taking good care of her. You didn't lose another child?"

"No."

"Miscarriage?" George pressed. "Did you have a miscarriage?"

"No."

George was clearly puzzled, since the information from the other side clearly indicated otherwise. "Why does your daughter have children around her who have passed on?"

Again Jeannie fell silent.

"Does the name Elizabeth mean anything?"

"I have a daughter whose name is Elizabeth."

"She's calling out, 'Elizabeth.' "

"Yes."

"Your daughter, Maria, passed on recently. This year."

"Yes."

"Did it rain on the day of her wake?"

"It rained the day she was buried."

"Oh. Because she's showing me rain. I wasn't certain if it was on the day she passed or was waked. It was on the day of her funeral, then, she shows me."

"Yes."

"Are there any youngsters around her when this [her death] occurs?"

"No."

"It's driving me crazy. I'm just going to give up on it. I keep seeing other children around. I'll have to let it go."

Although George was accurate in his interpretation of the message he was receiving without Jeannie's acknowledgment, it was impossible for him to go any further in translating it. One can't help but wonder what else the miscarried baby, the nephew, and the grandson might have relayed through George had Jeannie been able to acknowledge him at this point. The fact that George returned to these questions several times suggests that there was some urgency to their message.

"She says she's fine and at peace. She only went over [to the other side] a few months ago. This is May."

"She died in February."

"She says God has given her the chance to come through with her two grandfathers. . . . Now your daughter calls out to her father again. 'Definitely tell Dad you have heard from me,' she says."

"Okay." At this point Jeannie noticed that Katy was calling her father 'Dad,' not 'Daddy,' as other young children would.

George had paused momentarily to listen. "The car was going at some speed!" he said. "It looks like this is near a main highway. It seems the car is going at tremendous speed. It's as if whoever is driving doesn't even see her. It happened so quickly."

Jeannie nodded.

"She seems to appear right over here," George said, pointing behind where Jeannie was sitting. "She says the cause of her passing was being hit by the car. But would she have seen it coming?"

"I don't know. The coroner didn't know."

"Because it happened too quickly to see it coming. That's why I said before that she had a rough time prior to her passing. There's a momentary feeling I can't move, and *boom*! She's says it's an incredible hit. She doesn't even know what happens. It all happens too quickly, she says. Just continue to pray for her and know that she's all right. She says she's okay and at peace.

"You have other children."

"Yes."

"Because she keeps calling out to family. Is she the youngest?"

"Yes."

"Because she keeps saying she's the baby. She tells me she was here when I was talking to the couple just before you. Because I kept getting information that I felt was going to you. It's like cross-information. I could have gotten crossed wires earlier. You don't know each other, do you?" George asked.

"No," Jeannie replied.

"Oh, okay. I was just wondering why I got some confusion earlier. You have another daughter."

"Yes."

"Was she [walking] on a blind side [when she was hit]?"

"She was walking on the shoulder."

"Because it just seems that the driver goes off the road. That's what I see. It all happens so quickly, it's hard to see myself. The car makes a turn. It goes out of control. She's hit and thrown."

"Yes."

"But she doesn't blame anyone. It happened. And now she has to go on with her life in the next stage, as you must here."

Jeannie simply cried.

"She knows how much you miss her. She knows how you're suffering with grief. But she wants you to move on as she must, until you're reunited someday. Meanwhile, she understands your grief and your anger. It seems the driver wasn't in the right frame of mind. Something's wrong [with him]."

"He was drunk."

"Well, you certainly have the right to be angry. But she says it won't bring her back. Just know that she's closer to you than you can imagine. She's around a sister of hers like a guardian angel."

"Okay."

"I think she's going to step aside now. She sends her love to you and her father. Why does it feel like he's not with you?"

"No, he's with me. At home, that is."

"She shows me purple."

"Yes. It was her favorite color."

"She shows me herself in what looks like a purple dress. Didn't I say purple or some color like it to the [previous] couple before?"

"Yes. But she was wearing a purple dress the day she died."

"Who's Katherine or Kate?"

"That's Maria! That was her middle name. *I* called her Katy!"

"Oh, because it sounded like it was her voice saying, 'This is Maria.' But then I heard 'Kate.' "

"Yes, Katy."

"Well, she's going to step aside so others can get through. She definitely sends her love and asks that you continue to pray for her."

Jeannie's head throbbed with pain until she began to feel ill. George had moved onto other subjects, so she quietly slipped out of his house and stood in the cool evening air. As she looked up at the starry sky, she thought about going straight back to her motel. But something drew her back inside. She was standing in the foyer; the readings were going on in the family room to her right. As the evening concluded, George asked the group of subjects if any of them had since recalled any of the names that were not acknowledged before.

"Does the name Cindy mean anything to anyone?" George asked, staring directly at Jeannie.

"Cindy! Yes!" she exclaimed.

"It's right at the center of the room, again. Is she passed over?"

"Yes."

"Because I just heard somebody say 'Cindy' right over here," George said, pointing to the part of the room where Jeannie had sat earlier. "She knows your daughter."

"Yes."

"She says, 'Cindy.' Did she pass on before your daughter?"

"Later."

"Because your daughter says Cindy is with her."

"Yes."

"Was Cindy hit, also?"

"Yes."

"They were together."

"Yes."

"Cindy calls out to *her* family. But she's there [on the other side] with Maria. Was she watching your daughter that day?"

"Yes."

"Is she a child?"

"No."

"Why did I think she was a child?" George asked, puzzled.

"I understand why. But she's not a child," Jeannie answered, realizing that Cindy could seem very childlike.

"So the two of them passed on together," George said.

"Yes," Jeannie answered.

"Cindy says, 'I'm glad I passed on. I would not have wanted to live with this on my conscience.' Were they walking hand in hand?"

"Yes."

"They were walking hand in hand on the side of the road. Cindy is a friend of the family."

"Cindy cared for my children when I wasn't there," Jeannie explained.

"Because she says she's a friend of the family and a baby-sitter."

"She was like a grandmother, too," Jeannie added.

"Some things never change. She says she cared for your children here and she still does in the next stage. She says, 'Maria is with me.' "

Jeannie nodded.

"Why does it seem like she's a mammy? She gives me the impression she's a mammy." George was clearly confused; this was a new, and odd, image. "She's a mammy. A governess." He went on to say that he was seeing Cindy in the costume of an old-fashioned mammy, with an apron around her waist and a bandanna wrapped around her head.

To say the least, this psychic symbol was enigmatic.

Jeannie at first didn't get it, either. Then she remembered
a New Year's Eve several years earlier when Cindy was
baby-sitting for the Marshalls. They returned home several
hours earlier than expected to find Cindy with her hair set
up in bobby pins and covered by a red bandanna. Always
self-conscious, Cindy was initially embarrassed, but she
just laughed and quipped, "Oh, well, I guess I look just
like an old-time mammy. But that's what I am: I am a
mammy." Only Jeannie and her husband knew of this, and
after hearing George describe Cindy as a mammy, she was
certain this was Cindy's special way to let her know it was
really her.

"Cindy says be at peace knowing that she's taking care
of your daughter just as well in the next stage of life as she
did when they were on earth," George said to Jeannie, who
was weeping again. "Cindy says they're both all right. She
asks that you forgive her, but she couldn't help it. They
didn't even know what hit them. And again she says she
would have much rather sacrificed her own life than to have
to tell you that your daughter passed on. She says it would
have been like her own child had passed on.

"So she says she feels God was merciful letting the two
of them go together," George said. "And, again, she says
pray for them. She says, 'This is Cindy going back. I'm
going to take Maria back with me now.' They send their
love to everybody. They say God is calling them back."

Jeannie returned home to Kentucky knowing in her heart
that she had touched Katy again.

Jeannie's reading, as remarkable and reassuring as it was,
did not alleviate all her grief. Certainly bereaved parents
and other loved ones usually come away from a reading
feeling relieved or comforted. But, as George is quick to
point out, grief is a process all bereaved must go through,
and readings provide no shortcut.

Jeannie slowly emerged from her depression and began
volunteering her time, first with an organization that locates
missing children, then with various church groups, then
working with the bereaved. In the three years since her

daughter's death, she has come to see the grieving process from not only her personal perspective but society's as well.

"I think that grief is quite possibly the most misunderstood ordeal that we go through," she reflected. "You can't mourn, because people don't want you to mourn. They want you to start laughing again and act like nothing happened. And you can't do that. Also, you can't mourn until you can talk about it and publicly express your grief. People who've suffered a loss need to talk. But it's hard to do that when you're grieving. People don't want you to talk. As a society, we don't want to face death. But we need to look at death as a natural part of life.

"When someone like Katy is killed, at only eight or nine years of age, that's not natural, no," she went on. "But dying is part of life. And those who are going through a loss need comfort and support, particularly from friends and even from employers."

Jeannie's life was changed forever. "Things that used to be so important to me are not so important anymore," she said. "I got to the point where I realized that the only thing that made me feel good anymore was to know that I had helped someone else. When you're hurting so badly and your cross is heavy, you pick up someone else's cross, and they both become lighter."

Seven months after her first reading with George, Jeannie returned to Long Island with Dwight. In that session Cindy came through to say that she and Katy care for children who arrive on the other side disoriented and frightened. It would not be farfetched to say that Katy and Cindy do on the other side what Jeannie does here: help people with the transition.

People go to George hoping to hear from their beloved on the other side. But when we say "hear" from them, what do we really mean? Except for some direct-communications experiences in which people actually hear a voice as if that person were standing near them, no one but George actually hears anything. As George relays the messages he receives to the subjects, he is repeating what he either psychically hears, feels, senses, or sees.

Since George is not channeling the deceased person's voice and speaks in his own, what is it about the experience that makes so many people leave feeling certain that they did in fact hear from spirits on the other side? Subjects often say that the message "sounded just like" their loved one.

While George obviously cannot mimic the voices he hears or senses, he does relate expressions, manners of speaking, and tone accurately. In Jeannie Marshall's reading, both her daughter and the baby-sitter came through with specific identifying facts about themselves and their deaths. But what truly convinced Jeannie that the messages were addressed to her and her alone was the way George described Katy's and Cindy's personalities as he perceived them.

One of thousands of examples of the spirits maintaining the subtleties of what we could call personality—and George receiving them—is the case of Alexander Volpe.

"From the time he was a baby," Alexander's mother, Michele, recalled with a smile, "Alexander never slept through an entire night. He was so active. He bossed everybody around. When he was only a year old, I bought him a T-shirt that read, THE BOSS. I teased him and called him Napoleon. He was my firstborn, very domineering and rebellious but also smart and precocious. By kindergarten, he was reading, and he had a large vocabulary for his age.

"He was quite a character," she continued. "He had an unbelievable personality. He was small and thin, with dark hair and dark eyes. We used to call him 'the thirty-year-old midget.' He was always on the go, always doing ten things at once." His two-and-a-half-year-old brother Michael could not have been more different: easygoing, quiet, obedient. Despite their opposite personalities, the two boys got along beautifully and were quite close.

Typically, not even a slight fever kept Alexander from running around during a weeklong bout of chicken pox. The boy's pox had dried up, and he seemed fully recovered.

In fact, Michele was considering sending him back to school the next day.

That night, however, Alexander awoke complaining of a headache. Michele gave him some Tylenol, and he went back to sleep, but the next morning Alexander was uncharacteristically lethargic. His temperature was under 100 degrees, so Michele saw no cause for alarm. She called the pediatrician, who prescribed a sinus medication and assured her Alexander would be all right.

But as the day wore on, Alexander became more and more listless, alternating between screaming, "Mommy, my head hurts!" and falling off into a deep sleep. When Michele mentioned Alexander's condition to a neighbor, a biology teacher, the woman immediately remarked that Alexander's symptoms sounded like encephalitis. She urged Michele to seek further medical attention immediately.

Concerned, Michele again phoned Alexander's doctor. He listened, then brusquely replied, "Alexander does not have encephalitis." He did suggest that if the symptoms persisted, the boy should be seen in his office the next day. The doctor's response was rather puzzling, given the fact that virtually every medical source from medical school texts to common child care books specifically warns that encephalitis is a possible complication of chicken pox, requiring immediate emergency care.

That evening Alexander's condition deteriorated markedly. Several times that night he woke up crying, "Mommy, my head's screaming!" before dropping back to sleep. By morning he could barely open his eyes, and the excruciating pain of the headache had spread down his spine. When Michele realized that he could not walk, she phoned the doctor.

He urged her to stay calm and call again that afternoon. Michele listened, but she knew something was terribly wrong. Next she called her husband, Alex, Sr., and cried, "We've got to do something! I know there's something the matter with Alexander!"

"Let's just take him to the hospital," the boy's father replied.

Before Michele packed up the boys for the trip to the emergency room, she placed a call to another family physician. This doctor had never seen Alexander; he wasn't even a pediatrician. But after hearing Michele explain Alexander's condition, he snapped, "It sounds like he's got meningitis. You've got to get him to Children's Hospital!"

At the hospital a spinal tap revealed that Alexander did not have the more common form of meningitis, bacterial. But all of his symptoms and the fact that he was getting over the chicken pox clearly indicated a diagnosis of encephalitis caused by viral meningitis. Unlike the bacterial form, viral meningitis does not respond to antibiotic therapy. At most, the patient can be observed for further complications and kept comfortable and well hydrated.

Alexander was placed on antiviral medication. The doctors, assuring the Volpes that they had treated similar cases, promised that their son would be fine in a few days. "The virus just has to work its way through his system," one doctor explained to Michele and Alex. With his words, they felt greatly relieved, certain that their son would be up and creating havoc again before long.

But less than twenty-four hours after being admitted to the hospital, Alexander suffered a brain seizure. He lapsed into a coma and had to be placed on a respirator. Within the week Michele and Alex heard the shocking news: Alexander was brain dead. He would never walk, talk, or play again. He would never even open his eyes.

One month before Alexander's sixth birthday, his parents gave permission for life support to be withdrawn, and he was soon pronounced dead.

"The shock was terrible, especially when you had a kid in the house who was constantly on the go," Michele recalled. "He cooked. He made pancakes, chicken cutlets, French toast. He had to help me wash and vacuum. He was under my feet all the time. Suddenly the house was very quiet. Too quiet. It was very hard to be in this house every day.

"I had a lot of help from people. And I started reading a lot. I had trouble sleeping."

Alexander was deeply missed. Michele heard from his teacher, who, interestingly, never saw his aggressive, overly energetic side. "In school, he was very polite. He was very good and very bright. His teacher was very upset about his passing." One day she told Michele that she saw a vision of him sitting right in front of her in the classroom. "She said that she used to feel him in the class."

When Michele and Alex learned of George's work with bereaved parents, they were determined to see him. In this reading Alexander comes through exactly as his parents knew him.

"Your two grandfathers have passed over," George began.

"Yes," Michele said.

"Because there's a strong fatherly presence around you."

"Okay."

"Your mother's still living."

"Yes."

"Your grandmother's gone over."

"Yes."

"Your dad is still living?"

"Yes."

"A young male close to you has passed on."

"Yes."

"It's a young male. He's family. A very outgoing, anxious guy! He says, 'Let's not waste time. Don't analyze anything. Just tell her what I'm saying. She'll know it's me.'"

Michele started to cry.

"He passes young," said George. "He's a feisty character, isn't he? I don't mean to sound disrespectful. But he is a little pain—"

At this Michele broke into a smile and nodded at George.

"I'm telling him to slow down and wait a minute. He's not an infant. He insists he's grown up. But he's not adult grown-up. He's a youngster."

"Right."

"He's the son. Is he your son?"

"Yes."

"A granddad [of yours] is with him, because he's saying that he's with him. He's the one who called him in [to the hereafter]. Your son must have been a handful here. Because he must be quite a handful over there, too! He must have been a very hyper child."

"Yes."

"He's always got ten different things going on at once. One thing I can assure you is that he's not bored over there. You know in your heart he's all right, but this is a reassurance. You've dreamt about him, or he's done something to let you know before today that he's okay. You will see him again someday. He really wants to sock it to you now, to let you know that he's near. Did he talk fast?"

"Yes."

"Gosh, he's hyper! I'm telling him to slow down. Take a Valium over there! Do something, but slow down!" George jokingly pleaded with the spirit.

"He's very anxious. He's like a child. His turn has come. Now he can come in. He's very good with other children? Because he says he works with children in the next stage. He helps them to find themselves, he says. Because, it's funny, even though he's a youngster, he's still very mature and has a big heart. He's a very good-hearted child. Very close with you."

"Yes."

"Not that he's playing favorites here, but he singularizes his dad because he knows men suffer in silence more. He knows that he's Daddy's boy in a special way. Do you have a daughter?"

"No."

"Well, was your son very close to a female? Someone like a sister? Because he's speaking of someone who's like a sister. So I assumed you had a daughter. But it could be somebody who's a friend or another relative, like a cousin."

"Yes."

"One that's here."

"Oh, yes."

"Because he calls out to her like a sister. . . . Now, all your grandparents have passed over," George observed.

"Yes."

"Because there are people around you claiming to be your grandparents. One grandmother was close to you."

"Yes."

"One stands out or singularizes herself. She says that your son is there with her. She's a very motherly woman. She doesn't mean this to be uncaring: She says, 'Your loss is my gain.' She says she doesn't mind that he's a handful. He keeps her going."

Michele listened and cried.

"Now your son is calling out to your dad. He's having a little trouble with his health?"

"Yes."

"Pretty noticeable."

"Yes."

"I'm not saying he's going anywhere, but, to be honest with you, I'm concerned. Your son brings up that your dad doesn't feel well. But he might be keeping it to himself. It may be worse than he knows, or he's keeping it quiet. They call out to him in concern. Is your dad hospitalized?"

"He was."

"He might be again. I keep seeing him in a hospital. Now your son's showing me that he could have been in the hospital."

"Yes."

"Your son tells me to say it exactly as I'm hearing it. There is reason for concern. Your dad is having health trouble. He's told to watch his diet. Is he having trouble with his eating?"

"Yes."

"Your dad's trouble is in his blood. I was getting concern around his heart because of the blood."

"Yes."

"But to a degree, with your father, it goes in one ear and out the other."

"Yes."

"Your mom's still living, also."

"Yes."

"Your son is calling out to his grandparents. Tell them you've heard from him. I'm sure his passing is a shock to the family. Because there's a lightning bolt in front of you [psychically]."

"Right."

"Did your son pass tragically? Age as well as circumstances?"

"Yes."

"He says it's nobody's fault, though. Does that make sense? Did he have an injury to his head?"

"Probably. But it was not a blow."

"There's an injury to his head internally."

"Yes," Alex acknowledged.

"Because your son says, 'It hurts in here,' " George remarked as he pointed to his own head. "An injury to the head. Something must have popped. [Something involves] the blood going to the brain. [It feels like] some sort of stroke or injury to the head."

"Probably. Yes."

"Does the name Frank mean anything?"

"Yes," Michele said.

"Passed over?"

"No."

"I just wanted to make sure, because your son is asking how Frank is. Has everything been okay with him?"

"No."

"Is he having health trouble, too?"

"Not that I know of."

"It's around. If it's not physical, it could be emotional. He's not in good shape. Your son gives me that feeling. With him, things seem to get worse before they get better. Do you have other children?"

"Yes."

"You have another child."

"Yes."

"He calls to his brother. Is his brother graduating, or changing schools or something?"

"It's his first year of [a new] school," Alex answered.

"It could also be a symbol that he's moved up to the next step in school. That's probably what your son means."

"Probably," Michele said.

"Your son thanks you both for being so good to him prior to his passing. In whatever way, I don't know. I'm not interpreting it, and I won't argue with him. It's safer that way."

Michele laughed softly.

"Your son keeps saying, 'Joe is with me.' A fatherly figure to your son. Like a great-grandfather or uncle. Do you smoke?" George asked Alex.

"Yes."

"Someone's telling you to quit."

He nodded.

"Your son says you smoke more because of nerves than anything else. He says you're not breathing well in your sleep, and he tells you to give it up. I don't think he's the only one who's on your back about it, either. He says, 'Maybe you'll listen if you hear it from over here.' I mean, you're not going to die of lung cancer tomorrow, but he tells you to quit. He's loud and clear. Your son says do it for him. Does the name Ron mean anything at all?"

"Yes."

"Passed on or living?"

"Living."

"There's concern around his health. I'll just leave it with you."

"Okay."

"Are you having trouble in your stomach area?" George asked Alex.

"Yes," he replied.

"Watch what you're eating. Keep yourself balanced. Your work involves a lot of stress, according to your son. So you have to keep yourself in harmony. Make sure you're getting enough rest."

"Okay."

"You've been irritable lately."

"Yes."

"Because your son says you've been kind of grumpy."

Michele nodded in agreement.

"There's a birth coming up in the family. It's all around you. Could be a wedding or a birth [in your family]. You're hearing news up ahead of a white-lace celebration."

"Okay."

"Do you take the name David?"

"Yes," she replied.

"Living. Did your son have any friends by that name?"

"Yes."

"It seems like he's calling out to a friend David."

"Okay."

"Your son have health trouble? But it came upon him very suddenly?"

"Yes."

"Now I understand. I'm glad you didn't say anything before. Your son kept saying it was an accident. You probably thought I was thinking that. But he says, no, it comes upon him suddenly, *like* an accident. That's why he described it that way. Did he have an aneurysm or something like it?"

"Something like that," she said.

"That's why it feels like something pops in his head. He says it's nobody's fault. You didn't know it was there. Your son was around five years old when he passed."

"Yes."

"It seems like I'm talking to a five-year-old."

"Yes."

"He'd be more grown up now, naturally. But he comes in as you would remember him, a five-year-old. Quite an active one, too."

"Yes."

"Do you take the name Chris?"

"Yes," she answered.

"Your son's calling out to friends. Chris or Christopher."

"Okay."

"Did you ever miscarry?"

"Yes."

"It's around you. It must be a miscarriage. I think you

would have had a girl. There's a strong female presence around you claiming she's the daughter you would have had if the cycle of the birth had continued.''

''Okay.''

''Did you lose a sister?''

''No.''

''Did your mom ever miscarry? Because there's also talk of you losing a sister in the same way, a miscarriage. There's somebody else around you who's a young woman had the cycle of birth continued.''

Michele nodded slightly but said nothing.

''Do you take the name Paul?''

''Yes.''

''Passed on.''

''Yes.''

''Do you take the name Michael?''

''Yes,'' the woman said.

''Your son is calling out to his brother: Mike, Mikey, Michael.''

''Okay.''

''Your anniversary coming up? Your son just handed you a lot of white and pink roses for your anniversary. Are we close to your birthday, also?''

''Yes.''

''He's also wishing you a happy birthday. Are you planning more children? I see Saint Philomena appearing over your head. It's a sign of a happy birth. You still look young enough to have children. Your son kept saying you have more. So that might be the case. There could be a birth up ahead. Even when I looked at you [earlier], I felt you were in the family way. I thought maybe you were and you're not showing it. There's the possibility of another birth. Are you afraid?''

''Yes.''

''Because your son says don't be afraid. Children are life renewing itself. It's your decision. But he encourages it. Because after what you've been through, it would be a positive shot in the arm. He says you're setting yourself up for tragedy before you even begin. But it's your decision. Does the name Philomena mean anything at all?''

"No."

"I just wanted to make sure. Because it's a sign of a happy birth. So you need have no fear. To be honest with you—I won't stake my life on it—you might have a girl. Your son gives me the feeling of a sister. He talked about a sister before; I thought he had one. So it's in the future. I'll leave it with you. Blame *him* if it's wrong." George laughed.

"Okay."

"Do you take the name John?"

"Yes."

"Passed over."

"Yes."

"He knows your son."

"No."

"Well, I guess he does now. Your son talks about John over there with him."

"Okay."

"I think this is a symbol: Do you take the name Gerard or Jerry?"

"No."

"Okay. Saint Gerard is over your head. It's a symbol of motherhood. There's also the name Al."

"Yes."

"Uncle Al. He's with your son. Is this uncle full of life?"

"Yes!"

"He's the life of the party. He and your son are getting along fine over there. Two hyper guys having a good time."

"Right."

"Is there a Dorothy?"

"Yes."

"I keep seeing Dorothy in *The Wizard of Oz*. I keep hearing Auntie Em calling Dorothy before the tornado. Your son keeps telling me to give out the name Dorothy. Was he fond of the movie?"

"Yes. I used to sing that song to him all the time," Michele explained.

" 'Somewhere Over the Rainbow,' " George said.

"All the time."

"Oh, okay."

"Then one time we had a tornado," she added.

"Oh, no wonder your son showed me the tornado scene. Now it makes sense! Very interesting. He says, in his case he's literally over the rainbow. 'There are [other] children here with me,' he says. There are no Munchkins, but the landscape [in the hereafter] looks like what they portrayed in the movie, in the sense of color and scenery."

The film had additional significance for Michele and, obviously, Alexander. She later recalled an incident that occurred before the reading: "I'd gone shopping, and a group of people were looking up at a beautiful rainbow that went across the sky from one side to the other. An elderly man said he'd never seen a rainbow like that. And I thought about it, and looked at it, and for some reason it just put me in a better mood. It was exciting, because I'd never seen a rainbow like that, either.

"Alexander always loved *The Wizard of Oz*, and I thought about that when I saw the rainbow. It made me think of him. Could it have been a sign from him? Whatever it was, it helped me."

The reading continued, with George correctly divulging the names and relationships of three deceased friends and relatives. Then he said to Michele, "You'll never get over your son's passing, but don't put your life on hold. You want to have another child. Go ahead. He's pushing this. Life goes on. You'll be with him again someday. He's in another stage of life."

She nodded, and George continued. "I think this is symbolic: the name Theresa."

"Yes."

"Passed over."

"No."

"I see Saint Theresa over your head. I'm going to take it as a symbol. It means faith, strength, and endurance. Also the name Anthony or Tony. Somebody keeps calling Tony. It seems to be somebody here.''

''A friend,'' Alex answered.

''I think this is a symbol: the name Gloria or Grace?''

''Grace.''

''Did she pass on?''

''No.''

''I'll leave it as a symbol. Gloria. Graceful. It's the announcement of good news or a blessing to come. A wedding or birth. Something of that nature. News of a happy event. There's definitely a birth around you.

''Your grandmother passed before your son.''

''Yes,'' Michele acknowledged.

''When your son came over [to the other side], he was a little frightened at first. Your grandmother calmed him down. She crossed him over. He didn't know what to expect. They kidded and told him he had gone to Oz, over the rainbow. That kind of made him feel better. Your son knows he's not in Oz now. But he says that's how they handled it; in a childlike way, so he wouldn't be afraid. [He knows he'll] be able to see you in the next stage of life. He is near you spiritually, he says. Under the circumstances, it's stupid of me to ask, but you're having a tough time emotionally.''

''Yes.''

''You're out of harmony with yourself. Try to let yourself live. You're too wrapped up in fear. Your son is saying that.''

''Right.''

''Do you take the name Tom or Thomas?'' George asked.

''Yes,'' Michele replied.

''Anybody close?''

''Yes.''

''Your uncle and your son call out the name. 'Tell Tom you've heard from us.' I'll leave it go. Is there a Rose?''

''Yes.''

''Passed over.''

''Yes.''

"They say Rose is there."

"Okay."

"If there's truth to reincarnation, your son must have been around before," George commented. "He's a mature soul in a little boy's body. I think they're going to step aside now. Your son, your grandparents, the others, they all send their love and ask that you remember to pray for them. 'Until we meet again.' With that, your son and the others all go back."

4

Without Warning

For parents the years their children spend as preteens and teenagers are perhaps the most anxiety filled. As kids grow older and begin claiming their independence, few mothers and fathers survive that transition without a few close calls. Each generation, it seems, faces its own challenges and problems, but for kids today growing up is harder than ever before. Drug and alcohol abuse, car accidents, violence, and suicide occur most frequently in the teen years. Car and bicycle accidents, the number-one killers of young people, claim 27,000 annually. Because older children are most likely to be out of the home and away from adult supervision, they are also more prone to injury and death due to other, nonvehicular mishaps.

Experts agree that a parent's response to a child's death is in part shaped by the age of the child and his relationship with his parents. All parents experience periods of ambivalence about parenthood. There probably isn't a mother or father who has not in a moment's anger just wished the kids would go away, and this is certainly more common as they start to come into their own. In the necessary struggle for psychological independence young people commonly cross their parents; there are disagreements about everything from hairstyles to sexual behavior. While most parents understand that letting their children grow up means letting go, trusting them to their own judgment, it remains a difficult and sometimes confusing process. How far is too far? How responsible is responsible enough? How will my child fare?

When a youngster dies unexpectedly during adolescence, grieving parents face a host of unique issues. If death occurs as the result of an accident, there is the issue of blame. Some parents may feel that there was something they might have done to prevent the tragedy. The parents of a child who dies in a car accident, for example, may experience tremendous anger at whomever they believe was responsible, perhaps a drunk driver. Sometimes the grief is complicated by the fact that the blame for the accident lies with the child himself.

Anytime anyone dies in an accidental or unexpected way, survivors feel vulnerable and insecure. We are able to function in our daily lives because we assume that things will work properly and go according to plan. If we stopped to contemplate the possible dire consequences of our every action, we would be unable to get out of bed. Few of us truly believe in our hearts that disaster will ever occur to us or someone we love. Denial in adolescents, notorious for their sense of invincibility, is yet stronger. When an older child dies suddenly, without warning, it's almost as if the parents' worst fears have been confirmed. It is not only the grieving parents' nightmare that has come true, but the nightmare shared by almost all parents. For this reason, parents of deceased adolescents may be avoided by other parents. While almost all new parents know of and fear SIDS, for instance, statistically so few of these deaths occur that the chances of your knowing someone whose child died that way are fairly small. In contrast, we hear about young people being killed or injured in car accidents in our communities nearly every day. When other parents turn away from the bereaved parent, it is often because the tragedy struck too close to home and they can identify with the bereaved parent to a degree that they find uncomfortable and frightening.

In each of the four families we will profile in this chapter, the parent-child relationships were quite strong. In fact, these parents had come to think of their child as a friend as well. Each of the children return that friendship and respect in their concern for the families they left behind.

Chris Torchiano lived with her fifteen-year-old daughter, Lisa, and twelve-year-old son, Peter, in a bustling North Bronx, New York, neighborhood. A single parent in her late thirties, she did her best to see that her kids grew up right. Although the Torchianos' working-class neighborhood was considered safe, as Chris's children neared their teens, she worried more about their safety.

Like most single parents, Chris had a full plate. She and the children's father had been divorced only about a year when he died in an accident at age thirty-nine. Although Chris had to work full-time to support her kids, she made being a mother her top priority. She was close to both, but shared a special bond with daughter Lisa. At night Lisa would come into Chris's room and say, ''Mom, let's talk.'' She would then lie down on the bed, and they would recount the day's events. Chris felt lucky to have her.

Lisa, a petite, very pretty girl, had long thick black hair, blue-gray eyes, and freckles. As she grew into her teens, Chris naturally became anxious about her daughter's activities and whereabouts. Both Lisa and Peter were always mindful to call and let her know where they were, when they arrived, when they were leaving. Overall, Chris felt secure in knowing that she had raised two intelligent, sensitive, and responsible kids. Lisa was never permitted out on school nights; on weekends she was home promptly at eleven.

One February afternoon Lisa was getting ready to go out with friends, while Chris drove her brother to a party. Thinking she would be back in just a few minutes, Chris didn't say goodbye to Lisa. When she returned much later than she expected, Lisa was already gone. For some reason Chris could not figure, the idea that she had not said goodbye to her daughter left her feeling uneasy.

When Peter had not called from his party by four, as
Chris had asked him to, she grew nervous. She tried to
reach him at a number he had left, got a wrong number,
and inexplicably burst into tears. First about Peter, then
suddenly about Lisa. Although she reminded herself that
Lisa was nearly sixteen, that it was still daylight, and that
her daughter was responsible, nothing calmed her. At
around five Peter did call, and she picked him up and returned home.

As evening fell, Chris vacillated between hope and despair. If Lisa had gotten sidetracked somewhere with her
friends, it would not be the first time. She was a good kid,
but, like many in her circle, capable of misbehaving at
times.

At around eight-thirty the doorbell rang. It was four of
Lisa's girlfriends, all crying. "What happened?" Chris
asked. "Where's Lisa?"

"I think Lisa was in an accident," one friend answered,
trying not to look at Chris. Chris, panicked, asked the girls
for more information, but they would not or could not divulge anything further. After they left, Chris comforted herself with the thought that perhaps Lisa wasn't involved, and
if she was, it was only a fender bender.

But as the night wore on with no word from her daughter, Chris began frantically calling each area hospital. When
she reached someone who did know of an accident, the
news was bleak: several teenagers killed, including two
young women. Beyond that, there was nothing the person
at the hospital could say, and she would not release names.
Chris drove to the hospital but was told that the bodies of
the dead had been moved to the medical examiner's office.
She returned home more distraught than ever.

Chris's mother came to stay with her that night. A priest
from the local parish came to visit for a few minutes. He,
Chris, and her mother prayed, but he had no information
about Lisa, either, except that some neighborhood kids had
told him she was in the accident. Then at 3:30 A.M. two de-
tectives rang the doorbell. They asked her several cryptic

questions about Lisa, then abruptly left without ever clarifying the situation. Perhaps they thought Chris already knew; Chris, in her shock, was not thinking clearly enough to ask.

By morning, however, there could be no question as to Lisa Torchiano's fate. Chris and Lisa's uncle went to the medical examiner's office, where he made the identification. He emerged from the morgue, looking ashen. Chris began screaming, "Is she that bad? Why can't I see her? Was it her?"

Averting his eyes, her brother nodded.

As Chris and everyone in the New York area learned, Lisa was one of six young people who were killed when the car in which they were riding took a curve too fast and slammed into a tree. The force of impact was so great that the car literally wrapped itself around the tree; shards of flying glass still remained embedded in its trunk. The police found beer bottles in the car, and forensic tests revealed that the eighteen-year-old unlicensed driver, Daniel Moriarty, had a blood-alcohol level twice the legal limit. In addition to Daniel and Lisa, Lisa's close friend Ann and three other young men died.

But how did Lisa come to be in that car? Chris had warned her repeatedly about riding in cars, telling her that she could not know whether or not someone was a good driver. Apparently as Lisa and Ann were leaving an afternoon football game, the boys, whom they knew, offered them a ride. They were on their way to a fast-food restaurant when the accident occurred at 3:20 P.M. Ironically, Lisa belonged to her Catholic high school's chapter of SADD, Students Against Drunk Driving. Chris firmly believes that Lisa did not know Danny Moriarty was unlicensed and drunk when she got into the car.

Today, over two years after the accident, the tree remains a neighborhood focal point, a place where makeshift memorials, bouquets of flowers, candles, stuffed animals, and notes to the victims are placed. A wooden cross and a hand-painted sign that reads FOREVER YOUNG and lists the six names hang on the tree.

Lisa's death devastated Chris. "It was like I went into a

coma,'' she said. ''Everything that I found comfort in was gone. There's nothing that can ever replace her. Even now, if I'm having a decent day with my boyfriend and my son, there's always that feeling of something missing in your heart. I'm always thinking about Lisa.''

Lisa's brother, Peter, also suffered after her death, and the stress of their grief caused a rift between him and his mother. ''Right after Lisa's death,'' Chris recalled, ''I think Peter knew I didn't care about anything. I didn't tell him what to do. We didn't talk to each other for four months. I just didn't want to talk to anyone. And I think he felt the same way. He'd be very angry with me. Sometimes I'd scream at him, '*I* didn't do anything!'

''I think he blamed me for not being the mom that he'd had. I changed so suddenly, so drastically. I would just curl up on the couch and lie there in a daze. I can't function like I used to. I can't figure out and recall the simplest things, sometimes. I used to have a very quick wit. One night at my bereavement group I said something funny, and everyone laughed. I said, 'I'm getting my wit back. Now I'm a half-wit.'

''Peter is fourteen now,'' she continued. ''We're doing better. We're not doing great. We're doing better. Peter and Lisa were pretty close. He misses her, especially at night. They would watch movies together. Now he has no one. I feel bad for him. He's been very strong for me, too. There are times when I'd be in my room crying hysterically, and he would just come in and put his arms around me.

''Peter doesn't pray. He's very mad at God. He doesn't talk to anyone about it. There are no support groups around here for children. I pray. I'm not mad at God. I just try to tell myself that if God did have something to do with it, then I have to trust His reasons were very good. And my reasons, compared to God's, are very small. If God didn't do anything to cause this, then He was there for her. So either way I go, I have to trust in Him.''

Chris brought her mother to George's house for the reading. This reading is an unusual one in that the majority of it concerned Lisa's giving advice to her mother. It also dealt with the complex feelings Chris had about the fact that Lisa was on the other side with her father instead of here on earth with her.

George began by saying, "First, there's a strong male presence. . . . ''

"Well, I'm going to say yes, because I'm sure there is," Chris replied.

"And there's also a female, too, a female . . . Wait a minute," said George. "There is a male presence. Your dad passed on? Okay, because your father is here. Wait. Your mother and daughter? Okay, because he claims he's your grandfather, so I assume they're either that or niece and aunt." George turned to Chris's mother. "Your parents have passed on?"

"Yes."

''Because both of your parents are present. That's one of the males and the females. There's a younger female. There's somebody else with them, and she's obviously another generation and much younger when she passes on. And she is your family, also, yes?"

"Yes," Chris answered.

"Because she's between the two of you; she has her arms around the two of you. Very close with you? Not that she's playing favorites, but you're good pals as well as however you're related, because she just gave you a big hug. She comes to you with that emotion of sisterliness . . . closeness. Let me leave that open until I figure out how she means it. She gave me a strong sisterly feeling toward you. But it's obviously not your sister, but the closeness is there. But there is a reason she's closer to you? Because she keeps saying that you'll understand why she is singularizing your daughter. Yeah, because you were not only related, but you were friends."

"Yes."

"And you were starting to really become great friends. Your parents passed before her?" George asked Chris's mother.

"Yes."

''Because your parents claim that they were there to welcome her into the light when she passed on. So she doesn't want you to think she died alone. They were there for her in the hereafter. Her passing is tragic?''

''Yes.''

''It's beyond her control, yes?''

''Yes.''

''It's like this,'' George said, snapping his fingers.

''Yes.''

''She says she's gone in an instant. She's here in an instant and gone in an instant, you know, it's that quick. But it's no one's fault, she says. Does that make sense?''

''No.''

''Well, that's what she wants to declare, so I have to go by what she says. Feisty little character, anyway.''

''Yes.''

''You know, because she comes across like: her way or no way. So she's being very feisty in that respect. She talks about being a daughter. Is it your daughter?''

''Yes,'' Chris replied.

''Oh, geez, that's what's throwing me, because she says, 'I'm the sister, I'm the daughter.' Do you have other children?''

''Yes.''

''Oh, that's why she's the sister. But she had a closeness to you like that, that she said, 'I'm the sister, I'm the daughter.' And 'I'm the daughter' again; that's your granddaughter. So yes, she is the daughter. A bossy little child?''

''Yes.''

''Because she comes in like a little storm trooper, you know, bossy little child but a sweet child. . . . She gives me the impression that the short time she was here, she knew how to get her way. Her passing is accidental?''

''Yes.''

''Again she says it was beyond her control. Not that she has to apologize, but she apologizes to you especially because of what you had to go through. Because you're living in this grief of her loss, and there are days that it's literally driving you out of your mind. She says to try to put yourself at ease about it, knowing that she's still with you. Physically she's not here, but spiritually she is closer to you than you can imagine.

"Did you feel you didn't protect her at the end?" George asked.

"Yes," Chris answered, crying.

"She keeps saying, 'It's not your fault, [yet] you feel you didn't protect me. Why are you punishing yourself?' She certainly doesn't hold anything against you. She says however the tragedy occurred, she holds nothing against anyone. And she realizes it's not going to change anything. . . . But again, you feel—you were not with her?"

"No."

"She's saying that you feel if you had been there, you could have protected her, you could have stopped it, you could have saved her. And she knows you would have gladly sacrificed your life on her behalf. But she says it didn't happen that way. So she says please put yourself at peace.

"She certainly knows you grieve, and she certainly understands what you're going through. And she says [to] please try to put yourself at peace and go on with your life. . . . 'I know you'd much rather have me here on the earth than where I am; I can't turn the clock back.' A very smart child?"

"Yes."

"I feel like I'm talking to somebody older."

"Yes."

"Even though it's obvious she's very young. She's 'aged in wisdom,' as she puts it. . . . Is she your only daughter?"

"Yes."

"Yeah, that's why. Because that's another reason it hits home so badly. She's not only Mommy's girl, but she's also, as I said, like your best friend. . . . Another aspect of the death that hits home, you were just starting to get to know each other even better. You know, you were starting to . . . become good friends, like sisters, as she stated.

"Now, you and she were close, also, yes?" George

asked Chris's mother. "Because she keeps calling out to you with love and embraces you. She's directing the attention to her mom, but she doesn't want you to think you're being left out. So she keeps saying that. And she thanks you for being a tremendous support to her mother since she passed on, that you've been emotionally there for. . . . Her dad is still living, yes?"

"No," Chris answered.

"He's passed on?"

"Yes."

"Oh, she kept saying [something] about her dad, and I said, 'Oh, I guess she's calling to him.' Did he pass before her?"

"Yes."

"Then apparently he's with her, because he must have been there for her when she passed on. She kept saying, 'Dad, Daddy,' and I said, 'Oh, I guess she's calling to him.' I figured he was here. Again, I guess I judged by age. I figured the person's too young. He passes tragically, also?"

"Yes."

"Age as well as circumstances? Your daughter puts Virginia Slims over your head: It's a symbol [that] you've come a long way, baby. In other words, you've been hit double barreled: You lost your husband, and you also lost your daughter. She was close to her dad?"

"No."

"Because she says they're very close in the hereafter. So fortunately that's improved. She says that he was there to cross her over. He did abandon her?"

"Sort of."

"Yeah. She says, 'He did abandon me emotionally,' but, again, she doesn't hold anything against him. She says that he's there with her in the hereafter. He also apologizes to you. He was inclined to be a real S.O.B., as he puts it?"

"Yes."

"Did you and he end your marriage?"

"Yes."

"Because he says that you were married, then you divorced or ended your marriage. But it's not like you didn't hang in there and try to make it work. And he recognizes that. He feels bad for you only because he knows . . . you know your daughter's with him and you have to admit there's that feeling of resentment knowing that. Both your husband and your daughter say it's okay to feel like that.

"You brought her up, you were the heart and soul of the home, and now you've lost her and she's there with him. You know, it pisses you off. And as your husband says, 'I understand that you're justified how you feel—and your daughter feels the same way—it's okay to be pissed off.' And then you kind of get mad at yourself that you feel that way.

"But your daughter says, 'Mom, you have a justified gripe. It's okay to feel that way, because you feel that you put so much into things and now you've lost me.' She says, 'You haven't lost me, I'm still here.' She in some sort of accident?"

"Yes."

"Because she said she dies in an accident. And she wants to let you know she didn't suffer prior to her passing, that she is all right and at peace, in spite of the circumstances, the ugliness of the circumstances. I see a vision of Saint Joseph, which means a happy death and peace.

"Your husband basically abandoned you, yes? You know, emotionally and such. You called it quits, but he gave you a run for your money before you [did]. And he does apologize to you. Because that resentment and bitterness has been with you lately; they know that. He's got her, or she's there with him, yes, and you have to do without.

"Your daughter definitely embraces you again in a sympathetic way, that she knows you're bitter and resentful about that and you're justified. Because in essence—and your husband says you're right—you might have felt that your husband was never really a good parent to her to begin with, and you who were, she's been taken away from.

"Your daughter also tells you not to mess up your own head. Don't think you did something wrong, or you didn't do something right, or you failed her somehow. She said if she could be back here tomorrow, she would choose you as a mother without a moment's hesitation. So she says don't think that you did anything to deserve this. It's an unfortunate tragedy that's happened and you did not do anything to deserve it, nor have you ever done anything to deserve this.

"Are you thinking of moving?"

"No."

"Do you live in the metropolitan area? Because you might change residences up ahead. . . . Up ahead of you can be 1998. I'll leave it with both of you because it seems like there's a change of residence. Your daughter talks about how up ahead your life's going to start moving. And you're going to think you don't have the right to go on. You're going to feel like you're leaving her behind. She talks about it now because, as bossy as she can be, she demands that you go on with your life. She expects you to. If you go on with your life, it doesn't mean you're forgetting her, and it doesn't mean you're leaving her behind. It doesn't mean you don't love her anymore. You have the right to go on with your life. She says, 'Our lives run parallel now. Mine is spiritual, yours is material or physical.' But she will always be with you.

"You were home when this tragedy occurred?" asked George. "Because she states that spiritually she was next to you when you received the news of the tragedy. She was there, and she said the experience [was horrible] for her as well for you, because she's there next to you spiritually, and she's alive and all right, and you're hearing that she's dead, and you're freaking out.

"She says that she's there trying to let you know that she's all right and she's with you, and she knows you can't hear her. You're so wrapped up in your grief, which is justified, you don't hear her. And she says that's how she knows it's a terrible ordeal for you to have to go through.

"Do you have a brother?" With this question George entered an exchange that became quite confusing for him until Lisa straightened him out. "Close with you or close with your daughter? Living on the earth."

"None of my brothers was exceptionally close to her."

''Well, she calls out to one of her uncles, but [you're] hearing of some sort of happy news with him up ahead. Even if you're not that close, obviously I'll just leave the message with you in any case. . . . You have other children?''

''Yes.''

''Yes, because there are other children around you. You have more than one child?''

''No,'' Chris answered, thinking George meant children still on this plane.

''But counting her, you have children?''

''Yes, one.'' Again Chris's acknowledgment was misleading. As far as Lisa and George were concerned, if Chris had a child still on this plane, she had two children, not one.

''Okay, so you have one surviving. Because it seems like she's calling out to like a sister or something. Wait a minute, wait a minute, I'm mixed up. You have a son?''

''Yes.''

''Okay, she's obviously calling to her oh, that's what . . . she's talking about: her own [brother]. How old is he?''

''Thirteen.''

''Is he starting a job or something?''

''Oh, yes.''

''That's why. I was talking about *your* brother and the job. And it didn't seem to be making sense. Your daughter would be older than him?''

''Yes.''

''Yeah, because she's saying she's the elder child. Which is another reason it hits home. She's your first child, she's your elder child. Before, when I started asking about your brother and working, you said you knew your brothers weren't close with her, I said, 'Gee, what's going on here?'

''Then she kind of said to me in a polite way that I screwed it all up. And she said, 'Start over again.' She said, 'Ask about the brother.' And I said I did. And she said, 'No, I meant *my* brother, not hers. . . . '

''As your daughter says, with yourself, work on your

resentment, on the fact that you're downright pissed off over this tragedy. You're justified in that. But . . . try to let a lot of this anger go, she says. Because it's only going to make you feel miserable. And she says it's going to make things worse with you because it's a no-win battle. There's nothing you can do about it, and it's driving you crazy.

"She says she knows that if God told you tonight you were going to die, you couldn't care less. But she says you've got to go on with your life. You're here for yourself, and you're here for your other child. Your family. And she says, 'Someday we will be together again.' . . . She says you have to wait out your time and 'know that we'll be together again.'"

"One thing about your daughter," George remarked, "she tells it like it is?"

"Yeah."

"She's very to the point. She says she's not going to give me or you a line of bull, she's going to lay her cards out on the table. But on the other hand, this does not mean that—and she emphasizes this strongly—she does not want either of you to think that because she's being so blunt she does not understand what you're going through.

"She says, 'I certainly know how you feel, and I know how much you miss me, and I know how much you love me. I know how much you wish I were there again physically. I can't be, but I am there spiritually.' You've felt her around. You've dreamt about her. She's definitely let you know before tonight she's there. She's got that personality, so I'm not surprised.

"Now, right, she is in a car-type accident? You do feel the need to blame someone?"

"I don't know if I feel the need."

"But you're not happy with, obviously, somebody's behavior. She said, 'Don't blame anyone, it was an accident. It certainly was not done deliberately; nobody wanted to hurt you or kill me.' And she says, 'Unfortunately, wrong time, wrong place.'"

"She kind of did resent her father?" asked George. "I think she kind of did resent him for herself and also the way you were treated. She admits she resented it, but they've settled their differences over there. She says he's done a lot of growing up. He had trouble with drink?''

''No.''

''Was he kind of bad-tempered, then, or something?''

''He could be.''

''Seems like kind of crabby, bad-tempered. That could be the symbol that I saw, also. Without telling me, your daughter was called by a nickname? Like a breakdown of a formal name?''

''Yes.''

''Wait a minute, the nickname ... would be approximately five letters?''

''Less.''

''She keeps cutting it down. She says, 'Well, maybe I could expand it to five somehow by the way I spelled it,' but she said it would be less. Her actual name is a short name? Yes?''

''Yes.''

''Yeah, that's what it is. Her actual nickname and full name is four letters?''

''Yes.''

''That's the formal name.''

''Yes.''

''But I can shorten it, yes?''

''Yeah, oh, yeah.''

''That's what she's saying. You could, but it's not normally done. . . . For instance, someone's name is Diane, they can call you Dee. She says you can cut the name down. Lee? Lee or Lisa? Is that her?''

''Yes.''

''Yeah. She might have been called Lee at times.''

''Lis.''

''That's probably it, because she keeps shortening it down. She gave me the example—Dee, Diana, whatever— and then she said to me, 'Okay, now just be quiet for a minute and listen.' And I was quiet and I listened, and she said, 'Lee-sah,' like that. She kept saying you can shorten it down. . . . Is she in the car when this occurs?''

"Yes."

"But she's not driving?"

"No."

"Yes, I take it somebody else is, obviously." George then went on to ascertain that the accident had occurred in New York City, of which the Bronx is one of five boroughs, that six people were in the car when it crashed, that two were female, that they were out joyriding, and, most stunningly, that the car had wrapped around the tree.

George ended the reading by saying, "Again, she embraces you with love because she knows this is by far the worst thing that's ever happened to you in your life. And she says, ironically, 'You could say to yourself, "Now I've already gone through the worst. Now what's the worst life could do to me?" ' "

"I've said that," Chris admitted.

"Right. Are you inclined to be a little overprotective?"

"Yes," Chris answered, laughing.

"With good reason. She says you're going to have to kind of give him [Peter] breathing space. You're just so petrified this could happen again that you feel if you're overprotective he'll be safe. But she says up ahead it could cause, unfortunately, a lack of communication."

Following a few more unrelated exchanges, Lisa went back. Chris asked George, "Will my daughter forget me if I don't die soon?"

"No, she won't," he answered. "Not any more than you'll forget her, which you won't."

Later Chris said of her reading, "It helped. I play a tape of it every now and then and listen to what Lisa said through George. But everything that does help only helps a little and for a very short time. I don't think of it now as healing. I think about it as coping.

"I once heard someone on television say something that stuck in my mind: You have to accept things the way they are, not the way you want them to be."

•   •   •

Despite it being Lisa's time to go, Chris Torchiano was not necessarily wrong to think that someone was responsible for her daughter's death. Society places upon parents an awesome responsibility for their children's well-being. Regardless of their child's age, there are few conscientious mothers and fathers who do not think, even if only for a moment, that there must have been something different they might have done to spare their child's life. In the case of Helena and Tim Wresch, their decision to have their son undergo a relatively new heart operation that he may or may not have been a good candidate for led to his death. Even though the damage his heart sustained over his lifetime certainly would have ended his life in early adulthood, the Wresches still felt in hindsight that the surgery was perhaps a mistake.

The heart condition that plagued Timmy was congenital. Within his first twenty-four hours of life, doctors discovered that his heart had only two chambers instead of four, with only one valve dividing them rather than two, and the pulmonary artery that carries blood from the heart to the lungs for oxygenation had not narrowed, so that there was always the possibility that Timmy might succumb to congestive heart failure. In addition, other organs were adversely affected, and he was born without a spleen.

Doctors were so certain that Timmy would die within months of being born, they warned the Wresches not to even take him home. Yet he grew to be healthy, bright, and active. Except for a couple of early bouts with pneumonia and routine medical care and medication, Timmy participated in almost everything except very strenuous sports.

Timmy's life was, at least outwardly, so normal, few of the Wresches' friends even knew of his health problems. The only visible difference between Timmy and his peers was his stature. In the ninth grade, he was only five feet two. But nothing seemed to deter him.

"I think Timmy needed to feel important and needed to feel like everybody else," Helena recalled. "So he joined everything, and he was good at everything he did. He was the kind of kid who, even if he was short of breath, wouldn't say anything. The great loves of Timmy's life were playing in Little League and building remote radio cars, which he raced with his friends. Later he played trumpet in the high school band, studied piano, and bowled, a sport he took up after his father and I had to tell him at seven that he couldn't play soccer.''

Timmy's outlook on life was one we could all learn from. "I'm not going to sit back and wait to die," Timmy would say. "Believe me, if it's going to find me, it's going to find me whether I'm healthy or not. If I'm going to die, I'm not going to worry about it. Life goes on."

"So Timmy just went on with his life," Helena said. "He always played down his condition. He just wanted to be treated like a normal kid."

When Timmy was still a baby, the Wresches had taken him to the renowned Mayo Clinic in Rochester, Minnesota. There doctors examined the boy and consulted with the Wresches' physicians at home on Long Island. In the spring of 1991 doctors from the Mayo Clinic contacted the Wresches through Timmy's cardiologist. They felt they had made significant technical advances in cardiac surgery and that Tim was an excellent candidate for the "Fontan procedure." As Helena explained, "Simply, the idea was to reroute the plumbing, so to speak. We knew there was some risk. But for some reason we felt confident because Timmy was always so healthy. I felt the doctors were saying this was his only *real* chance to live into adulthood."

"What did the doctors say they were going to do to me?" Timmy asked his mother.

"Well, I think they might make another heart chamber," she answered.

"Three chambers? Well, I guess I'll be an amphibian," Timmy retorted.

"What are you now?"

"I'm a bird," he replied.

In preparation for the trip to Minnesota, Timmy prebowled fifteen games for a bowling tournament he would be missing. "He didn't want to let his team down," Helena recalled. "That's the type of kid Timmy was."

Helena recalled Timmy leaving their house, sports bag filled with schoolbooks, balloons for water balloons, and *Mad* magazines. "Let's get this over with," he said.

"My husband and I just felt secure that the miracles would continue for Timmy."

But shortly after the operation things took a wrong turn. Because the heart had to be stopped for a period during surgery, Timmy was placed on life support. When the surgeons tried to restart his heart, it did not resume pumping normally. They were surprised to see the toll fourteen and a half years of supporting Timmy's body with only two chambers had taken. Timmy's heart was incredibly enlarged.

Helena, Tim, Sr., and their daughter, Christina, were at Timmy's side almost constantly over the next several days. Because he had a respirator tube in his throat, Timmy could not speak. He was also taking morphine for the surgical pain. No doubt sensing that something was wrong, the boy refused to close his eyes. "Timmy was determined to show us that he would pull through this operation," Helena said. "We had discussed earlier that if he couldn't talk, he should blink his eyes to communicate or try squeezing our hands. In spite of the morphine and the other drugs, he jerked his foot whenever he could to convey the message that he was fully cognizant of what was going on around him.

"The doctors had placed him on a mini heart-and-lung machine, which they had hoped to wean him from slowly. But by then, I guess, his heart was giving up. He just kind of went to sleep."

At one point the doctors attempted to revive Timmy by manually massaging his heart, an extreme measure. The Wresches waited in another room for about an hour, praying that Timmy might be saved. "Then the doctor came out and said they'd done all they could. It just didn't work." Five days after the operation Timmy Wresch died.

"I was in shock. It was as if he'd gotten hit by a car. He walked into the hospital, and he was shipped home in a box. It was torture. It didn't make any sense," Helena said.

"Without the operation, Timmy wouldn't have lived," she acknowledged. "He might have had another year or so, but we would have watched him suffer. This way he didn't suffer. Maybe it was never an operation for Timmy. After he passed, we racked our brains: Did we go too late? Should we have taken him earlier? Did something go wrong? My husband feels we should have taken Timmy for surgery years before we did."

After attending meetings of the Compassionate Friends, Helena, Tim, and Christina had their reading with George during a group discernment. For the first several minutes Tim received a long, personal message from his own father.

"Your son passes tragically?" George asked, then went on. "He's close with the three of you. I'm sure that as parents you had your ups and downs; that's normal."

"Very close," Helena answered.

"But he still knows his parents and sister love him very much, and the feelings certainly are mutual. You obviously pray for him, because he keeps thanking you for your prayers and asks that they continue. You pray for him in your own way, yes?"

"Yes," Tim replied.

"Because you're a typical guy: It's all inside. But he knows you send prayers to him. You're not doing it publicly. It's all within yourself, but your son says, 'I'm receiving your prayers, and I want to let you know that it's a very personal exchange between you and the hereafter.'"

"Okay."

"He had a vehicle-type accident?"

"No."

"Did he pass very suddenly, then?"

"Yes," his mother confirmed.

"That's what he means. Because I'm beginning to realize now that there's a new meaning for a vehicle accident. It can mean an accident. But it can also mean the person passes suddenly. Wait a minute: Is his passing accidental?"

"No."

"Wait. I think I know what he's doing. He doesn't pass from a health problem."

"Yes."

"Does it come upon him suddenly?" George asked again.

"Yes," the woman acknowledged.

"That's what he means. Because he's telling me there's health involved, it's accidental, and it's very sudden. He showed me a car accident. But he says, 'It's not a car accident.' However, he says it's very sudden, accidental. And then he started talking about his health. I thought he was trying to tell me he *didn't* pass from a health problem. When you said he did, he said 'Yes, it comes upon me suddenly, accidentally.' It was there for a while [the health problem], though?"

"Oh, yes," Helena said.

"It's there, but you don't know about it, or you don't know the severity of it. Your son just wants the three of you to know, as his family—particularly his parents—that just because you're parents doesn't make you infallible. You almost think you should have known something was wrong."

"Yes."

"He says no. He didn't even seem to know he was ill. His illness affected him in the head in any way? Internally. It also affects his breathing," George said.

"Yes, more of that," she acknowledged.

"Because I'm not getting enough oxygen to the brain. That's probably why he's saying it's affecting the head. Is it more in the lungs? Because it's in the respiratory or lung area."

"Yes."

"It was diagnosed as not being serious? He's giving me that impression."

"Yeah. He didn't make a big deal out of it," she said.

"Exactly. It's almost as if I have bronchitis, and then I find out later that I have deadly pneumonia. But I wouldn't think [at first that I was that sick]."

"Right."

"It seems your son's not as ill as you would think."

"Possible."

"By the time it does manifest itself wholly, it's almost too late. It becomes worse. Did his lungs fill up? Because I feel like there's a lot of fluid, a heaviness in the chest."

Again: "Possible."

"There's pressure on the heart, too. Because your son tells me that his heart gives out," George said.

"Right," she acknowledged.

" 'Just don't feel that you've failed me,' he keeps saying."

"Yes."

"He keeps saying, 'I know you didn't fail me. You didn't fail me. Just because you're parents doesn't make you infallible.' So he says to let go of that despair. . . . Because, again, as normal parents, you may feel had you known better, you would have done something. But you didn't know, and your son didn't know.

"You and he very close?" George asked Christina. "Because he feels close to you. I mean, I'm sure as brother and sister you had your ups and downs. Everybody does. But the thing is, you were starting to become closer in the sense of understanding each other. Probably with time that would have been achieved."

"Yes."

"You and he were becoming closer, also," George told Tim, Sr. "Not that you weren't close to begin with. But you were getting closer because you were seeing things more from a man-to-man point of view, and not from a man-boy point of view."

"Right," he acknowledged.

"Your son does thank you for all being good to him while he was passing. When things got that bad, he says he knows that you certainly did your best to help him and do the best for him. But he goes off into a sleep at the end. I see a vision of Saint Joseph, which means a happy death. He passes peacefully into the hereafter,'' George said.

''Okay.''

''Did your son pass in the hospital?''

''Yes,'' said Helena.

''He said his grandmother [about whom George had spoken earlier in the reading] was in the hospital room, spiritually. Because he says he was talking to her in this sleep state. He says that she knew he was coming over, and she said to him, 'If you're ready to let go, I'm here for you. But the time [to pass] is when you decide you're ready.' Your son says that your mother crossed him into the light,'' George explained.

''Do you take the name Ron,* or Ronald,* who's passed on?''

''No [not passed on].''

''Maybe your son knows him. He's asking how Ron is. Are they friends? Well, I won't even try to figure it out. He's not telling me what it is,'' George said.

''I'd tell you,'' the boy's mother said, ''but I don't want to.''

''Your son says, 'Tell Ron you've heard from me.' I'll leave it at that. He keeps calling out to Ron. He's a friend of the family?''

''Yes.''

''He says it's a friend of the family. He's also a fatherly figure.''

''Oh, yes.''

''Oh, he's talking about a priest!'' George exclaimed.

''Yes!''

''I keep seeing a priest in front of me [psychically], and I know he's not passed on. Your son calls out and says, 'Tell Ron you've heard from me. He's been praying for me.' He thanks him for it. Your son also thanks Ron for

---

*This name has been altered. Everything else in this story, however, is true.

being a tremendous spiritual support to all of you since he passed on. That's the important thing. He says some clergy don't go out of their way, and Ron has gone out of his way. So your son thanks him for that.''

''Yes, he has been a tremendous support to us,'' Helena confirmed.

''Without telling me, your son was called by a nickname.''

''Yes.''

''It's a breakdown of his formal name.''

''Yes.''

''It's a short name.''

''Yes.''

''It's five letters or less.''

''Yes.''

''Your son's formal name has seven letters,'' George said.

''Yes,'' she answered.

After several minutes of trying to psychically decipher the spirit's name from the symbols and clues he was hearing clairaudiently, George said, ''Don't mind me laughing, but he just said to me, 'If you think about who you just spoke to that you didn't like, you'll find out what my name is.' ''

George thought a moment. ''Is it Timothy? Timothy, Tim, or Timmy?''

''Yes,'' his mother acknowledged.

''It's funny,'' George explained. ''I just had contact with somebody by the name of Timothy, whom I don't like. And that's what went through my head. And your son said, 'Right!' I thought at one point he was saying 'Jimmy.'

''Do you sing?'' George asked Helena.

''Yes.'' She was a music teacher and singer.

''Not professionally, but you do.''

''Yes.''

''I mean, you're not onstage at the Metropolitan Opera.''

''Right.''

''But you do sing in church or something like that, because your son keeps telling me about your singing. You offer up your singing on his behalf," George said.

"Yes."

"He says he hears you singing around him. . . . Was he fond of that character from *Dumbo*, Timothy? I keep [psychically] seeing that little stuffed animal floating around you."

"Yes."

"He had one, right?"

"Yes, he did."

George paused, then returned to the subject of the priest, Ron.

"You still have contact with him," he said. "Whether he's open or not [to George's psychic-mediumistic ability] is not the point. Your son says to tell Father Ron you've heard from him, and he thanks Ron for being so supportive to all of you. It's the message in the reading we want to get through."

"Yes."

"But Timmy says to both of you, don't ever feel that you didn't do the right thing. . . . As ironic as it may sound, it was his time to pass on. In the back of his mind, it was his time to go. He says it always seemed that he was going to be here a short time to achieve as much as he could. It always seemed that Timmy had a lot to get done."

"Right."

"You've dreamt of him?" asked George. "Because he says he's come in dreams. Your son says to let you know that it was him. . . . Also, do you belong to a support group?"

"Yes."

"Your son is glad. Because there are times that he's seen you have your days when you can deal with it and days when you can't. So it's good that you have somebody to talk to about it."

George continued, "Timmy says he's very close to you around special occasions and holidays: Mother's Day, birthdays, Christmas, things of that nature. Is your birthday coming up?"

"Mine just passed," Timmy's sister said.

"Because your brother wished you a happy birthday. He extended white roses to you from the hereafter. . . . Was your son very athletically inclined?"

"He loved sports," his mother replied.

"Because it seems he's more physical-looking than I would be."

"Yes."

"Timmy's fine and at peace. He wants to assure you all that he is closer to you than you can imagine, and that he certainly is aware of the grief that you are going through.

"Timmy wants you to know that the tragedy that occurred to him was certainly like an accident. It just happened suddenly. It was no one's fault, no one's responsibility. It just happened."

The couple nodded they understood.

"Maybe that's why your son stated it was his time to pass on. He also says your going over [his passing] is not going to bring him back. But he says he knows it's easier said than done. He's close to you. He says, 'I'm there spiritually.' But you don't see or feel him as if he were here physically. When the day comes that you're there with him, you'll understand exactly what he's talking about. It's hard for our physical consciousness to comprehend what they're trying to say sometimes, because we see things from a certain perspective."

"Right."

"They want you to know that they understand what you're going through and that they care. That way it makes it easier for them. They can do something about it in a caring sense, as best they can. But on the other hand, they do want you to realize that unfortunately there's only so much they can do. They still want you to go on with your lives. They are near, and you certainly will be with them again someday, your son says."

"Yes."

"There's also a Helen," George said. "Passed on."

"My friend," Helena answered.

"Your son is saying that Helen is with him, also. She's present and is well.

"I think with this he's going to step aside, because he withdraws along with all the others. He sends his love to the three of you and asks that you continue to pray for him. He sends his love to you all, and the others do the same."

Not every reading yields the answers subjects seek. In the case of the Elwell family, however, the reading provided hope and, in the case of Travis Elwell's father, a new perspective on death. The tragedy of Travis and his best friend, Ron Cook, Jr., also shows what can happen to families when grief is not dealt with effectively.

Travis and Ron, Jr., were the very best of friends. Coincidentally, both their fathers and their paternal grandfathers had been close friends as well. They had graduated high school only three months before and spent most of their time hanging out together in Seacaucus, New Jersey. Travis lived at home with his parents, a brother Jason, nineteen, and sister Alexis, fifteen. Along with his three brothers, Travis's father Dennis operated the trucking business his father founded years before. Travis was anxious to join the family business.

One evening in early September Travis and Ron were en route to meet friends at a local fast-food restaurant. They came to a railroad crossing. Ron, the driver, pulled around the lowered gate, putting the car directly in the path of an oncoming passenger train. Both boys were killed instantly.

For Annette and Dennis Elwell, the news came as a complete shock. First police told them only that Travis had been in an accident. Although the officers assured the couple that he would survive, Annette had a strong feeling he would not. Soon they were informed he had died.

Both parents were overwhelmed with grief. Although Annette took solace in her religious beliefs, Dennis had nothing to hold on to. "Before I went to George," he said, "it was black and white to me: When you die—you die. That's it. My opinion was always that when I die, it's going to be like it was before I was born: nothing.

"After my son was killed, I cried a lot. I cried a lot alone. I do a lot of long-haul trucking, often alone. That was probably my most difficult time. Because that's all my son ever wanted to do, to work with me. So when I'd drive, that was my difficult time. But when I had to cry, I cried.''

Complicating the Elwells' grief was the lack of hard knowledge about the accident. How had the boys come to be on those tracks when the train came? "We never knew exactly what happened," Annette said. "Because in the first report, they told us that the train had passed, and for some reason the gate just didn't go up. And then when the boys proceeded to drive around the downed gate and across the tracks, another train came from the opposite direction—which they obviously did not see. A police officer initially told us he thought there was a parked train on the tracks nearby that may have blocked the boys' vision. However, when we got the written police report, that wasn't mentioned in it.''

Did the boys simply ignore the downed gate and drive around it? If so, why? Were they speeding? Were they careless? One of Dennis Elwell's primary reasons for going to George was to resolve these questions. But more important, as he said, "My wife and I needed to hear that somewhere my son still existed.''

The Elwells did attend a bereaved-parents support group and took some comfort in that. Dennis's good friend, Ron Cook, Sr., however, was simply inconsolable. His grief plunged him into a deep, intractable depression from which he never emerged. Unlike Dennis, he believed in an afterlife, but he was so distraught over whether or not his son was all right there, he took it upon himself to find out the only way he knew how: He shot himself in the head and died at age forty-five.

Three months after Travis's death the Elwells had an experience that suggested that perhaps there really was life after death. Donna,* a girlfriend of their son Jason, phoned Annette to tell her of a dream in which Travis appeared to

---

*This name has been altered. Everything else in this story, however, is true.

her on a motorcycle. "He looked good," Donna told Mrs. Elwell. "He was smiling and wearing a green sweatshirt and black jeans." As we later learned from Annette, green and black were Travis's favorite colors, and he'd always wanted a motorcycle.

In Donna's dream, she said to Travis, "Come on, let's go, Travis. You have to take me to the dentist."

"Okay, Donna," Travis replied. "I'll take you, but there's one thing you have to promise me."

"Sure. Anything."

"You have to promise me that you're going to get in touch with my mother. You have to tell my mother and father, Jason, Alexis, and my grandparents that I'm fine and happy where I am. But tell my mother I'm with John. He's taking care of me."

"Travis, can you do me a favor?" Donna then asked. "Can you tell me something that only you or your mother know, so that when I tell her, she'll believe me." That's when the dream ended.

"Annette, I woke up suddenly and started crying because Travis never got a chance to tell me," Donna told Travis's mother.

"But, Donna, he *did* tell you," Annette replied.

"How?"

"Because he told you he was with John." As Annette explained, her grandfather—whom the kids knew only as Grandpa—was named John. She is certain that none of the children knew their great-grandfather's given name. Annette was sure that Donna's dream proved that her son was still alive somewhere. In the reading with George, Travis came through and confirmed that Donna's dream had been no dream at all. Further confirmation that Travis was in communication from the other side came by his mention of two recent suicides: Ron, Sr.'s and that of Joe, Travis's girlfriend's father. The latter occurred just a week before the Elwells' reading.

"There are two males; one younger, one older," George said to Annette and Dennis.

"There's one older," she corrected.

"And there's one younger, too. I've got two different generations. Because it's two men. The younger one is closer to the two of you, because he came in immediately. He's the first one. Did your dad pass on?"

"No," she replied.

"Yours is still living, too?" he asked Dennis. "Because he keeps saying 'Grandfather' is with him. So apparently he's trying to tell me it's a grandfather to one of you. . . . You lost a son," George said.

"Yes," she answered.

"He passes as an adult. Young, obviously, but he's an adult."

"Just about."

"He certainly is beyond the age of thirteen."

"Yes," answered Dennis.

"Because he says he passes on as a young adult. Did he know your grandfather? Were you very close with your granddad?"

"I never knew him!" Annette replied.

"It's funny," said George, "because your son keeps insisting that your grandfather was one of the souls that was there to meet him when he came over."

"I got that in a dream!" she exclaimed.

"Oh, okay. He keeps insisting that I tell you that."

"We got the message in a dream," Dennis confirmed.

"Then this is a reassurance of the message you both received. Because he keeps insisting I say that. But he says your granddad was there to meet him when he came over. You might have been afraid he didn't know anybody over there. But that [the dream] was to assure you that even though he didn't know anybody personally, that certainly didn't block out the family connection.

"You do pray for him, needless to ask, because he thanks you for your prayers," George continued. He addressed Dennis. "You and he very close? Because this is a daddy's boy. He keeps coming over to you, and you're not only father and son, but you seem to be best friends as well. You have a very nice, close relationship, the two of you.

"He's not shy about showing affection to you. I keep feeling you're being hugged. You know how some young people, when they get older, don't show it as much to their fathers as to their mothers. . . .

"He very athletic? He's very athletic-looking. He's definitely broader than me."

"Yes."

"But then," George joked, "so is everybody. In any case, he is very athletic-looking. I'm sure you won't challenge me on this, but he does come across as the son every parent would be glad to have. That's the feeling I'm getting. He kind of gives me the impression that he's the All-American Boy type.

"He also passes tragically. It's beyond his control, he says. He goes tragically, and the reason it's even ten times more shocking is that I feel like I'm dealing with someone who's got a real head on his shoulders. There's a loss of control, you know, and it's beyond his control.

"He apologizes for this happening—not that he has to—but he sees the grief you two are going through, and it's a frustration from over there, because he feels helpless to do anything about it except to let you know that he is okay. And he also claims he didn't suffer prior to his passing.

"Yes," George went on, "he's definitely been trying to send signs, somehow. The dreams, familiarities, anything. . . . He says how it can be very frustrating for them in the next stage, that they're trying to let you know they're all right, and they know you can't hear them.

"Was he in his late teens when he passed? Because I feel he's around eighteen. He says he's over sixteen, and then he said he was eighteen."

"Just eighteen," Annette said.

"Was he still in school?"

"No," her husband answered.

"Just graduated," she added.

"Okay. Because he talked about graduation, so I assumed he was just about to graduate or something. Now, this can be symbolic, but: A vehicle involved in his passing? Because there's a vehicle-type accident.'' Both parents nodded.

"Very popular individual."

"Yes," said Dennis.

"And everybody likes him," George went on. "I just get the feeling that he's very friendly, outgoing, and makes friends easily. Very fair, nice guy. You might have been afraid he didn't know anybody over there, but I see he's made plenty of friends. You know, I feel like I'm very well liked in the next stage, even as much as I was liked here.

"He does pay you a nice compliment. He says he's heard rumors about reincarnation. If they're true, he's going to choose you as his parents again. Not that he's playing favorites, but he's kind of partial to his father, so he says he definitely wants him as a dad again. He doesn't want to hurt your feelings, but he knows you kind of know that anyway. This is definitely Daddy's boy, that's for sure.''

George paused, then asked, "Is he your only son? And your youngest?''

"He's our youngest son," Dennis answered.

"Thank you," said George. "That's what I wanted to know. He keeps telling he's the younger son. . . .

"Does somebody say the rosary for him?''

"I do," Annette said.

"Because he keeps showing it, and I thought, Well, wait a minute, you might not relate to that if you're not Christians, but it's a spiritual thing to me. In any case, he does thank you for it and asks that it please continue. He asks that his father do so, too.''

"He's got to learn," Annette explained.

"Because your son says it's a very powerful form of grace in the next stage. . . . His grandparents are still living? Because he keeps calling out to grandparents. So apparently the grandparents that are there are your grandparents; *his* great-grandparents. Because he keeps calling out to the family.

"Does he have a sister he's very close to? Not that he's playing favorites again, but he definitely calls to a sister. They were like best friends. And he keeps saying to tell her you've heard from him. But he states again that the two grandparents were certainly there for him when he crossed over.

"Was he in a vehicle when he passes? Is he driving? Because he keeps saying he passed in a vehicle or some sort of vehicle-type accident. Again, he claims he doesn't suffer prior to his passing. He seems to be out of it," George explained.

"Good," Annette replied with a sigh.

"So even if he was alive, he's not conscious of any type of pain or suffering. I don't know, he just says, 'I'm out of it,' and he seems to pass on pretty quickly. But as parents I'm sure you worried about whether he suffered prior to his passing. I see the vision of Saint Joseph, which means a happy death. He also sustain injury to the head?"

"Yes," said Dennis.

"Because he says it's like, *pow*!, a blow to the head, and 'I'm gone instantly.' He literally doesn't know what hits him. But he's somebody that would adapt to any situation, any circumstance. So when he got there, your grandfather came up to him and explained, 'You've been in an accident, you've passed on.' And he came back to your grandfather and asked, 'You mean I'm dead?' And your grandfather said, 'Well, yeah, but you're not, you know,' and he tried to explain to him. Then your son adapted very nicely to the situation.

"Is there a Joe who passed on over there?" George asked.

"Living. My father," Annette acknowledged.

"I heard him call to Joe. Is everything okay with him health-wise? He seems to be concerned. I'm not saying anything terrible is happening, but he calls out to Joe. So I'm going to leave it with you."

"There's also a Joe that just passed on," she said.

"Well, he did say Joe, Joseph, so that could be my clue for two. He did talk about your father's health. But then on the other hand, he was also saying, 'Joe is here with me.' And that's evidence of the two of them together. Did this other Joe pass young?"

"Last week," Annette answered. "No, but—"

"But young by today's standards?"

"Yeah," she agreed.

"Oh, so that's what he means, because he seems to pass on young by today's standards. Is he kind of like an uncle figure to your son?"

"His girlfriend's father," she clarified.

"Yes, then he would be. Because he said he's a father figure to your son. His girlfriend still living?"

"Yes," answered Dennis.

"He started talking before about a girlfriend, and I kind of said to myself, 'Yeah, I know, I'll get to that.' But that's when he cut in with Joe. So he might be trying to say that he met Joe when he came over. . . . You still have contact with his girlfriend, because he's asking for her. Also tell her that her father is there with him now. Because he says, 'Joe has crossed over.' I think the reason he's pushing this is to give you alternate proof that—"

"That he's there," said Annette, finishing George's sentence.

"Yes, that he's there. He says Joe is there. But he does bring up about your dad, the concern with health. . . . Was he fond of hockey? Did he watch it or something? Because he seems to like that. He's on a team, though."

"Yes," Dennis responded.

"He definitely is on a team, some sort of sport. I've got to be honest with you, the only sport I excel at is sleeping, so I wouldn't know one from the next. . . . All right, the name Sean or John?"

"John is my grandfather," answered Annette.

"Passed on. Okay, I couldn't tell if he said Sean or John. So apparently he said John; that's why I gave out both. That was the one that met your son when he came over, because when you said grandfather, he said that's the one that met him when he crossed over, and he says *he* met Joe.

"He's right, technically he [Joe] is a father figure if they'd gotten married. He would have been his father-in-law, so he was right when he said he was a father figure, like an uncle.

"Joe's wife is still living? Or has she passed? Because I heard Joe start talking about his wife, so apparently he's trying to tell me she's there," George said.

"She died before him," Annette explained.

"It's funny. It's like one couldn't live without the other, because if she went first, it's as if he almost just let go to make sure she was all right. He couldn't live without her."

"He killed himself," Dennis said.

"It's interesting, too, because not that they'd recommend it—I certainly would never recommend it to anybody—but there doesn't seem to be a penalty on the other side when you kill yourself under those circumstances. But they still say it's not the right thing to do. In any case, he's with his wife. Because it's obvious they loved each other so much, and this man just couldn't live without her.

"He does admit it was not the right thing to do, but he's certainly not being punished like somebody who commits suicide for selfish reasons. . . .

"Did your son pass before his girlfriend's mother? Because he also claims he met her when she came over, and then the father followed. Also, Joe does call out to his daughter and family. He does apologize for taking his own life. It was not the right thing to do, especially with them having just lost their mother. So he asks that you tell them that. But the three of them are together, in any case.

"Your son says the minute you go home, call her and tell her 'You heard from us.' She's been hit with a triple whammy—parents, boyfriend—and she's in the worst state possible. That's why he wants to let her know that they're still with her. You do have another boy?" George asked.

"Yes," Dennis acknowledged.

"Okay, because he does talk about his sister. Not that he's playing favorites, but he's very close with her. Counting him, you would have had three children?"

"Right."

"Because that's what he's telling me, that there are two children surviving. And I take it he's in the middle?"

"Yes."

"He calls to his brother, but his sister definitely is taking his passing very badly. Do you take a 'Paul'?"

"Paula," Annette corrected.

"Living?"

"Deceased."

"All right, I'll go with it. I thought he said Paul, but Paula is close enough; I just could have missed a letter. She is family? Or just a friend or something?"

"No. It's the mother of someone I met in the cemetery."

"It's funny," George remarked, "because he said, 'I know who Paula is.' He didn't know her at all?"

"No."

"She passes on as a youth."

"Yes."

"Because he says, 'I know who Paula is.' He's met Paula over there."

"He must have met her since [she passed on]," Annette remarked.

"The fact that you've met the parents or know the parents, it makes sense that the message would come through. Otherwise I'd say it has no purpose. So I'll leave it with you.

"Is there a Denny or Danny?" George inquired.

"Dennis?" Annette asked.

"Passed on."

"Danny," she said, nodding. "Yes."

"Wait a minute," said George, "did I hear him say Den or Denny?" He looked at the man. "Now, *your* name is Dennis."

"Yes," he acknowledged.

"But there's no Dennis passed on?"

"Not that I know of."

"Okay, because he must have been calling out to you, and I'm not surprised. You're number one in his life. But he did say, 'Danny is with me, also.' So apparently Danny is there with him as well."

"My uncle," Dennis explained.

"Your son is pretty broad-shouldered," George remarked.

"Yes."

"He looks like he's a football player. Because he looks like he's in a football uniform now, and he keeps showing me the pads, or whatever they put on their shoulders."

"He played football," he said.

"Okay, that's probably what it is. Because he told me before that the sport he's involved in was kind of a rough, physical sport. And that's what made me jump before at hockey. I don't know one from the other. I see him in a football uniform. He was officially on a team."

"Yes."

"Yes, he keeps saying Danny is there, and Margaret, also. Is she a great aunt?"

"Grandmother," Dennis corrected.

"His *great*-grandmother," his wife chimed in.

"He keeps saying Margaret is there with him, also. He says you can sleep at night if you just know he's all right. Well, he's all right. He's closest when the need is greatest. It's like he's gone to another country and lives with the family there. But he says he certainly is alive and at peace.

"A very giving soul. He has a nice compassionate air. And he says he's been trying to help out Joe over there, too, because he kind of went over there restlessly under the circumstances [suicide].

"Who is Bob, or Robert? A friend; again, I'm going to leave it as a friend. And you did say he had a friend Girard?"

"Yes."

"Because he is calling to Jerry or Girard, Gerald, whatever his name was. He calls out to a lot of friends over here. Because everybody seems to have been at his wake and the funeral," George said.

"Yes," the boy's father replied.

"That's probably why I think he's trying to incorporate so many different people. You still have contact with Girard and some of his other friends?"

"Yeah."

"Like they're linked to him."

"Yes, all the time."

"That's why he's glad that they've become like your adopted children in a lot of ways, because they're linked with him, and he says definitely tell them you've heard from him. . . . I think he's going to step aside, because he says there's somebody else trying to get through behind him. But he does say to go home and have a good night's rest and know that he's all right, and he sends his love to the two of you, his brother and sister, and his friends and family. Just know he's okay and continue to pray for him, particularly through the rosary. Only because, again, it's a very powerful form of grace.

"I'm trying to figure out whether we're being cut off or . . . There's also a Mike?"

"Mikey?"

"Has he passed on?"

"Yes, my cousin," Annette answered.

"Because I got cut all of a sudden," George explained, "then I heard somebody say 'Mike, or Michael, is here with me.' So it must be. He also passed on very young?"

"Yes."

"He comes through now, and he greets you. Again, to give you evidence that your son's not alone."

"Okay."

"Because you might have been worried that your son didn't know anybody there, but he seems to know a lot of people.

"Also, Ron?"

"Yes."

"Passed on."

"Yes."

"Because he says, 'Ron is here with me.' They passed together," George stated.

"Yes," Annette acknowledged.

"They were the two that were killed in the accident."

"Yes."

"Because he says, 'Ron, or Ronnie, is here with me, also.' You know his parents?"

"Yes."

"Do you know if they can deal with this? He calls to them. Just let them know that he's okay."

"Okay."

"He said Ron *and* Ronnie?" Dennis asked.

"Ron and his father," Annette told George. "His father killed himself after that accident. So *both* Rons."

"Wow," George remarked, "you've had plenty of tragedy in your lives. Now, Ron's mother is still living."

"Yes."

"Ronnie, I guess, is the boy. I'm glad you picked up on that."

"*Ron* is the son," Dennis explained, "Travis's friend. *Ronnie* we all knew as his father."

"Oh, because your son said, 'Ron, Ronnie is here with me,' and I just thought it was the same person. I didn't pay any attention to it. You have contact with the mother?"

"Yes."

"If you think she could deal with this, both call out. The father seems to take his own life . . . as if he wanted to find out his son was all right, and that was the only way he could do it. It wasn't just for selfish reasons, but he was so upset by the passing, I'm being told, he figured the only way he could find out if his son was okay was if *he* died, too. And apparently, since it wasn't his time to go, he forced it.

"Again, he says it's not the right thing to do. This is not what he should have done, because now his wife is left in despair. You know, you uphold one and sacrifice another. He says that he should have remained.

"If you can call this lady, and you think she could deal with it, tell her that the two of them are together, that her husband reports back that yes, his son is 'alive' and so is he. He seems to be a little restless because he knows he put his wife through a double tragedy. But that's the reason that he did take his own life, and I think she knows that anyway.

"Ronnie, Sr., says the two of you don't have to worry

about dying, because your son's all right. They can tell you that he's all right.

"And, with that, I think they're going to step aside. Again, your son sends his love to both of you. Remember to pray for them all, especially through the rosary. Don't feel you're wasting your time. Because you say it faithfully every day, so he thanks you for it. Dad should learn.

"He says, 'This is something you can do for me in the next stage as well as for yourself.' You want to do something special for him since he's passed on. He says, 'Well, this is it.' Just pray daily, and, again, it's not a Catholic suggestion, it's a spiritual suggestion. With that they all step aside, because a whole mob is going back, and they call out to people that are here. He sends his love to both of you, and he calls out to his sister and brother. He says you won't mind if he says he loves Dad best of all?"

"No," Annette answered.

"Okay. I didn't know if I should say it or not. I said I didn't want to hurt anybody's feelings, but he said, 'You won't mind that, will you?' Because he's definitely Daddy's boy. Okay, he steps aside."

George took a deep breath and exhaled.

"So, what a group of tragedies: your son, the suicide, this one, another suicide."

"It just snowballed; it just kept going and going and going," Annette said.

"And I think *I* have problems," George remarked.

"Oh, there's worse than us," Annette said. "There's worse than us."

Months later Dennis had this to say about the reading: "The visit to George was probably the only thing that helped me. But I'm not going to say it made everything okay. George never said it would. But the reading made me realize that my son still existed. Now I feel I'm not alone. I can talk to Travis when I need to. And he hears me. That doesn't always do much good, but it's certainly better than what it was before that.

"I don't believe Travis and Ron knew whatever hit them.

George couldn't get that out of them. For all the many things they told George about themselves, they couldn't tell George what killed them.'' However, in a later reading for the Elwells, the boys came through and said they were killed by the train, though the exact circumstances surrounding the accident remain a mystery. In a further example of cross-confirmation, Ron, Jr.'s grandmother went to George anonymously; he had no reason to connect her to the Elwells. In her reading, Travis, Ron, and his father all came through with specific details.

5

Even When You Know

For the vast majority of parents, a child's death occurs with little or no warning. Accidents and acts of violence claim many more children than do terminal illnesses. But while illnesses such as cancer and leukemia, chronic or congenital diseases, and AIDS still account for the smaller percentage of all children's deaths, their numbers are growing.

Each year thousands more children are diagnosed with cancer; while the rates for cure grow at an impressive rate, so do the number of victims. Worldwide, the World Health Organizations predicts that 10 million children will be infected with HIV. According to the Centers for Disease Control, over 22,000 young Americans are HIV-positive; another 200,000 may be so and not even know it, raising the possibility that by the turn of the century tens of thousands of babies may be born with AIDS. Due to advances in neonatal and pediatric medicine, babies born with severe congenital defects and illnesses live months, sometimes years beyond doctors' expectations.

For these children, part of their lives and their family's will be consumed by the day-to-day struggle of coping with the stress and demands of their illness. Hospitals, medication, surgery, doctors, and nurses become as much a part of their daily routine as watching *Sesame Street*. As diligently as parents and other concerned adults might try to make these children's lives as normal as possible, studies show that a child diagnosed with a serious illness usually senses that *he* is never really the same child again. Parents, siblings, grandparents, aunts, uncles, teachers, friends—virtually everyone the child has contact with—treat him differently.

While it may take time before that child understands the meaning of his illness, almost all seriously ill children are remarkably cognizant about how others regard them. These youngsters know when they are being lied to, for example, and usually, whether their parents choose to tell them or not, that they are going to die. In these and countless other ways, terminal illness forces children to grow up prematurely.

Parents who are suddenly hurtled into a bewildering world of hospitals, tests, and medical jargon usually come to understand the ramifications of their child's illness only over time. Most describe the time between the moment of diagnosis and their child's death as one in which everything else in their lives went "on hold" while the illness ravaged their family, their resources, their lives.

Often, toward the expected end of the child's life, most parents experienced what is called anticipatory grief: mourning not only the death to come but what has been lost (for example, their child's "normal" childhood) and what will be lost (for example, the chance to grow up). In the case of a terminally ill child, the parent also mourns at each stage of the body's deterioration; for example, the loss of motor control or vision.

For some, anticipatory grief makes dealing with a loved one's death somewhat easier. But it is a mistake to assume that simply because a parent knew that her child was going to die that she is any better "prepared" for it than the parent whose child dies in a sudden accident. Yes, parents of terminally ill children have the opportunity to discuss death with the child, say goodbye, develop private rituals, be more conscious of the words and events that will one day make up their memories. But even when a child's death is expected, most parents admit that they never really believed it would occur. And when it does, it rarely occurs as they imagine it. Parents who believed they were emotionally prepared for a child's death are no less overwhelmed and surprised by the depth and persistence of their grief. While a mother or father may come to accept the idea of a child's death, it does not blunt the pain of returning home to the child's empty bedroom.

Through the months or years of treatment there are alternating moments of hope and despair, countless opportunities for second-guessing and self-blame. As parents strive to do the right thing, make the best decision, they often face conflicting opinions and emotions. As the end draws near and the child's suffering increases or her quality of life diminishes, parents may find themselves wishing it would all be over, that their child would finally be delivered from her suffering. These feelings can then result in a complex web of conflicting emotions that are difficult to reconcile.

In this chapter we will examine three readings for parents of terminally ill children. In each case the child's death was anticipated (in one instance almost from birth). Nevertheless the parents did literally everything in their power to prolong their child's life. As you will see, each family's feelings about their child's death and how they have coped with it is unique.

Becky was Shelly and Ted Jackson's only child.* At just three years of age she was charmingly precocious. Becky adored dressing up in frilly outfits, her long blond hair decorated with bows, and when anyone complimented her, she would reply without hesitation, "I know I'm gorgeous!" Self-assured beyond her years, Becky had a way about her.

*At the request of the subjects, their names have been altered to protect their identities. Everything else in this story, however, is true.

As her mother recalled, "She wouldn't walk into a room, she would *march* in."

One day Shelly noticed that Becky seemed dizzy, unbalanced, her gait unsteady. Within a few days the Jacksons learned that Becky had a tumor on her brain stem. Surgery to remove the tumor and subsequent chemotherapy and radiation seemed to clear the malignancy. The family rejoiced, certain that Becky was cured.

But within several months, Shelly remembered, "We noticed that Becky wasn't herself again." The tumor had reappeared, and this time the prognosis was very bleak. The survival rate for brain-stem cancer is approximately 25 percent. Becky again underwent surgery to remove the tumor. The operation itself was a success, but while in the recovery room, Becky began to hemorrhage. Doctors halted the bleeding but warned the Jacksons that their daughter did not have much time left and that she would probably eventually become paralyzed as the tumor metastasized.

To everyone's surprise, however, the little girl rallied to defy predictions that she would never walk again. "She did walk with a limp," Shelly recalled, "and she couldn't run. But I would always tell her, even as her condition worsened, 'Baby, you're going to walk again. You're going to run again.' Becky would look at me and say, 'I know.' " Her parents and her maternal grandmother, Eileen, often reassured Becky that she would also someday regain the beautiful long blond hair she had lost during treatment.

Over time, however, Shelly noticed certain changes in Becky. She seemed to be at peace with her situation. "She taught us how to accept her death," Shelly said.

Several times she asked her grandmother, "Who will take care of my puppy when I'm not here?"

"Well, Becky, where are you going to go, honey?" Eileen asked, unaware of the depth of Becky's understanding.

"Oh, when I go away," the little girl replied softly.

"Grandma will take care of your puppy," Eileen answered, somewhat stunned by her granddaughter's words. "Don't you worry about it."

Another time Becky asked Shelly, "Mommy, will you

love me forever in your heart?''

''Of course,'' she answered.

''I'll always love you in my heart, Mommy.''

One odd thing, Shelly recalled, was Becky's sudden insistence on being called ''Katy.'' ''We don't know exactly why,'' Shelly said. ''We think she had a near-death experience.'' That is one possibility, for, as Dr. Melvin Morse demonstrated in his study *Closer to the Light*, near-death experiences are common among children. Perhaps Becky saw a child or someone else named Katy during her NDE. Another, more earthly explanation is that Katy is the name of the little girl in singer Michael Jackson's video *Moonwalker*, of which Becky was fond. Whatever the reason, her family complied.

For nine months after her second surgery, Becky struggled with her disease. Shortly before death came, Shelly called her Katy, as she had been doing for months. Becky looked at her sadly and shook her head. ''Mommy, I'm not Katy anymore. I'm Becky. That's the name I'd like you to use. I'm Becky.''

Shelly and her mother recalled the last days of Becky's life, spent at home. ''We were all doing our part, real calmly. There was no hysterical screaming or crying. Just love and acceptance. It was like we couldn't believe this was really happening. At some level I think Becky understood what was going on.''

''And she was so ready for it,'' Eileen added. ''We knew it couldn't be such a horrible thing that was actually happening to her. There was something greater than everybody in that room. There was something much greater than us.''

Becky slipped into a coma as her family kept a bedside vigil. ''When we knew she was having trouble breathing,'' Shelly remembered, ''I asked my mom what to do.''

''Pick her up,'' Eileen said. ''This is what we're here for. Hold your baby and help her.''

''I picked Becky up in my arms and told her I loved her and that it would be okay. And I told her to go toward the light. We let go, and we told her it would be all right. I said, 'Baby, let go. Go to the light. Go to the light. Keep going.'

"With that, she took her last little sweet breath and just sighed as if to say, 'It's over, guys. I'm going home.'

"To be able to hold your child and be with her that closely—the same way she was brought into the world—to help her out, is so much better than to have had tubes and medical equipment and the tears and the screaming at the hospital."

Despite the closeness the family felt during Becky's illness, the Jacksons divorced not long after her death. Unlike many bereaved parents, Shelly found no comfort from the support group she attended. "Maybe I picked the wrong group," she said. Deep depression and thoughts of suicide prompted her decision to travel to Long Island with her mother to see George.

George began Shelly and Eileen's reading by discerning the presence of Shelly's grandfather and a younger female.

"A young female calls you 'Mom.' Is it your daughter?" George asked.

"Yes, that's my daughter."

"Because she keeps saying, 'Hi, Mom. Hi, Mommy.' She says not only are you mother and daughter, you're also good friends."

"Yes," Shelly agreed. "Good friends."

"She's coming to you like a sister."

"Yes."

"She's obviously passed on as a young person."

"Yes."

"She's a very courageous child."

"Oh, yes."

"I keep seeing the Cowardly Lion [from *The Wizard of Oz*] behind her, which would symbolize that she's achieved courage," George explained.

"Oh, yes," Shelly answered with a slight laugh.

"She embraces you with love," he said to Eileen. "You're her grandmother. However, it's obvious why she came in first to her mother."

"Sure," Shelly's mother replied.

"Earlier when I felt a young female [spirit] come into the room, she gave me the feeling of a child running into the room."

"That's her," said Shelly.

"And then she went over and hugged you. She said she was here, and she'd been waiting. Although your daughter passed on as a child, I thought I was talking to an adult," George said.

"Yes," Shelly answered.

"Because she's young in body but older in mind."

"Right. That's right."

"She has wisdom for her age, she says," George explained.

"Yes."

"She says the first thing she wants to tell you is that she's all right. That's the main thing on your mind: Is she all right? She keeps saying, 'Tell my mommy I'm all right.' So I said, in my mind, 'Well, every parent wants to know that.' And she said to me, 'Don't think that; just say it. My mother wants to hear me say that I'm all right.' That's number one.

"Number two," George continued, "she knew that she was going to pass on."

"I think so," Shelly answered.

"She says she's not shocked by death. Because I see a vision of Saint Joseph, which means a happy death. She tells me she passes peacefully into the hereafter."

"Yes."

"She suffers courageously."

"Yes."

"But inside herself."

"Yes."

"She's more concerned about what you're going through than what she's going through. Again, I'm talking to a child, but I feel like I'm talking to someone who has the wisdom of the ages because she seems much more mature. So she says she is all right, and she's made it. At the end, when she passed, she might have been in a coma or asleep.

Because she tells me she was out of it. She was asleep, as we'd understand it. That could be a coma. But she knew you were there.

"Were you holding hands?" George asked.

"Yes," Shelly answered emotionally.

"Because she says you're holding her when she passes. She says she knows you are. She had a great sense of humor for a youngster."

"Oh, yes."

"Because she made a joke: She says you wouldn't even go to the bathroom. You were afraid to go out of the room for even a second. You wanted her to have a happy death in the sense of being with you. She says she made it. She said to herself, after she passed on, that she knew you were very upset, but she joked, 'At least you'll go to the bathroom now.' "

Shelly smiled.

George addressed Shelly's mother. "Your father took her passing badly because he says it was very heartbreaking."

"Yes."

"Obviously you pray for your granddaughter."

"Yes."

"She thanks both of you for your prayers and asks that you please continue praying for her."

"Okay."

To Shelly, he said, "She says that more than anything, you constantly took care of her. There was no sacrifice you wouldn't have made for her."

"Yes."

"She doesn't want you to think it was in vain, although obviously you'd much rather have her here than there. You'd have preferred her to get well, but in her wisdom, she says it just didn't go that way. She says your prayers have been answered in one respect: She's not sick anymore. She says that she's completely fine and normal; one hundred percent the child you knew and loved. She says that's another answer you wanted to hear: that she's free from any illness or suffering."

Shelly nodded.

"It's the strangest thing," George remarked. "When she was born, it was as if the two of you already knew each other. If I didn't know better, I'd think you'd lost your best friend. The feelings of love and companionship are very strong."

"Yes."

"You're still angry about losing her. She's telling you to let it go. She says, 'I'm not dead, I'm alive. I'm closer to you than you can imagine.' One thing about your daughter, she's got personality."

"Yes."

"I feel you've gotten the signal that she's been near you before tonight," George said.

"Oh, I have," Shelly agreed.

"She comes in a dream. You feel her around. You've experienced a certain scent that connects you with her; a song on the radio."

"Yes."

"Anything like that. She's given you more than ample signals that she's around you."

"Oh, yes."

"Because she says, 'I don't want you to think I'm over here just saying I'm at peace. I'm fine. Too bad that you're in grief.' "

"Right."

"Anyway, she just wants to let you know that she definitely is with you. You are not alone. You're struggling with loneliness, anger, and bitterness. And you didn't do anything wrong. You might be thinking you did something wrong, and this is punishment for it. She says that is complete nonsense. I agree. It *is* complete nonsense. Total superstition," George said.

Shelly listened quietly.

"Your daughter says you'd much rather have had her here for the short time you did than not at all. She knows how much you loved her. She says sometimes when you get your down days, which is normal, you're going through the worst thing anybody could experience."

"Yes," Shelly admitted.

"She says you've been through the worst now. She says not to make yourself crazy thinking you did something wrong. . . . Everything went the way it was supposed to go. As upsetting and as tragic as it turned out to be, there still seems to be a tremendous lesson in love from the experience. Because it still left you with incredible memories, and you've gained incredible strength from her. Your daughter is saying that a little child shall lead us. Was she very fond of the movie *The Wizard of Oz?*" George asked.

"Yes!" Shelly answered, remembering a night in the hospital when Becky sat in her bed transfixed by the film.

"Because I keep hearing the song 'We're Off to See the Wizard.' She says there was more to why she put the Cowardly Lion behind her [psychically] to symbolize courage. She tells me that the dimension she's in resembles Oz. Except there's no Tin Man or Munchkins. But she says it's very much like that in its essence. In its beauty."

"Okay."

"She says she knew she was going to pass on. Yet she always hoped that she was going to pull through. The only thing that kept her here for as long as it did was her wanting to endure for you. Because even if she was ill, she was still here. And she says she hung on for as long as she could. She says that she knew in her heart that she was going to go someplace, but she wouldn't be here physically."

"Yes."

"Was your daughter less than ten when she passed over?" George asked.

"Yes."

"I knew I was talking to a child, but again, she had an older person's mind. She seems to be around you a great deal, and she's very concerned about you being very lonely. It's as if she was all you had, and now you have nothing. But your daughter says, 'You still have me. I'm still here.' She's come to you in dreams. She's talked to you. You feel her there."

"I do," Shelly acknowledged.

"You just know she's there. Sometimes you might say it's your imagination or just wishful thinking. She says,

'What makes you think I'm not there?' She says you talk out loud to her as if she is there. Why can't you accept, then, that she's there? She says the essence of her that you knew and still love very much is very much alive and with you. The physical body has died and departed.

"She says, 'You didn't love my body. You loved me.' And that's what survives physical death. Her body was suffering, but she's out of it now. She's completely fine, she says.

"Your daughter says you've had a hard enough life to give up emotionally. She was the greatest gift in your life and yet the greatest tragedy of your life."

"Yes."

"That's why she says don't think that somebody 'over there' singled you out for all this difficulty. She says there is a purpose to it. There is a lesson. You may not understand it now. But someday you will."

George continued. "Why is there a lot of purple around you? Did your daughter like the color? She has purple light around her. Violet light . . . She wasn't afraid of the dark [when she first passed over]. Then, she says, the tunnel of light was there, and lots of animals came up to her, and she went to them. She trusted them.

"Did your daughter dance at any time? Or did she want to?"

"No," said Shelly, confused.

"Why does she look like she's in costume?"

"She had a cute little ballerina costume," Shelly's mother explained.

"That's what it is! She's in a ballerina costume. . . . She had a cute way of talking," George commented.

"Oh, yeah."

"I keep hearing her talk like a little girl, but in a different way. There's just something cute about it. I wish I could explain. . . . Your father says he could have been closer to you. Is that true?"

"That he felt that way?" asked Shelly. "Yeah, probably."

"Because he feels he abandoned you emotionally, and

he apologizes for that. He was there but he wasn't there. And he doesn't want you to think you did anything to deserve that. That's just him. I can't explain it any other way. He admits he was like a boy trapped in a man's body a lot of times. When he got over there, he realized there were certain things he'd overlooked [on earth].

"He says that even later on in life, he tried to be closer to you, and he always seemed distant. He apologizes for that. He also apologizes to your mom. He could have been closer to her, also. He's sensitive, but he didn't know how to express it."

"Yes."

"Your daughter does something with the alphabet. She's showing me letters. She's talking about her name. Without telling me, was she known by a nickname?"

"Yes."

"Because she keeps saying a name and then breaking it down. I just sense that it's a breakdown of her formal name."

"Yes."

"She does love the children up there [the other side], also. Even though she's a child herself, she's wiser than they are. So she helps them through her wisdom," George said.

"Are you Eileen?" he asked Shelly's mother, who answered that she was.

"There's no Eileen passed on, is there?"

"No."

"Okay, because I heard her say Eileen," George explained. "So obviously she's calling out to you." George spent the next several minutes attempting to decipher Shelly's daughter's name from the psychic communications he was receiving. He had described this process as something akin to playing "spiritual Scrabble."

"She will tell me the name in time," he said. "She told me to think about the name Kathleen or Kathryn."

"Right."

"And that's what I did. I said Kathy or Kathryn. She

tells me I'm in the neighborhood. Is it Katy?'' George asked.

"Yes!" Shelly acknowledged.

"Now, is that your daughter?"

"No," she explained. "It's what she wanted to be called for a while."

"She's saying, 'This is Katy.' "

"She named herself that after she got sick," said Shelly.

"Oh, okay. Then it makes sense. That's all I need to know. It was her voice that said her name was Katy. I understand why she said it to you. It's something only the two of you would know about her."

"Yes."

Several minutes passed while the spirit psychically showed George the letters that would spell her real name. "Now she's trying to break the alphabet down," he explained. "It is not an *L*."

"No."

"Okay. She wanted to show me [that part of the alphabet]. There's no *K* in her name?"

"Yes."

"There is. That's what it is. She keeps pushing me at *K*. She heard me saying the alphabet, but she slowed me down at *K* and *L*. Then she said, *K*. There is a *K*."

"Yes."

"It's something, the vowel, then something again and then *K-Y*. I can't figure it out! She seems to like to play with letters. She's saying, *A, B, C, D, E*. There must be an *E*. There's a *B*. Her name begins with a *B*. The second letter is *E*. *B, E* . . ."

"Becky!" George exclaimed.

"That's it!" said Shelly. "Yes."

"She just said to me that her name is actually Rebecca."

"Right. Rebecca."

"You call her Becky, or Beck."

"Right," Shelly answered.

"She's saying, 'This is Becky.' . . . She says to keep going on with your life. Are you afraid to have [another] child?"

"Yes," Shelly admitted.

"She's telling you not to be afraid. She says there's another child there, even if you adopt. I don't know exactly what she means. But I see Saint Philomena over your head, which is a sign of a happy birth. Becky says don't be afraid to be with another child. Because there's at least one child ahead. Unless you marry somebody who has a child. That could be it, also."

"I don't know if I can have more children now," Shelly said.

"Would it be risky?"

"Right now."

"Yeah, she talks about that. You could have another child, but it's risky presently. But perhaps not up ahead. Becky feels badly, because you've always tried so hard to make sure everything worked. And she says it just seems that every time you surmount one obstacle, fifty more appear, and they're harder than the previous ones. But she says, 'Just don't give up the ship yet, Mommy.' She says you've been through a lot, and you'll surmount it yet again."

Shelly nodded.

"You'll always have the grief," George went on. "You will always feel Becky's loss, but she still wants you to go on with your life. She sees that you have days when you want to go on and other days when you don't. But you've got to go on with your life, for your sake as well as for those around you. You have a purpose and a mission here, and you haven't fulfilled it yet. You have to go on. Becky says, 'Just think, when the day comes, I'll be waiting for you.' That's a guarantee.

"Here's the answer to question number three," George said. "Becky wants you to know she's safe. She says, 'I can guarantee that without a doubt. I'm all right. I'm free from all suffering. You will see me again. I'm still your best friend, but I'm in the hereafter.'

"It's funny," George said. "Your dad is with her, yet she's very independent. . . . Becky's throwing a little ball.

Did she have trouble with her legs? She told me she's now walking fine."

"Yes. She had a limp after she became ill."

"No wonder she performed in front of you," said George. "She's telling me that her legs are fine. Did she also have trouble with her eyes?"

"Yes."

"She's telling me her sight is now fine. Her hearing is fine. Even her speech is. Everything is back to normal. The illness obviously affected her tremendously all over."

"Oh, yes."

"Her breathing, too," George continued. "She's completely fine. Becky says, 'I'm not suffering at all. I'm happy now.' She feels a little self-conscious, saying that she's happy and at peace when she knows what you're going through. . . . Now, your name is Shelly?"

"Right."

"Your daughter showed me the number six. When did she pass? A couple of years ago?"

"Yes," Shelly answered. "That's why."

"That's why she's showing me six circles. Now I understand: She says, 'I would be celebrating my sixth birthday.' She passed at the age of four. Four going on twenty-one," George remarked.

"Yes."

"Did she call you Grandma?" George asked Eileen.

"Yes."

"I thought I heard 'Nana.' "

"She called me another name because she couldn't say Grandma," Eileen explained.

"Oh, maybe that's why. Because she called you Grandma, but it seems she was calling you by another term of endearment for grandmother, and I couldn't figure it out. So I said it could be Nana or Nanny, or something like it," George said.

"Yes."

"She knows you're certainly quite broken up over her passing."

"Yes."

"She admires you because you stayed in the hospital and held her. Even against the rules, you were there."

"Yes. Oh, yes."

"I don't blame you," George said. "Because Becky says a lot of times the doctors might have been trying to bully you around."

"Oh, yes."

"You told them to go take a walk."

"Yeah." "Right," both women acknowledged.

"You were very firm, and your daughter's happy that you held your ground, because you knew there was nothing they [in the hospital] could do. So what difference did it make if you were there? If anything, it would have made more of a difference if you weren't there. Whether your daughter was unconscious or not, it meant something to her that you were there. She says now you know where she got her courage from. That you held your ground. You stayed in the hospital by her. They didn't have the courage to remove you because you would have raised quite a stink," George said.

"I think so," both women answered.

"Becky got a laugh out of that. She said she's happy that you stayed where she wanted you to be, no matter what."

"Yes."

"Your dad apologized to you. He knows you understand, but he wants to say it anyway. He wants you to know that he was wrong, and he realizes that now. He says he's doing his best to take care of your daughter in the hereafter. But he says now it's the other way around: She's taking care of him!"

"Yes. I think we knew that," Shelly answered.

"Becky's an old soul. It's almost as if she's been around before. He says if anything, he's learning from her example, not the other way around. Your grandparents have passed over? She talks about other people that I think are her great-grandparents. She talked about a great-grandmother that might have been very close to you many years ago. Is your husband open to this?"

"Oh, yes," Shelly replied.

"Good. Because she said that the minute you get home, call him. She just wants to let him know how much she loves him and that she's all right. She says to tell him, 'I know he's suffering and that he's brokenhearted.' That's what makes her sad. She says he's also putting himself through an un-necessary guilt trip [because your marriage failed]. She says it has nothing to do with what happened. She sees things from a perspective in which there is hope. She says, again, 'Someday we will all be together again.' She says it doesn't necessarily mean you have to get along in a marriage. She says you can all be friends. You and he [the ex-husband] ba-sically are still friends?" George asked.

"Oh, yes," Shelly answered.

"Yeah. You still have a nice relationship, even if you're no longer married. He's kind of on a guilt trip, because he feels things went the wrong way. But as your daughter says, it happened. He didn't fail as a father or as a husband. It just didn't work out."

"Right."

"And it was better to divorce than to go on resenting each other and not getting along.

"Did Becky have a teddy bear?" George asked, chang-ing subjects. "I'm sure she did. She talks about her stuffed animals."

"Oh, yeah," Shelly acknowledged.

"So there must be a number of them in her room."

"Yes."

"She describes the hereafter as a nondimensional type of existence. It's not physical or dimensional. . . . She says those in the hereafter are not there to tell you what to do as they would on earth. They let her find things out by herself. She says that's what the learning process is all about on the other side," George explained.

"Is there a George?" he asked. "A Ted? Theodore?"

"Yes. Ted. Her father," Shelly answered.

"I just heard your daughter call to George. Then I said to myself, *'I wonder if she's trying to get my attention.'* Then all of a sudden she said yes, she was. And she told me to say 'Theodore, Ted.' So she's calling out for her daddy. She's saying Ted. She says he's hurting.''

''Right.''

''She's just trying to call him right away. She says you'll certainly all be together in peace [in the hereafter someday]. She says, 'Just think, I'll have plenty of time to say good things to all of you.' But in any case, she embraces the two of you with love. Not only as a granddaughter and a daughter, but as good friends. Your daughter says continue to pray for her. Know that she's all right. She signs off with love.

'' 'This is Katy going back,' she says,'' George concluded.

''Bye, Katy!'' Shelly called. ''See you later.''

''We really thought we'd never have children,'' is how John George described the years with his wife, Lorraine, before their only child, Jason, was born.

''We waited thirteen years. We didn't think he'd ever come,'' Lorraine recalled. ''And then when he was three, I had a hysterectomy for cancer, so of course I could never have any more children.''

John and Lorraine cherished Jason, a cute little boy with dark hair and skin. He was a happy child whose best friend was the family's dog, Christopher. A few months before Jason was born, Lorraine was shopping when a badly mistreated black puppy collapsed at her feet. The little dog had been burned in spots and suffered from mange. She took him home, got him veterinary care, and then she and John adopted him, naming him Christopher because she found him on Columbus Day. He grew to weigh eighty pounds, a gentle giant who let Jason race his toy cars along his back.

Almost from the moment Jason was born, he and Christopher were best of friends. One day Jason told his mother, ''Mommy, I don't want you to feel hurt, but I have to tell you something.''

''What?'' Lorraine asked.

''I love Christopher Dog.''

"I do, too."

"Yeah, but I think he's my brother," Jason explained.

"Well, I think he's *like* your brother," Lorraine replied.

"No, you don't understand, Mommy. I think Christopher Dog *is* my brother."

In September 1988 Lorraine noticed that one of her son's testicles appeared unusually descended. Fearing he had developed a hernia, the Georges immediately took Jason for an examination. The doctor confirmed that there was something wrong with Jason. Yes, he did have a hernia, but the doctor also suspected neurofibromatosis (also known as "Elephant Man's disease") and a malignant spinal cord tumor.

Jason underwent an eight-hour operation to remove the tumor. Within two days he was up and walking again, much to his doctors' surprise. But before too long, the tumor, which was difficult to excise completely because of its location, began growing again. Shortly after Jason complained of pain and weakness in his legs, he became paralyzed. Lorraine was at her child's bedside when he awoke one night screaming, "Mommy! Mommy! I can't feel my legs! I can't move my legs!"

Despite massive doses of radiation, the malignancy continued its invasion until Jason was paralyzed from the upper chest down. He had some use of his right hand and arm. Still, he never once complained.

"The nurses would come in to take care of him, and he'd say, 'Hi! How are you doing?' " Lorraine recalled. "His nurses would say, 'Well, we want to know how *you're* doing.' And when they asked him why he wanted to know all about them when they were there to find out about him, he replied, 'Because I want *my* nurses to have a good day.' "

Before long, Jason also lost his ability to speak, see, and hear. Later it became difficult for him to even breathe. Lorraine fashioned a card containing the alphabet so that Jason could communicate by pointing to the letters. But as his disease progressed, even that became an exercise in frustration as he grew too weak to point. Shortly before he lost his speech, one of the last things he said was, "I don't want to die. Mommy, I don't want to die."

"We had never discussed it, but he knew he was going to die. We answered him; I consider it poorly [now]," Lorraine said. "I told him that he wasn't going to die, that my husband and I would die first. And I'm not too thrilled with that answer. Looking back, I'd tell Jason differently.

"At the time, I said to him that we all die. But if somebody you know is there [where you go after you die], you're not going to be alone. And eventually we're all going to be together. As long as somebody's there—a grandparent, for instance—we're not alone! But how can we imagine what that would mean in a nine-year-old's head?

"Jason's brightness and maturity is what was frightening to him. Because he wasn't in fantasyland. He was in reality, and yet not sure about what we're saying and what's going on. He believed in heaven and an afterlife. He prayed to God. He had faith; he had strength. He believed in God and the angels."

When it became clear that Jason was terminal, doctors advised the family to take him home. "The hospital couldn't be bothered," Lorraine recalled bitterly. "As far as they were concerned, he was dead already. They would take me into this room and say, 'You have to understand: Your son is going to die.' And I answered, 'Look, I know science has done all it can. Now we're turning to God.' "

In an act of desperation and of faith, the family traveled to Medjugorje, in the former Yugoslavia, where an apparition of the Blessed Mother has been reported to have appeared to several children in recent years. For the faithful, the site has become a place of prayer and of miraculous healings, not unlike Lourdes or Fatima. In February 1989 the Georges took their son, "wheelchair and all," Lorraine recalled, on the trip overseas. They climbed two mountains with their son in a custom-built litter. Despite the bitter cold, the family stayed there for a week, kneeling for hours on the church's cold marble floor.

Not long after they returned from the pilgrimage, Christopher the dog suddenly fell ill with terminal cancer. That

April Jason's best buddy died.

The Georges took care of Jason at home in a room set up like a hospital room. Nurses came in daily to perform medical procedures, and the boy left home only to go to the hospital when he needed blood transfusions. On Easter Sunday he went into cardiac arrest. Technically, he was dead; emergency workers revived him with CPR and oxygen. Although John and Lorraine both knew that the inevitable was close at hand, "I didn't want to let him go," she said.

Jason lingered, his condition deteriorating rapidly. On the day before Mother's Day he went in for a blood transfusion. Lorraine and Jason wanted nothing more than to be together at home for Mother's Day; they knew it would be their last. "I didn't want him to pass in the hospital," she said. But shortly after midnight—on Mother's Day—Jason died.

"We haven't joined any bereavement-support groups," Lorraine said. "We felt we have had enough therapy. We've been in it, and we understand the levels of bereavement. I might be selfish, but I really don't want to sit in a group and share the pain of other people. I can't handle it.

"Right now I'm angry," she admitted. "I was willing to accept Jason in a wheelchair and do whatever was necessary to help him through his life. It may not have been a quality of life for him, but I was selfish. I wanted him nonetheless. I guess I'm still angry at God, because who else am I going to put my anger on? I mean, it wasn't God's fault, and I don't intellectually blame God. But I'm just angry, because I did pray and I didn't get what I wanted. In reality, it was probably better for Jason [to pass on]."

"Whatever I say, please just answer yes or no," George told John and Lorraine before their reading began. "Now, you lost a son?"

"Yes," John replied.

"That's who's between the two of you. He's the one who's [speaking] about the happy trip up ahead."

"Okay."

After a long and accurate message about Lorraine's

health, George asked her, "You work with colors?"

"Yes. My business is called Flying Colors," she replied.

"Are you expanding in your work? There's expansion. I feel like I'm teaching or sharing. I almost feel like I'm in a class. Well, I'll leave it with you for up ahead. That's how your son describes it."

"Okay."

"You just had a bad time over the holidays."

"Yes."

"He's kind of kidding you that you made it. You made it through the holidays, which is one of the worst times of the year. Because you felt the emptiness ten times more than at other times of the year. But your son just wants to let you know that he was with you spiritually because they're always encouraged to be closest when the need is greatest. Of course, at the holidays, the need is greatest. Not only for you, but they [on the other side] also like the connection. Has your son's birthday just passed?"

"Yes."

"Because he keeps wishing himself a happy birthday. I guess it was in December."

"Just before Christmas," John answered.

"Because your son keeps saying his birthday just passed. He was born a few days before Christmas?"

"He was born December fourteenth."

"It's as if your son was a Christmas gift the year he was born. That's another reason why the holidays can get to you. It was not only his birthday, but he came during a time of year when you looked upon him as a cherished gift. That's why, since he's no longer here physically, it makes it all the more difficult."

"Right."

"Your son passed from health trouble."

"Yes," Lorraine answered.

"He passes from illness within the past few years."

"Yes."

"It affects his blood."

"Yes."

"Because I see blood cells [psychically]. Is it leukemia?"

"No."

"It's a form of cancer."

"Yes."

"He has a rough time prior to his passing."

"Yes."

"Do you take the name Paul? Wait a minute. It's not Paul. It's Peter. Does the name Peter mean anything?"

"Yes."

"Passed on."

"Yes."

"I saw a Mounds Bar in front of me and I jumped at the name Paul. Then I heard your son say I got the wrong name. So I said it must be Peter, then," George explained.

"Right."

"He's family?"

"No."

"Like family?"

"No."

"Does he know your son?"

"He's a young fellow that passed on. He was a friend of a fellow who worked for me," John explained.

"Oh, now I understand why he said there was a family connection. Through your family there is a connection. Peter states that he and your son have become friends over there. Did Peter pass young, also?"

"Yes."

"Did he pass on after your boy?"

"No."

"He *did* go first. Okay. Because he claims that the two of them are friends. They've met each other over there. . . . Who's Sam?"

"That was a nickname for me," Lorraine replied.

"Because I heard your son call out 'Sam.' That's interesting. He didn't say anything with it. I asked him, 'Who's that?' He said, 'Just call it out!' Did he used to call you that? Or did somebody in the family?"

"I don't even think he knew it was my nickname," she replied.

"Well, I guess he does now! He's apparently aware of it. I would take that as evidence of his presence in the room. Because that's something that you would know that he didn't know. He knows it now."

"Right."

"Is there a Josephine passed on?"

"Yes."

"Someone in your family."

"My grandmother," Lorraine said.

"She says, 'This is Josey or Josephine.' She's there, also. The two of them are present."

"Okay."

"Because they say that your son kind of lives with them over there, or he spends a tremendous amount of time with them."

"Okay."

"Your son would be about twelve years old now?"

"Yes."

"Because I feel like I'm talking to somebody who's a preteen. He says he would have been twelve now if he had remained on the earth. Was he around nine or ten when he passed?"

"He was nine and a half."

"He says he was only supposed to come to the earth for a short time."

"Oh!" his mother cried out.

"Were you kind of left out this holiday season?"

"I guess you could say that."

"It's as if people were not around you. I feel there were people who contacted you or kept in touch, but there were also people who didn't bother. And your son feels badly about that. Yes, some people were kind enough to remember, such as some of his friends. Some people contacted you because they know you feel very empty at this time of year. And yet some other family members were at a distance. They kind of excluded you. But not that you've missed anything, in your son's opinion. He says not to take it personally.''

"Okay.''

"Are you having a lack of communication with a brother?'' George asked, turning toward Lorraine.

"Yes.''

"It's been going on for a while.''

"Yes.''

"Because your son gives me the impression 'So what else is new?' It's been going on for a period of time. Is he [your brother] a very negative person?''

"Yes.''

"It seems that he's kind of unhappy. But it's almost his own fault. He's a negative individual. Your son says he's learned, since he's gone over, that there are some things you cannot change. I keep hearing that prayer, 'God grant me the wisdom to change the things I can . . . ' You know how it goes. The next step is to accept the fact that you can't change it and just let it go. It has to work itself out.''

"Yes.''

"Does the name Cheryl* mean anything at all? Cheryl or Sherry? Or Cher?'' George asked.

"Yes,'' John responded.

"She's living,'' George said.

"Yes.''

"Maybe your son's calling out to Cheryl. Is she someone close with him?''

"Cheryl was one of his baby-sitters,'' Lorraine explained.

"Because he's asking me to ask you how Cheryl is.''

"Okay. I saw his buddy Christopher today,'' Lorraine added.

"So far your son brings up Cheryl, Sherry. He does call out to Christopher. Probably because you just said that you saw him today.''

---

*This name has been altered. Everything else in this story, however, is true.

"Well, it was his birthday today."

"Christopher's birthday?"

"Yes."

"Because your son is saying something about seeing him, and he calls out."

"Okay."

"Your son says he's taking a vacation from his work over there through the holidays to be near the two of you twenty-four hours a day. He took his break because they know [on the other side] that this time of year is a very difficult obstacle. . . . Do daisies mean anything? Because your son keeps handing you daisies. I'm just going to have to say that's he's doing it. I'm just trying to make sure it doesn't mean anything specific."

"Oh, yes. It would make sense because it's my birthday."

"What does that have to do with daisies?" George asked. He was a little surprised to see daisies, since when a spirit "gives" flowers from the other side, the visual cue is usually roses.

"Because he used to pick what he called daisies. You know the dandelions? He used to call them daisies. He would bring them to me when he was younger. When he was little. He'd be playing. He'd stop and hand them to me. He'd call thcm daisies. So I guess what he's doing is giving you daisies."

"It's funny that you should say your son gave you daisies when he was a youngster," George commented, "because I saw him much younger than twelve years old. Again, I argued with him. He said to me, 'No. Tell her what you see. She'll understand.' So I did."

"Right."

"Did you do something with your son's photograph over the [Christmas] holidays?"

"Yes," John answered.

"Do you understand what he means?"

"Yes."

"Okay, I won't argue with him again."

"What did he say?"

"He showed me a picture of himself. I should say, I thought I saw a picture of him. He said, 'Ask them about the photograph.' I asked him, 'What about it? What does it mean?' He answered, 'Just ask them. They'll know what you're driving at.' Did you put his picture somewhere? Don't tell me. Just say yes or no."

"You have to ask him—one or many," John replied carefully.

"Was it given out? You did something with his photograph."

"Right."

"Because I keep feeling that more than one person got a photograph."

"Yes."

"But there was also one photograph that was memorialized."

"I did a lot with [many] photographs. It's my hobby," John explained.

"With him, though," George stressed.

"All with him. I gave something to his uncle. I gave a lot to his mother."

"Wait. There was one [picture of your son] used on a card," George said.

"Yes," Lorraine acknowledged.

"Because he says the one on the card is the one he's talking about."

"That's the one!" John exclaimed.

"He's playing the piano," his wife added.

"Was it a Christmas card?"

"Yes!" John responded.

"That's what he means," George said.

"It's to me from him," Lorraine clarified.

"Because your son keeps telling me he was memorialized. He says that you gave out many photographs. Then he said there was a photograph with a card."

"Okay."

"He says *that's* the one he's referring to. Because I saw [the picture] framed. It looked like it was on a card. So your son's aware that you gave his mother a Christmas card, from the two of you, that had his photograph on it."

"Yes."

"Because I see white roses around [psychically], which would be a symbol that your son knows spiritually that you did that. You felt so bad about his not being here physically during the Christmas holidays. So he's giving you unique evidence to prove to you that he was there spiritually. [The information] about your blood pressure, about seeing his friend Christopher, about Cheryl. But most specifically about the Christmas card that was exchanged. Because as he says to his mother, the card not only came from his father, it came from him, also. Your son was physically there in the picture, but spiritually there during the exchange.

"The little guy knows what he's talking about!" said George. "I keep arguing with him about certain things, and he keeps saying, 'I know what I mean.'"

"What went on Christmas Eve? Did you dream about him around Christmas? Unless you don't remember. Because your son says his presence was uniquely close on Christmas Eve. Something went on that would make you think about him. What does he mean now? Did you put up a Christmas tree?"

"Yes," John replied.

"Did you put something on it?"

"Yes."

"To do with him?"

"Oh, yes."

"*That's* what he's talking about. I keep seeing somebody decorating a Christmas tree. It stood out for some reason."

"We set a place for him for dinner," Lorraine offered.

"On Christmas Eve?"

"And had conversation about him and his grandma and grandpa being there."

"Because he says it was something about Christmas Eve when he was closest. That's what he means, then."

"Yes. Specifically we felt that he was there," Lorraine said.

"Okay," George said.

"Because he used to have Christmas Eve with Grandma and Grandpa," she continued.

"I took a picture of the table and the three seats, and I almost felt sure he would come out on the photograph," John added.

"Oh, okay. That's probably why your son's saying he was *uniquely* there on Christmas Eve. Even if he didn't come out in the photograph, he still was uniquely there. He showed me the Christmas tree and decorations on it. Then he kept showing me something about Christmas Eve."

"Right."

"Did you go to his grave around Christmas?"

"Yes," John acknowledged.

"You also left gifts there, or something was left behind. Even if it was in the emotional sense. Did you put flowers on the grave?"

"Flowers," John replied.

"That's the gift. I don't mean a wrapped gift. But he says you're at his grave around Christmas, and he says you left flowers there or Christmas mementos of some sort."

"Right."

"You put a Christmas tree up for him," George said.

"His grave is near a pine bush, and we put a little ornament on it for him, besides the Christmas blanket I made for his grave," the boy's mother explained.

"Your son brings all these things up. You know you did them. This is to give you evidence that *he* knows you did them, so you don't feel you just wasted your time. He did receive and see what you were doing. Because he says he was with you twenty-four hours a day around the Christmas season. He says he took his break from work, so to speak. He took his 'Christmas holiday.' It's as if he'd been away, and he'd come home for Christmas. That's exactly what he did."

"Okay."

"Does the name Jack mean anything?"

"Yes."

"Passed on."

"Yes."

"Because your son keeps saying Jack is with him. Your son's name also begins with the letter *J*?"

"Yes," John said.

"Don't say it. But I saw a *J*. Jay. Jason."

"Yes."

"Now, Jack was like an uncle?"

"*My* uncle," Lorraine clarified.

"Okay. Because your son keeps saying, 'Uncle Jack is here with me.' Then he said his name also begins with a *J*. But it's not John or Jack. He said it's Jay. Then I saw it spelled out in front of me. Occasionally, he was called Jay."

"Yes."

"No wonder he just showed me the single *J*. As time goes on, some of his friends are starting to drift."

"Yes."

"Just don't take it personally. They have to go on with their lives, too, your son says. But he just doesn't want you to get your feelings hurt any more than they already have been. Not from his friends, just from life in general. But your son says that a lot of his friends, as they get older now, might start to drift. Because they're going to start to come into their own lives. He says just don't feel that you're left behind. Some of them are reaching their pre-teens, as he would have now."

"Right."

"I see Gloria* around you. Does the name Gloria mean anything?"

"Yes."

"Passed on, though?"

"I don't know. It's a girlfriend."

"Oh. Did your son lose a pet?"

"Yes."

"Because he keeps talking about a pet dog being with

---

*This name has been altered. Everything else in this story, however, is true.

him. Why does he bring up a cat? You didn't lose a cat, also, did you?"

"No, but he loved cats," his mother said.

"Because he has cats all around him. And he tells me that his pet dog is with him. The dog passed on first or around the same time as your son?"

"Just before. The dog died one month before our son did," John explained.

"Because your son says it's almost as if the dog had to be there to welcome him over. The dog kind of sensed. You know how animals have a keen instinct. Your son was ill. When the animal passed, your son was about ready to let go. He says that the dog was there for him when he came over. The dog deliberately died for that purpose: to meet your son. And he says that the dog was there for him when he came over."

"The dog was also nine years old and also died of cancer," John said.

"But your son says, 'I also have pet cats.' He seems to be surrounded by cats on the other side as well."

"We put a little porcelain figure of a cat on the Christmas tree. Jason was allergic to cats, so we couldn't have a real cat," Lorraine said.

"Over there your son has a number of pet cats. There are no allergies [in the hereafter]. He can have them now. Because I feel like they're kind of sitting around me, and it's fine with me," said George, a cat lover himself.

"Does the name Alice mean anything?" he asked.

"No."

"He didn't have any friend by that name?"

"Not that we know of."

"Do you take the name Sarah?"

"Yes," John answered.

"Passed on."

"Yes."

"He must have made friends over there with some girls by the names of Alice and Sarah. He says, 'My friends Alice and Sarah are with me,' " George said.

"Alice might be a girl from school who passed over just

before Jason. I don't really know,'' Lorraine said.

"I'll have to leave it. But Sarah you know."

"Yes, Sarah we know," John answered.

"Jason knew Sarah here."

"Yes, they were in the hospital together," she explained.

"I was going to ask, Were they in the hospital together? Because he says he knows her here [on earth]. They went through illness at the same time. They had familiarity here on earth. Now they're linked together again. These two girls [Sarah and Alice] were with their families during the holiday season. They were definitely present."

"Okay."

"Does your son play the piano?"

"Yes, he did," John said.

"Because I hear a piano. I mean, Jason's no Liberace, but he plays. Because I can hear it being played in the background."

"Right."

"It's funny," George remarked. "He was older than his years."

"Yes," he said.

"He seems like a youngster, but his mind is more mature. He'd be twelve years old now, but he seems older in this thinking."

"Right."

"Does the name Andrew mean anything at all?"

"Are you saying Andrew?" John asked.

"Wait a minute. No. Because your son did say Andy."

"Right."

"That's my mistake. I did that. Because he called to Andy, and I made it Andrew. Is there any Andy, living, though?"

"Yes," Lorraine responded.

"That was his nurse," her husband added.

"Because Jason keeps calling to Andy here. I take it her name is Andrea."

"Yes."

"She was very special to him," she said.

"Do you still have contact with her?"

"No."

"He does call out to her. Maybe that's why. Because she was good to him at the time and very special to him."

"Right."

"You still technically do celebrate Christmas? In your own way?"

"Yes," John said.

"Because your son is glad that you do. He says many parents put everything on hold. He's glad you celebrate because he says, 'I do come home, spiritually.' Jason says there could be cynics who think it's all in your mind. Well, that's fine for them. But he says he does come home at Christmas. Not that he's ever far from you. And the evidence he's told you tonight is evidence that he's there. He's glad you celebrate, and he is there spiritually. When some families lose their children, they just don't want to be bothered anymore."

"It's very difficult. But we do it for him," Lorraine said.

"I'm sure it is difficult. But your son wants you to know that he is there and that [he knows] you still include him. You celebrate the holidays for him, and he wants you to continue to do that. Not only for your own benefit, but for his as well."

"Okay."

"Did you say some special prayer for him during the holidays? You do always pray for him, which he thanks you for. But you did something more specific, in a spiritual or prayerful sense."

"Yes," she said.

"He doesn't seem to go into detail about it. But he says it was a private, spiritual prayer experience done on his behalf."

"Yes."

"Did you light candles?"

"No, but we went in to visit the church. And there was absolutely nobody there. There was a priest in the confessional. But there was no mass or anything going on. We just made a specific visit into church."

"Oh, okay. That could be why your son is saying it was

very private. Because the two of you did it and there was really nobody there. He says, spiritually, he was there with you.''

"Okay.''

"Wait a second now. His first name is Jason. His middle name is Phillip?''

"Correct,'' John replied.

"Okay. Because he keeps saying Phillip, and he's not saying anything [else]. But he's putting it after his own name. So it's obviously his middle name.''

"Yes.''

"Again, spiritually, he plays the piano as a sign of harmony. It's to let you know he's in harmony and that he's certainly around you harmoniously during this time. He says you've surmounted the obstacle, though. He kids the two of you. He's very proud of you that, yes, it's a very lonely, very empty, down time for you, the holidays. But you overcame the obstacle and kept moving ahead. He says that's what he wants to see.''

After a moment of silence George continued. "Does the name Beth* mean anything at all?''

"There was a little girlfriend,'' Lorraine said.

"That passed on?''

"I don't know. I would hope not. But I don't know.''

"Because I don't think so. I don't think she has. I heard Jason call out to Beth.''

"She was young. It's somebody he liked.''

"He just asked me, 'How's Beth?' To be honest, I'm not going to ignore it, because he seems to be delving into things that are specific about him.''

John then said, "You know why? Because I'm redoing all the old [home] movies. And Beth, she's in all the movies. I'm transferring them to video.''

"Oh, maybe that's why,'' George said.

"That's what I just did.''

---

*This name has been altered. Everything else in this story, however, is true.

"Your son keeps bringing up Beth, and he's asking how she is."

"We called her his first little girlfriend. You know, they played together," Lorraine recalled.

"Does the name Buddy mean anything at all?" George asked.

"No," John answered.

"He has a buddy," his wife added.

"Don't say anything. He keeps talking about Buddy. Did he call a pet Buddy?"

"No."

"His pet *was* his buddy," John explained.

"Oh. That's what I need to know. He said to me, 'The dog is my buddy.' He called the dog his best buddy."

"Yes," he said.

"That's what he means. He's referring to the dog as Buddy."

"Right."

"Why does he show me a chess game? Chess or checkers? Does that make sense?"

"We used to play," John replied.

"But I'm also thinking it's a sign of moving, too. Checkers move. Chess moves. Making moves in life. Again, it could mean you're making specific moves or changes," George explained.

"Okay."

"Do you take the name Marcus*?"

"Yes," Lorraine acknowledged.

"Living or passed?"

"Both."

"Is there a Marc?"

"Yes."

"Living? There is one your son calls out to: Marc, Marcus. I feel like it could be in his own age group. It could have been a friend of his. But he also claims that Marc is

---

*This name has been altered. Everything else in this story, however, is true.

with him. So is there one passed on? Is he family?''

"It's my mother's brother," she said.

"Because Jason says there's a Marc or Marcus there with him as well."

"The Marc that's here is a little friend."

"Again, your son is going through his childhood. He's bringing up specifics that *you* would know but that nobody else would. They're all being done as forms of evidence to assure you that he was near."

"Okay."

"Because you know in your heart that you felt him near over the holidays. But still there's a part of you that says he's not here anymore, he's gone. You're frustrated over that. That's why he's trying to bring you evidence that he was there. So he can keep you moving on ahead."

"Okay."

"Now your son shows me tulips. Does that mean anything? He keeps showing me a field of tulips. I see him walking through a field of what looks like tulips in the hereafter. They're definitely a very rich golden-yellow color. I see [Jason] walking in the hereafter. I see him with pets and friends. The weather looks much nicer than it does here," George said, laughing. "It's very bright and sunny. It's vibrant-looking. There's also Steven with him. Steve."

"Yes," John replied.

"Your son talks about Steve being there. There are other relatives who are there. They don't want to take the 'microphone away from' him. They know Jason is obviously who you wanted to link up with. But in any case, they just want to let you know that certainly he's there with them."

"Right."

"There's Camille*?"

"Yes."

"Living?"

"Yes."

---

*This name has been altered. Everything else in this story, however, is true.

"Somebody I guess he knows."

"Yes."

"He keeps saying, 'Tell Camille you've heard from me.' "

"Camille's a friend; real close to him," John answered.

"And we saw her not that long ago," Lorraine added.

"Do you keep his bedroom as it is?"

"Right."

"But you brought something in? Knickknacks or something, you said before."

"Well, yes," she said.

"Because there are things added to his room. Additions. Did he like stuffed animals?"

"Yes."

"I see a number of them in his room."

"Right now they're all on the floor because I'm cleaning. I'm tearing the room apart," she explained.

"Maybe that's what he means. Because he told me there were changes in his room."

"Yes," John replied, "we just cleaned it up."

"I [psychically] saw stuffed animals all over the place, so obviously he knows you cleaned the room. It's concrete evidence. You know he's there. It's a minor point, but it means something to you. You have to be hearing it from him. You said you've left his room just as is."

"Yes."

"Someone gives you a hard time about it."

"Yes, his godfather."

"There are those who give you a hard time about how you should deal with bereavement. But they don't know what you're going through. . . . Does the name Jack mean anything?"

"My brother," John said.

"He was close with your son," George said.

"Yes."

"Your son is concerned about people. It seems he was a very loving child. A very affectionate child. He says he's here a short time. He shows love and affection as an example. Not to teach or force it on anybody, but to show by

example. That was what his mission was in life. He also
fulfills it because Jason certainly left an impression on you
and so many other people. So he says, 'See how much you
can achieve in a short period of time?'

"He says it's like he graduated from school. Be proud
to know that he achieved what he was supposed to in a
short time. As bad as his illness was, he always seemed to
be worried about everybody else. His concerns went beyond himself. He says that was his Christmas gift, spiritually and in the hereafter. He's told that he achieved what
he was supposed to. That people would learn love and affection.''

"Right.''

"Did he pass around Easter? He shows me Easter lilies.''

"He passed—died—on Easter Sunday. But he came
back to life for forty more days,'' John explained.

"So Jason had a near-death experience and then came
back.''

"Yes.''

"Your son was artistically inclined and creative.''

"Yes. He drew.''

"He had a good sense of humor.''

"Yes.''

"It seems like he's a lot of fun as well. Because he's
kind of kidding. He says, 'Well, the moment has come that
I have to walk into the tulip field again.' Obviously he
means that he's going to withdraw. All the other relatives
that were here are starting to [go back]. Your son and his
friends are withdrawing also. He says, 'Back into the tulip
fields!' They're going back into the light, they say. He
jokes. He says, 'It's the yellow brick road, but it's made of
tulips.' ''

The night before this reading, the spirit of a young boy had
appeared to George. He said, "My parents will be visiting
you. Tell them not to be angry with God or Saint Jude. My
passing was my destiny. Please give them your Saint Jude
statue.''

The next evening, after the reading, George asked the

Georges to wait. He got the statue of Saint Jude and gave
it to them as a gift. He then told them why.

John later explained the meaning behind George's allusions to Christmas and special photographs of Jason. "For
Christmas, one of my gifts to Lorraine was to go through
the old photos. I blew them all up and put together a cal-
endar. I was all done and then—out of nowhere—I got an
inspiration to put a photo of Jason inside a blank Christmas
card. It was a picture of him at his piano, which he loved.
Inside I wrote an inscription: 'To my mom, whose love not
only spans time and space but dimension as well. Love,
Your son, Jason.' And, of course, Jason talked about that
in the reading.

"There is nothing we wouldn't do for Jason when he
was here on earth. Now that he's in heaven, going to
George was a way we could communicate with him. This
is just another way of talking to my son."

Reflecting on how she and her husband prepared themselves and their son for his death, Lorraine said, "Whether
you're nine, nineteen, or ninety, there's the fear of the unknown. I think what would help both the parents and a child
who is incurably ill or dying is to feel that there's somebody's hand right there waiting for them.

"George told us that my mother's spirit was there in the
hospital room with Jason when he was in a coma. George
said Jason sensed that his grandmother was there holding
his hand to help him cross over."

John added, "The way I would teach a child or talk to
a child who's going to pass would be to tell them, 'We're
going to put you in the care and trust of someone you
know. And you will be with them for a little while. Then
we will come and join you very shortly."

"Some parents wish that their children grow up to be president, a football hero, a movie star, or something like that.
I was just wishing that my child could put her arms around
me, give me a kiss, and tell me that she loved me," Ivan
Whiting said of his deceased daughter, Shelby.

Shelby was born on October 11, 1981, apparently a

healthy, normal child. But at three weeks old, she began experiencing brain seizures. Doctors discovered that the baby's corpus callosum, the pathway that connects the right and left hemispheres of the brain, never developed. She was also found to have suffered optic nerve damage and was determined to be profoundly mentally retarded. Taken together, Shelby's problems were diagnosed as Aicardi's syndrome, a condition so rare that Shelby was only the fifty-third child so identified in the past two decades.

Children with Aicardi's syndrome rarely live beyond two years. The news so overwhelmed Shelby's mother that she abandoned her husband and child three weeks later. Suddenly thirty-one-year-old Ivan Whiting, a professional tennis player and instructor, found himself a single parent, the sole caregiver to his handicapped and mentally retarded daughter.

"Here I am, a professional athlete, and my daughter was confined to a wheelchair all her life. You couldn't even measure her IQ. She couldn't do anything because of her lack of motor ability. It just killed me, why I had so much and really wasn't worthy of having it all, and Shelby didn't have anything."

Shelby could not walk, could not even lift her head. She was fed through a tube surgically implanted in her stomach. She could not speak and, mentally, never developed beyond a two- or three-year-old's level. Because of her optic nerve damage, she probably saw only shadows and light.

Against the advice of family, friends, and doctors, Ivan resolved never to institutionalize Shelby. Instead he devoted his life to her care. "I was very, very close to her. Shelby was my world, and I was hers. She was so beautiful. She was very, very pretty with brown hair and brown eyes," he recalled. Ivan organized his life around Shelby, taking her with him to tennis lessons and tournaments.

Most nights Shelby slept with Ivan, who turned her several times each night, a simple task that she could not do herself. He also created an environment so that she wouldn't startle, something that might cause more seizures. Though Shelby could not speak, she did vocalize, and she and Ivan had their own language. "I knew when she wanted to be turned over, have her diaper changed, or if she was hungry. For example, Shelby would try to rub her eyes with her hands when she was tired or maybe if her eyes itched. But she couldn't do that. She'd rub her cheekbones instead. I would take my fingers and gently rub her eyes for her, and she would relax. It was exactly what she wanted done. That's the kind of relationship we had."

Once when Shelby was five, Ivan had to go out of town, so he left her with a friend overnight. When Ivan returned the next day there were several more friends at the home where Shelby had stayed. The moment he picked up his daughter, "It was wonderful," Ivan recalled. Just then someone asked Ivan to come into the kitchen. Within seconds he heard a bloodcurdling scream. He raced back to the living room, picked up Shelby again, and she instantly calmed down. Ivan finally knew for sure that Shelby knew who he was. "She just didn't want to be put down because she missed me so much. It was one of the best things that ever happened to me. She knew when I wasn't there."

Shelby was eight years old when she was first hospitalized for pneumonia, the most common cause of death for Aicardi's syndrome children. Remarkably, Shelby rallied, and a week later Ivan learned he could take her home soon. Her IVs were removed, and she was to have left the hospital the following day. But that night the hospital notified Ivan that his daughter had taken a sudden, surprising turn for the worse. At first Ivan was sure there had been some mistake. Then he learned that she had suffered a massive heart attack and kidney failure.

Ivan rushed to the hospital. "After the heart attack, I was with her every moment. I held her for several hours. What bothered me was that Shelby was conscious for some of the time, and she had tubes everywhere. It looked painful to me. She had to be uncomfortable. There was so much tape on her face to hold the tubes in place, you could just see her eyes. And she looked frantic! It still kills me to think about it. I have trouble when I remember it, and I have to switch to another thought. It's very painful.

"She looked at me as if to say, 'How are you going to take me out of this pain? How are you going to get this taken care of?' And, of course, I was helpless."

Shelby experienced a series of heart attacks. After each the doctors used electrical shock to revive her. "I think they brought her back three times," Ivan recalled. "The doctor took me aside and said, 'You know, you're not doing her any favors. She's probably in some pain. She's going to keep having heart attacks. You let me know what you want to do. It will happen again. You have to make a decision.'

"At that point I realized I didn't want Shelby to be in any pain. I loved her so much." He tearfully told the physician not to resuscitate her. "I feel like that was a big mistake on my part," Ivan said sorrowfully. "I felt like I had given up. And maybe my giving up is what killed her. *That's* been very hard for me to understand; why I did what I did."

Shelby died soon after. Ivan placed several of her stuffed animals in her coffin. Her favorite, a large teddy bear, did not fit, so Ivan took it home and kept it.

"I knew that at some point I was going to lose Shelby," Ivan said. "I knew it and yet I wasn't prepared for how to react. Even knowing eight years in advance that this was going to happen, when it finally did, I couldn't believe the hurt and the pain."

Ivan's grief was devastating. He feared that Shelby was alone wherever she was. All she had known in this life was him. Who was with her now? Was she afraid? He also wrestled with the injustice of it all. "I couldn't understand Shelby spending eight years in a wheelchair, being mentally retarded, eating everything through a tube, not being able to see or talk. I mean, eight years of that crap and then you die! And that's it?"

For the first year after Shelby's death Ivan hardly left his house. Concerned friends would knock at his door, and he'd refuse to answer. Finally he decided to be with Shelby the only way he knew how.

"I wasn't too bright about it," Ivan said of his suicide attempt. "I opened up some arteries, but I also took quite a few sleeping pills. I was found before I died.''

Several years after Shelby's death, Ivan heard about George and traveled from Florida to New York to see him. He approached the reading with skepticism and hope. "I always wanted Shelby to put her arms around me, to give me a kiss, and tell me that she loved me. But she never had the ability to do that. As a father, as a parent who really loved his child, that's what I wanted to happen. Before I left my hotel room in New York, I said aloud to Shelby, 'I just want a hug and a kiss.'

"I had a nickname for Shelby; I called her Bozo, like the circus clown. Well, while I was talking to Shelby before I left to go to George's house, I said to her, 'I'm going to go see this George Anderson. But you and I will have a code [word] and you know what that is; your nickname, Bozo. That'll be our code. If I hear that, I'll know it's you. I'll know you're there.' ''

Ivan's reading raises some intriguing questions. George has done many readings in which the spirits of people who were mentally retarded, comatose, or otherwise intellectually compromised came forth with knowledge of things that those around them here could not imagine they would know. Shelby's case is unique in several ways. First, she was not only profoundly retarded but practically blind. In the reading, however, she comes through to George and proves that she had tremendous awareness of Ivan and many other things in her life.

We generally assume that the model for discarnate communications looks something like this: Here on earth we collect information with our minds. Somehow, after death, that information travels with us in whatever form we then take. We think of some of the messages that come through from the other side as reflections of the spirit's life here on earth. Shelby's case and those of other profoundly retarded people raises a question as to whether the mind is indeed the only means by which we collect and process information. Throughout Shelby's reading, you will see indisputable evidence that she knew and understood Ivan, his emotions, and his activities in a way that suggests there might be another part of us that participates in and records our experiences. Perhaps we have both a mental (i.e., brain or mind) intelligence and a spiritual intelligence. Was there, as Ivan so often wondered, more to Shelby's life here than was apparent? Did she know how much he loved her? From the other side, she answered, Yes.

"There's a strong male presence around you," George said to Ivan. "In fact, there are two or three male presences."

"That could be."

"They seem to be grandparents. Your grandfathers have passed on."

"Yes."

"There's also a female who's passed on."

"Yes."

"A very young female who's passed."

"Yes."

"Now she says she's the daughter who's passed."

"Yes."

"It's your daughter. Has your daughter crossed over?"

"Yes," Ivan acknowledged, his voice choking with emotion.

"Your father has passed."

"Yes."

"Your father comes through. That's the first male who was just around."

"Yes."

"He passes young by today's standards."

"Yes."

"His passing is tragic in the sense of age and circumstances."

"Yes."

"He passes accidentally."

"Yes."

"Vehicle involved."

"Yes."

"Your father wants you to know that he's sorry he didn't get to know you better."

"Yes."

"You could have known each other better. But he wasn't *allowed* to. He uses that word. That's exactly the way he says it."

"Correct. That's right."

"He puts it that way. 'I'm sorry I didn't get to know you better. But I wasn't allowed to.' Those are his words."

"Exactly."

"You're obviously young when he passed on."

"Yes."

"Your daughter passes as a child."

"Yes."

"She's showing me ten or eleven."

"She'd be around ten or eleven now. She was eight when she died. That's three years ago."

"Oh, okay."

"Also, George, my daughter's birthday was 10–11. She was born on October 11, 1981. I always referred to her birthday as 10–11. I wouldn't say October eleventh."

"Your daughter says you and she were pals. She's saying you *are* pals."

"Yes."

"She was everything to you, and you were everything to her."

"Yes."

"She passes tragically. Both age and circumstances."

"Yes."

"She passes accidentally."

"I don't know."

"Well, her death is a shock to you."

"Sure."

"She had lung problems? There's something in the chest," George said as he tapped his own chest where he felt pain.

"Yes."

"She has a heart attack. She does *not* pass from a lung problem. She's showing me that her passing has to do with the heart. I'm not getting enough oxygen from the lungs."

"That's right. That's correct."

"She dies from this heart attack."

"Yes. I should have been there," Ivan added. "I wish I'd been there."

"You shouldn't feel sorry or feel badly that you weren't there when she died."

"I *was* there when she died. She died in my arms. I wasn't there when she had the heart attack."

"Oh. That's my confusion," George said.

Ivan nodded.

"Your daughter passes peacefully. She says to tell you she didn't suffer. She doesn't feel any pain, even if it didn't look that way."

"Okay."

"Your father obviously passes before your daughter. Because he says he met her when she came over. He crossed her into the light. He's taking care of her."

"Okay."

"She says, 'I can see. I can see colors. My favorite color is pink,' she says."

"Right."

"She also says, 'I can speak.' She says to tell you that she can speak. Which I already knew, because I can understand her perfectly."

"Yes."

"And she says to tell you that her brain is . . . I'm searching for the right word. Well, I'll tell you just what she's saying. She says to tell you her brain is normal."

"Yes. I understand."

"Was she older than her years?"

"No, not really. Actually, my daughter was mentally retarded."

"Well, it just seems like she's very down to earth, with common sense. She seems older than her years."

At this, Ivan smiled.

"When she died, she left her physical body behind. Her spiritual body is what's alive and what's there. She says don't think about her illness or mental retardation. She says, 'That was my physical body. My spiritual body is here. And I can see, and I can hear. And my brain is normal.' "

"Good."

"Your daughter is calling out to her mother."

"She didn't know her mother. Her mother left when my daughter was about six weeks old."

"Well, she calls to her mother," George repeated.

"Why would she do that? She didn't even know her."

"Well, apparently, she wants to close that gap at this point. And your daughter just wants her mother to know that she's okay."

Ivan nodded.

"There's a lot of energy between you and your daughter."

"Yes."

"That's what made your relationship as good as it was. You and she were very close."

"Yes."

"You took her passing very badly."

"Yes."

"She knows that. She knows you took her loss very badly. It devastated you. After that [her passing], you haven't wanted to go on with your life. You're overwhelmed by grief."

"Yes."

"Your daughter says it makes her sad to see you enveloped in the grief of her passing."

"Okay."

"But she's fine now. And *you* need to go on with your life here as she must there."

"Right."

"You must know that your daughter is with you spiritually because you talk aloud to her. She tells me you do that."

"Yes."

"You must know—at least subconsciously—that she's with you, or you wouldn't be talking to her."

"Right."

"Don't blame yourself. You mustn't do that. There wasn't anything you could have done or foreseen. She says, 'Neither one of us could have. And if I tell you a hundred times, will you believe me? That you did all right by me.

You did good. If I had to choose a father all over again, I would certainly choose you.' That's what your daughter is telling me to tell you."

Ivan just nodded.

"Did you try to take your own life?" George asked.

"Yes," he admitted.

"After she passed."

"Yes."

"Because of that."

"Yes."

"She knows you did that. That you attempted suicide. But she says that's not the way to be with her. It's not the way to be together. She knows that if you died tonight, you couldn't care less. She knows how much you want to be with her. But it's not happening right away. Because it's not what you're supposed to do. You can't be with her that way. It would also make your daughter unhappy. If you [take your life], you don't fulfill your soul's mission here. Because your daughter says, 'Daddy, don't. You can't hurt yourself. Don't take your own life. You'll ruin the plan for your soul's mission, your soul's growth.' "

Ivan listened, then George asked, "You're spending a lot of time alone?"

"Yes."

"Too much time alone?"

"Yes, I am."

"She sees that, and she's very concerned about you. You definitely need to get out more, she says."

"I guess so, yes."

"She wants you to go on with your life here, as she must in the next stage. Are you alienating friends?"

"Yes."

"It's as if you don't want to be around other people. You don't want to do anything. You work and go home. That's all."

"Yes."

"You are employed?"

"Yes."

"Self-employed."

"Yes."

"But are you thinking about a job change?"

"Yes."

"But have you lost interest in what you're doing since she passed?"

"Yes."

"It's like you work because you have to work. But you don't really want to anymore."

"Right."

"Well, as your daughter said before, you've got to get on with your life. You've got to stop blaming yourself. There's nothing more you could have done for her. Did you know she wouldn't live long?"

"Yes, I knew that."

"You have no reason to be guilty. You shouldn't blame yourself. She keeps saying that."

"Okay."

"You've dreamt about her?"

"Yes, I have."

"Because she says she's come to you in dreams. You've heard from her before tonight."

"Right."

"She says, 'Just as you were my guardian angel in my life, now I'm your guardian angel.' "

"Okay."

"Did you take her to Disneyland?"

"No."

"Well, she's showing me Disneyland characters. Now she shows me cartoon characters; like clowns and things. I think it's a clue to her nickname. She had a nickname?"

"Yes."

"It's a term of endearment of some kind."

"Yes."

"She's trying to make me understand that this is very important to you. You need to know this. This is a code between the two of you."

"Yes."

"It's definitely a nickname."

"Yes."

"Is her first name uncommon?"

"Yes, it is."

"Why do I see scenes from the movie *Steel Magnolias*? I think it's some kind of clue to her name."

"Should I tell you?" Ivan asked.

"No. No."

"Okay."

"It's from *Steel Magnolias*. It's the daughter who dies in the movie. That's what she's showing me."

"Right."

"The character's name in the movie is Shelby. She's the daughter who dies. That's who I see."

"Yes."

"Is her name Shelby?"

"Yes."

"Your daughter says, 'This is Shelby.' That's her."

"Yes, that's her name."

"Now about her nickname. Whatever it is, this is really making my brain race. I keep seeing these clowns and cartoon characters from Disneyland."

"Right."

"Does her nickname have less than five letters?"

"Yes."

"It's four letters."

"Yes."

"I can feel it. But I can't hear it."

"Okay."

"Is it . . . 'Baby'?"

"No. Not Baby."

"I hear *B*."

"You're so close. Do you want me to tell you?"

"No, no. I want to get it from her."

"*B*. Baby. Bozo. Is it Bozo?"

"Yes!" Ivan exclaimed.

"That's why I see clowns. Like Bozo the Clown. That's what she's trying to show me."

"Yes!"

"And that's the code between just the two of you. Her nickname. It's Bozo."

"Yes."

"Your daughter says, 'Some souls come to earth to give love and some come to earth to get love. In my case, I was lucky. I got both.' "

"Yes."

"Your daughter says about her illness that you both chose to be in this situation."

Ivan said nothing in response.

"Do you take the name Bea?" George asked.

"No."

"Bea or Beatrice?"

"No."

"What about Jenny? Or Jennifer?"

"No."

"Phil or Philip? Does that mean anything?"

"No."

This exchange is a classic example of a subject temporarily blanking out. Ivan was so overwhelmed during the reading that it wasn't until later that he "remembered" that his sister's name is Beatrice* her husband's name Phil* and their daughter's, Jennifer*. He did not really forget, but he was unable to think of anything but Shelby.

"Do you take the name Chris?"

"Shelby's middle name was Christina. My confirmation saint was Saint Christopher," Ivan explained.

"She's giving you back a teddy bear. She's handing you a teddy bear. Does that mean anything to you?"

"Yes. When Shelby died, I wanted her to have her favorite teddy bear. I gave her some little stuffed pets in the coffin, but the teddy bear was too big for her casket. So I kept it."

"Well, she hands it to you now."

"Okay."

"And she has pets now [on the other side]. She's taking care of pets. And she's helping other children cross over

---

*This family's names have been altered to protect their identities. Everything else in this story, however, is true.

who are confused or afraid. That's her job in the next stage
now. To help other children, just like herself, who are afraid
or confused when they come over.''

"Okay."

"When you die—and it's not happening right away—
your daughter will be there to meet you when you cross
over. And you will be together forever.

"Your daughter wants me to tell you that she's getting
ready to leave. It's not because she wants to. But it's because she realizes what a drain this is on me mentally. She
wants me to tell you that she's in your lap. She has her
arms around you. She's giving you a kiss. And she says
she loves you.''

After the reading Ivan described his frustration over not
being with Shelby, but he added, "I'm more at peace inside
than I've been in a long time."

From a book of his poetry that he published, Ivan offered
this:

> I held you in my arms slowly,
> careful not to disturb the tubes and needles
> but wanting to be near you
> with all my heart.
>
> You always loved your daddy to hold you
> falling asleep every time.
>
> And I held you
> until you died
> never telling you
> that you were holding me.

6

When Love Is Not Enough

Throughout the book we have tried to demonstrate how different types of deaths affect bereaved families. While it is impossible, even pointless, to state that one type of death is more or less painful than another, among all causes of children's deaths, suicide is truly a singular phenomenon. Parents whose children commit suicide are profoundly affected by the simple fact that their children *chose* to die. Issues of responsibility, blame, and cause often become painfully entangled.

Even when the reasons behind the child's decision are clear, as in the first story here, parents and other family members cannot help but wonder how things might have been different if they had said this or done that. While whole families, sometimes even whole communities, are affected by and may feel they failed the child who committed suicide, parents must endure a terrible burden in this regard. Amid the myriad questions and concerns that arise after a suicide, it all seems to boil down to this: Wasn't my love for my child enough to keep her here?

The reasons behind suicide are individual and often complex. Experts in the fields of bereavement and childhood suicide very carefully point out how important it is for survivors to put the issue of blame into perspective. Contrary to popular belief, an act of suicide is not always preceded by a predictable telltale pattern of behavior and may not always be preventable.

We are in the midst of a teen suicide epidemic, with an estimated 500,000 attempting suicide every year and about 6,000 succeeding. Among children fifteen to twenty-four years of age, suicide is the third leading cause of death, after accidents and homicides, and the rate may be even higher, since it is very possible that a number of single-car crashes, falls, drug overdoses, and similar mishaps are actually suicides.

While the media focuses primarily on the problem of teen suicide, children much, much younger have attempted it and succeeded. Since most children under ten do not fully grasp the finality of death, it would not seem to present relief from desperation.

Surprisingly, however, an alarming number do see suicide as a way out of this life. It is the fifth leading cause of death among children between five and fourteen. According to Margaret O. Hyde and Elizabeth Held Forsyth, M.D., authors of *Suicide*, "Suicidal fantasies, acts, and threats must be taken seriously in children as young as three. . . ."

Our culture's attitude toward the act of suicide and those who commit or attempt it is often a mix of shock, ambivalence, and disgust. We search endlessly, often futilely, for the reason the suicide rejected life and, by extension, us. Many of us wonder why that person could not overcome or see clear of problems that we may feel we have all faced, leading some to conclude that suicide is an act of weakness.

If, as we know, bereaved parents as a whole feel ostracized, suicide survivors present an even more difficult case. For one thing, unlike most bereaved parents, the parents of suicides are often, however subconsciously, blamed for the act. Not surprisingly, many parents do blame themselves. "If only his mother hadn't gone back to work." "If only she hadn't fallen in with that crowd." "If only we had not moved to the new house." "If only we had seen the signs."

Despite the cultural stereotypes of suicide, experts are quite clear in stating that no one really knows what causes a person to take his life. Even when the suicide does leave a note the reasons are not always fully explained. Studies of people who have survived their suicide attempts show that each case is unique.

Sometimes a single event that would seem bearable taken alone adds to a cumulative feeling of failure or loss that becomes unendurable while in other instances the act occurs during a state of high emotion. Then there are situations like those in the two stories that follow. In one, a young girl carefully and methodically plans her own death; in the other, a young man acts impulsively, so much so that when he comes through to George he admits that he really did not expect to die when he did.

George is very careful about using his position as a platform to lecture on anything but what he has learned from the other side. He carefully takes no public position on a number of issues. But suicide is the one area in which he feels compelled to speak out. Anyone who feels that life is not worth living might well wonder, If life on the other side is all that George and others say it is, why shouldn't I go? Why shouldn't I end my own life?

"I will always say—because I've heard this time and again from spirits who passed this way and regret it—don't take your life," he said. "It may look like a shortcut, an escape from all the pain and problems here, but it's not.

"Now, I have to be clear here: I am not talking about someone who has a terminal illness and is choosing death because of that. That's a different issue, and one I won't get into. But while there is no judge and jury on the other side, there is one person who sits in judgment of what you've done, and that's you.

"Time and time again, spirits have come through to tell me that when they arrived over there, they were confused, and sometimes in a state of darkness. Contrary to the teachings of some organized religions, suicide is not a sin per se; those who die by it do not go to hell or endure a tortured existence as we have been taught to understand it. However, committing suicide does seem to set your soul's growth or development back.

"And—I've probably heard this from spirits a thousand times by now—you will suffer terribly over there when you see the grief and pain your death caused. Most times, spirits of suicides come through and, ironically, because of the outpouring of sympathy at their wakes and funerals, see that many more people cared about them than they realized. Also, virtually every spirit who has taken his or her own life has told me that now they see that they could have worked out their problems if they had given it more time here, and they are sorry they did not choose that option. For them, the most painful part is knowing that they chose to end their lives, and that now, as much as they may wish to, they cannot turn back time. It's too late."

As we wrote earlier, many experts believe that suicide is a widely underreported phenomenon. However, what George has learned through a number of readings, is that some apparent suicides are actually accidents.

"Sometimes spirits confess that they weren't in control of themselves or their senses at that moment. They say that it wasn't suicide, even though it looked like one. The difference there is that they really did not mean for it to happen.

"In one case I recall very clearly," George continued, "a couple came to me from Minnesota. For years they had thought their sixteen-year-old daughter committed suicide. The reason they believed this was that, while there was no suicide note, she had left her diary, in which she had expressed the normal frustrations and disappointments most adolescents have. She mentioned how hard a struggle she found life, and things of that nature. Years later, during the reading for her parents, she came through and said, 'I didn't commit suicide. I accidentally fell and hit my head.' It was in the dead of winter, and no one knew where she was, so she froze to death in an unconscious state."

Suicide has a long and fascinating history, but we are concerned primarily with the source of the shame that survivors of suicides feel. Ever since Saint Augustine took a stand against the act in the fourth century A.D., Church teachings have deemed suicide a mortal sin. Those who committed suicide might be denied full funeral rites, or their bodies might be buried away from consecrated ground.

Such attitudes are not as prevalent today, but even if we do not regard suicide as a mortal sin, we seem prone to viewing the act, at the very least, as a waste. One author remarked how hospital emergency room personnel were observed being generally less involved with, perhaps even less sympathetic toward, people who had attempted or committed suicide. Perhaps subconsciously, many of us wonder what was "wrong" with a person who just couldn't hack it. Ours is a culture that eschews weakness and surrender. It would seem that we do place blame on the person who commits suicide. Yet, why does practically every young person's suicide set off communitywide introspection? Clearly, our sometimes contradictory thinking about suicide makes the road for bereaved parents and others that much harder to travel.

The two readings that follow are a study in contrasts. In one an obviously troubled boy succumbs to problems he literally could not articulate. In the second, a young woman's suicide reveals the hurt little girl behind her happy, accomplished facade. It's important to note that in each case, parents and loved ones did their best to save these children. Perhaps more painfully than anyone else, the survivors of suicides know that sometimes love simply is not enough.

Pauline and Howard were in their late thirties when they were finally blessed with a child.* They showered Baby Stephan with love. When three years later a baby sister arrived, the couple felt their lives were complete. Howard was successful enough in business to allow Pauline to stay

---

*At the request of the subjects, their names and other biographical details have been altered to protect their identities. Everything else in this story, however, is true.

home and raise the children. Their sixth-floor Boston apartment was sunny and comfortable; their days seemed full and happy.

But Stephan was only a few months old when his parents noticed that he was different from other babies. Though alert and obviously bright, he hardly ever cried. At first they assumed this was just his personality. As the years passed, however, Stephan remained unusually quiet and withdrawn around everyone his age except his sister Denise. But most of the time he still preferred playing with, as his mother said, "anything mechanical."

"Even before he went to school, Stephan began to read. When he spoke to me, I'd have to laugh sometimes. He just seemed so much older. He had a wonderful vocabulary. He was a joy," Pauline recalled. "But then when we got around friends, relatives, neighbors—anyone not in our immediate family—I couldn't get him to say a word. Everyone would comment on how shy he was."

"His teachers couldn't say enough about how bright he was," Howard added, smiling. "But he had no friends. I thought we should have pushed him more to have friends."

"There was nothing seriously wrong with him," Pauline said. "He had mild asthma and allergies, for which he used medication and a bronchial spray. He also had a slight astigmatism and wore glasses. But he was a good-looking little boy. He had dark hair and dark eyes."

"As he got older, it became a no-win situation," Howard recalled. "If I yelled at him, he'd become more sullen. If I said nothing, then he never played with other kids or went out at all. He could be very stubborn. So as he got older, we locked horns, I admit."

"If we left him on his own, he'd read constantly, and he loved computers," his mother said. "Put him around anything with computers and electronics, and he was a genius. Every school he attended told us that his aptitude in science and math were exceptional."

"Yet, we just couldn't get him to talk about anything that was on his mind when he was growing up."

Pauline described their daily exchange: " 'How was school today?' I'd ask.

" 'Fine,' he'd answer.

" 'What did you do today?'

" 'Nothing.'

" 'Where are you going now?'

" 'My room.'

"And that would be the whole conversation. Still, I felt that he and I were very close."

"Oh, yes, Stephan and his mother were much closer, I admit, than he and I were," his father observed. "I'm sorry to say that we had our conflicts."

If Stephan knew any happiness, it was in his room, his refuge from the world. There he kept an extensive collection of computer components, a stereo system, and shelves groaning under the weight of technical manuals, Gothic, science fiction, and horror novels, and rock and jazz CDs. He also had a television set and a VCR, videotapes of science fiction movies, and posters of rock stars and faraway places. Directly over Stephan's bed hung a portrait of Albert Einstein alongside a *Star Trek* poster.

At the suggestion of Stephan's high school guidance counselor, he began seeing a psychiatrist, under whose care he remained for two years. Despite this, Stephan's relationship with his father did not improve. During his junior year of high school, Stephan seemed to be deteriorating.

"We were both alarmed," Pauline said. "It was just impossible to get him to speak. I'd say, 'Stephan, sweetheart, please tell me what's bothering you.' But he wouldn't answer. Once, I remember, we were sitting at the kitchen table. I thought he wanted to open up and tell me what he was thinking. He looked at me and started to say something. My heart started beating faster, and then the phone rang. I answered and hung up immediately, but by then— in a split second—he had gone into his room, and I couldn't budge him. He closed up again."

Stephan rarely shared with his parents what he discussed in therapy, and he balked at their involvement in the sessions. After Stephan spent the summer before his senior

year virtually secluded in his room, his psychiatrist prescribed Elavil, an antidepressant. Over the next several
months, as Howard remembered, "He actually started talking to us."

"He told us he wanted to go to college, to study computer science or engineering. We were thrilled," Pauline
added.

"One day the phone rang, and it was someone asking
for my son. Stephan told me later that he'd become friendly
with someone in school. That's all he would tell me, but it
was the first time he'd ever allowed someone to call him
at home," Pauline said.

"We thought he was coming out of his shell, finally,"
Howard added.

Stephan and his new friend went out and studied together. Then that winter he began talking about a girl he
was friendly with, too. His parents were happy and relieved.

"You know some people might have thought that we
overprotected him, or we didn't want him to go out. But
that wasn't true," Pauline said. "His psychiatrist never really told us what caused Stephan to be so introverted and
depressed."

"But you got the feeling," Howard added, "that maybe
the psychiatrist partly blamed us. I don't know. I got to the
point where I knew he was troubled. I never wanted to use
the word *sick*. But, honestly, we wanted him to get better."

Right before graduation Stephan inexplicably withdrew
again. He graduated the top of his class and planned to
attend college in Boston. But beyond that he seemed as
unfocused as ever. When Howard casually asked him about
his plans for the summer, Stephan just shrugged.

"Several days after graduation I was home. It was mid-
afternoon; a hot day," Pauline recalled. "Stephan came out
of his room. He stared at me blankly. He looked very depressed. I asked him what was wrong. He didn't answer.
When I asked him where he was going, he said, 'Out.'

" 'When will you be back?' I asked him.

" 'In a little while,' he answered. 'I'll be right back.'

"Several minutes later I heard sirens, but I didn't pay

any attention. I don't know how much time went by. Maybe fifteen or twenty minutes after Stephan left the house, a cop was at the door. He told me what happened: Stephan had gone up to the roof of our building and jumped, feet first. He plunged six stories. His body landed in a courtyard.''

"There was no warning," Howard said, still stunned by the events of that day. "We thought he was getting better."

"Where did we go wrong?" Pauline wondered. "We've racked our brains. What more could we have done? Were we too strict? Too lenient? We heard from his friend. He told us that he didn't know what happened, but one day a couple of months before he jumped, Stephan just pulled away. He didn't want to be friends with him anymore. We never heard from the girl he said he liked."

"Maybe I was too tough on him," Howard mused. "I don't know. How do you get into the mind of a seventeen-year-old boy?"

It was several weeks after Stephan's death before Pauline could summon the courage to clean her son's room. Her real goal was to find the suicide note she hoped might explain this baffling tragedy. What she found instead was a supply of his Elavil. Apparently he had stopped taking his medication. Later Howard and Pauline learned that severe, even suicidal depression can occur when the drug is suddenly stopped.

"But we don't blame the medication," Howard asserted. "Maybe he shouldn't have stopped taking it. But he was so stubborn. Would he be alive if he hadn't stopped the medication? Was there something I—we—did wrong? Was it just the way he was born? I have agonized every day and night about those questions. The guilt is terrible!"

Through a neighbor, they learned of George and traveled to New York for their reading.

"There's a male passed," it began. "Now there are two male presences."

"Yes," Pauline answered.

"One is older. The other is younger. They're of two different generations."

"Yes."

"Now, your mom's passed?" George asked her.

"Yes, she's passed on."

"The young male says he's the son passed on. 'I'm the son.' Does that make sense?"

"Yes."

"He's *your* son."

"Yes."

"You're his parents."

"Yes, we are," Howard replied.

"I asked you about your mom. She's passed. Your dad's passed over, also."

"Yes," Pauline said.

"And your parents have passed over as well, because he says all four of his grandparents are there with him."

"That's correct," Howard confirmed.

"Your son passes as a young man."

"Yes."

"I mean, he's not a young child."

"No, he's not."

"He passes from health troubles? Because he says he struggles with his health. Does that make sense?"

"Yes."

"Were you afraid that he was mad at you?"

"Yes."

"Because he says he's not. 'Tell my father I'm not mad at him,' he says."

The couple listened to the message but did not reply.

"There was obviously a lack of communication between you and your son."

"Yes, there was," Howard admitted.

"He says he forgives and he hopes you do, too."

"Yes, I do."

"Your son is very independent. That's the feeling he gives me. He does things *his* way. Boy, once he makes up his mind, there's no talking him out of [anything]."

"Yes. He was stubborn and introverted."

"You and he definitely had conflict."

"Yes, we did. Especially at the end."

"Well, he forgives and hopes you do, too."

"Yes," Howard answered as he began to cry softly.

"Your son say he's walking fine now [in the hereafter]. Does that make sense? I don't know what he means. So I'll say it to you as I hear it [psychically]." Stephan was referring to the fact his legs had been shattered in the fall.

"Yes, I understand."

"He definitely went over [to the other side] in a state of anxiety."

"Yes."

"When your son arrived, he went into what we would understand as a rest home. He was very lonely here. He's not happy here."

"That's correct."

"He says he can communicate better from the next stage than he did when he was here."

"Yes, I understand."

"Do you take the name Al or Alan? Albert? Something like that."

"Yes. There's an Al. It's short for Alan," Howard said.

"Living?"

"Yes."

"Your son knew him?"

"Yes. It's a friend of mine. My son knew him."

"Oh. Because your son calls out to him. He said, 'Al.' I formalized it. Al or Alan."

"Yes."

"Did your son have trouble breathing?" George asked as he felt the sympathetic pain.

"Well, he had asthma, but it was mild. He also had some allergies," Pauline explained.

"At the end, he just goes off into a sleep. Something makes his heart stop."

"Yes."

"It's funny. Within himself, your son is very emotional. But he keeps it all inside. I see a clown. It's my symbol that he laughs on the outside, but he cries on the inside. All of his upset he definitely keeps within himself."

"Yes," Howard said.

"Your son admits that he wanted to die."

"Apparently so."

"I see the Sacred Heart of Jesus. It has nothing to do with your religious beliefs. It's my symbol. He took his own life? That's what it means."

"Yes. He took his own life," Howard answered.

"Because he had to find himself. He didn't know how to do that here. He keeps his struggles inward. He's introverted. Self-contained. That's the reason why he went first to a 'rest home' on the other side, as we would understand it here. Someone takes care of him in the hereafter in order to help him find himself. Through the grace of God he'll find himself."

The couple nodded their heads, but neither said a word.

"Your son made things very hard on himself here."

"Oh, yes," Howard said.

"But he says, 'You *didn't* fail me as parents. You did your best as mother and father. There was nothing more you could do. You did your best,' he says."

"I'm glad to know that," Stephan's mother said.

"Only *he* is responsible for the choice he made. It was *his* decision. He's not playing favorites. But your son calls to you [mother]. It seems he was closer to you. It's like you and he were close friends, as well as mother and son. It's not that he doesn't love his father. But of the two of you, he felt closer to his mother."

"Yes. That's true," Howard replied.

"He says, 'Mom, you didn't let me down.' He just wants you to know that."

"Oh, good," she said.

"He's close to you."

"Is he close? I hope so."

"Definitely. He says closer than you can imagine."

"Can he see us?" Pauline asked.

"Yes, he can."

"Oh, thank you, George."

"Do you have other children?"

"Yes," she replied.

"Because he says he's your only boy. Your oldest. That

makes his loss even harder. He knows that now.''

"George, will he stay near us?'' she asked.

"Always. But remember, he's got to find himself, too, in the next stage.''

"Right.''

"Your son says to consecrate him to the Sacred Heart of Jesus. He asks that you light a candle.''

"Okay.''

"He had an emotionally hard life here.''

"Yes.''

"Your son just doesn't seem to get a break here. He always struggles, it seems. His life is empty and lonely.''

"Yes.''

"He had trouble finding a job? Because he says he had trouble holding a job here. He admits that.''

"Yes.''

"Then toward the end, he was getting a little better. He was finding himself a bit and doing a little better. But then he just didn't have the confidence, and he took his life.''

"Yes. It was sudden. That was what surprised us, too,'' Howard explained.

"Did your son take something? You know, a drug or medication?''

"Well, he was supposed to take medication, but he wouldn't.''

"Oh. Because he said something about medication. I thought he'd taken something. But he must have meant that he hadn't taken the medication he was supposed to. That was my misunderstanding.''

"Okay.''

"Do you take the name Steve or Steven? Something like that.''

"Yes.''

"Is that your son's name?''

"Yes.''

"Because it sounds like his voice. I heard him calling out Steven or Steve.''

"His actual name was Stephan,'' Howard explained.

"Well, he says he preferred to be called Steve.''

"Yes, he did."

"He says his actual name is Stephan, but most people called him Steve. That's why when I heard him say Steve, I formalized it and asked you if his name was Steven."

"We always knew that. He didn't like to be called Stephan. He wanted to be called Steve."

"He gives me the impression he was very smart," said George. "He's very creative in the area of his interest. He's scientific. And good with mathematics, too? Because I [psychically] see what looks like all kinds of computers and electronic equipment around you."

"Yes. He was brilliant with those things. Especially with computers. That was really his expertise," Howard said.

"Obviously he was in school. Was he changing schools?"

"Yes. Shall I explain further?"

"No, no. Let him tell me. He shows me eighteen. Was he around that age?"

"Yes. Close."

"Younger. Because he showed me eighteen. Then he dropped me in age. Was he seventeen?"

"Yes, he was."

"Because he said he was seventeen, but he would be eighteen on his next birthday. Had he just graduated?"

"Yes."

"From high school, he tells me."

"Yes."

"He says he was going to go to college, but he didn't yet."

"That's correct. He took his life a short time after he graduated from high school. He would have begun attending college in September—had he lived," Howard said.

"He still *is* alive in the next stage of life," George emphasized. "His grades in school were excellent."

"Oh, yes. Always."

"Because he says he was at the top of his class."

"Yes, he was. He was on the high school honor roll when he graduated."

"Yeah, that's the thing. Because your son is obviously

brilliant in his field. I don't get the feeling I'm dealing with a teenager when it comes to his subject; computers and mathematics. So his problem wasn't something intellectual. It's obvious that it's emotional. His struggles were with himself. Things that most of us would find difficult to comprehend in the fields of computers or electronics, he found easy.''

''Yes. That's him.''

''But he does realize now that he did the wrong thing by taking his life.''

''Oh. He does now,'' she replied.

''Your son stopped taking his medication, which contributed to his passing, but that did not cause his passing.''

''That's correct.''

''It's just that not taking the medication made him more depressed.''

''That's right.''

''It's too bad, because he seemed to be doing better in the last few months of his life. It's as if he's improving slightly, then suddenly he takes his life.''

''Yes.''

''Did something cut off his air? I feel like I can't breathe.''

''Yes.''

''Did your son get the information about how to take his own life from some book he read?''

''We really don't know.''

''It's interesting. Because he gives me the feeling that he read something, and that was where he got some ideas about taking his own life.''

''It could be. He read a great deal,'' Howard said.

''Does your son fall?''

''Yes.''

''He jumps.''

''Yes.''

''There are internal injuries, obviously.''

''Yes.''

''Because it feels like there's quite a severe impact when he hits.''

"Yes."

"Your son jumped. But to be honest, I don't think he actually expected to die. It's more like he figured that he'd be injured, but that he would live."

"Oh, God!" Pauline cried.

"I [psychically] see him jumping from a pretty good height."

"Yes, he did. He jumped from the roof of our apartment house. He threw himself off the roof. It was a six-story building. He landed in the courtyard below," Howard explained.

"It happens unexpectedly," George said.

"Right. There was no warning."

"This happens in Boston?"

"Yes."

"You've dreamt about him? Because Stephan—he corrects me; he'd rather be called Steve. In any event, he says he's come to you before this. He says this isn't the first contact you've had since he's passed on."

"That's right. He came to me one time in a dream. It seemed so lifelike. I kissed him and held him," she said.

"Did you lose a pet dog?"

"Yes, we did," Howard replied.

"The dog passed before your son."

"Oh, yes. By several months."

"Because the dog is with him now. The dog is with Stephan in the rest home, as we'd understand it. They're together in the next stage.

"Now, you said he was the eldest, I recall. But he calls out to someone who's like a brother?"

"No, he didn't have a brother."

"It's someone *like* a brother," George insisted.

"Oh. That could be a friend of his. There was one boy he'd been close to from school," Howard said.

"Is there any reason why this friend would be angry at your son? Because your son apologizes to this other boy. Did they have some differences that you know about?"

"I don't know."

"My son had been friendly with this other boy. I know

they'd studied together. Actually, it was the first friend he'd made," Pauline explained. "I was happy about that. But then Stephan pulled away. I asked him if they were still friendly. He said not anymore, but he never said why. My son was very quiet."

"That's the thing. It seems your son withdraws from their friendship. It's not like they had a big disagreement or anything. Your son just doesn't want to be bothered, and he pulls away from contact with others. He's withdrawn into himself. Although toward the end he seemed to be a little more talkative, he's still very lonely. He's very introverted."

"Yes."

"That's where you and he had conflict," George said, turning to Howard.

"Oh, yes," he replied.

"Well, he's apologizing for that now. He's saying he's not angry at you. Please don't think he is. And he also calls to that friend. He says they were becoming close like brothers. That's what frightened him. So he pulled back. He gave the friend the impression he was angry at him. But it wasn't anger. It was fear on your son's part. He wants that boy to know that. Do you have contact with that boy?"

"No."

"But we could," Pauline added.

"Oh, because if he's open to this, your son says, 'Tell him you've heard from me. I'm definitely not angry. You shouldn't blame yourself.' He's beginning to understand himself.

"Again, your son is coming along in the hereafter. He's *not* suffering in some horrible hell-like state. So don't worry about that. That's not the way it is. He's in a 'rest home,' where he's getting to know himself better."

"Okay."

"And, again, you did not fail him in any way as his parents. You're not at fault for any reason. He made the decision by himself [to take his own life]. But he says he certainly didn't mean to cause you such grief."

"I hope we didn't fail him," Pauline said.

"You were also worried that he was alone in the here-after as he was on earth."

"Yes. Yes."

"Well, he wants to reassure you that he's not alone in the next stage. Many relatives and friends came to help him when he arrived."

"Oh, good."

"So he's definitely not lonely on the other side the way he was here."

"Okay."

"He sees your grief, but he does want you to go on with your lives."

"I wish we could wrap him up and take him home," Pauline remarked.

"You can," George said. "Spiritually. Continue to pray that he finds peace and progresses further into the light. Please light a candle for him to the Sacred Heart of Jesus."

"We will."

"It's funny," said George. "Your son can accept help and friendship on the other side. But if it had been offered when they were both here on earth, he wouldn't have been able to accept it."

"That's right."

"So you see, your son is progressing in the hereafter."

"Right."

"Just don't feel your son is alone. He had a very lonely life here, but he's certainly not alone in the hereafter."

Months after the reading, Pauline and Howard shared their thoughts. "Next to the agony of losing Stephan, I needed to hear that he wasn't suffering somewhere," she said. "I had this fear from what I'd been taught growing up, that if one commits suicide, one is condemned to hell. I felt such a relief to hear Stephan tell us that wasn't true.

"Nothing can bring him back to us. I know that," she continued. "But I try to reassure myself that he's not alone now, and he's not suffering, here or there. I pray we didn't fail him. He said in the reading that we didn't. I hope that's true. How do you help someone you love who doesn't love you?"

Howard remarked, "I was very relieved, I admit, to hear my son say that he wasn't angry at me, that he doesn't blame us. But, believe me, there is still plenty of guilt and anguish."

"We mainly stay to ourselves now," Pauline said. "A lot of people are uncomfortable around us, I think. They offered their sympathies, of course, when it happened, but after that they kind of avoided us. They act like they're afraid to be around us. They don't know what to say, but they don't have to say anything. The way that people don't want you around only adds to our loneliness."

Stephan's parents never did find a suicide note, although they have since begun to wonder whether or not their son wrote such a note and filed it away on computer disk. Someday, neither Pauline nor Howard is quite sure when, they plan to look for it.

At forty-eight years of age Owen Miller was a charming, affable, gregarious man.* "A born salesman," was how most of his neighbors in his Oregon hometown would describe him. He had single-handedly built up a successful car dealership, and was regarded as one of the region's most popular and most prosperous businessmen.

What few outside his family knew, however, is that there was a dark side to Owen Miller. He was a manic depressive and an alcoholic. Manic-depressive illness—also known today as bipolar disorder—produces wild mood swings between mania and depression. Alcohol and drug abuse often become part of the picture as the manic-depressive attempts to "level out" his moods through "self-medication."

Manic-depression can be treated by psychotherapy and

---

*At the request of the subjects, all names and other biographical details and facts pertaining to their case have been altered to protect their identities. Everything else in this story, however, is true.

appropriate, prescribed medication. However, many manic-depressives, their thought processes distorted by a combination of the disease itself and whatever psychoactive drugs they take, do not seek or stick with treatment. In their quest to relieve their pain through drink and/or drugs, sufferers end up actually increasing the depth and severity of their depressions to the point that they engage in suicidal thinking and may even commit the act.

Aside from the havoc Owen's illness and his drinking wrought on his wife Penny and their children, Andrew, twenty-three, Cynthia, twenty-one, and Rebecca, nineteen, it appears to have left a tragic legacy for Rebecca, whose behavior and subsequent suicide suggest that she may have inherited a genetic predisposition for the disorder from which Owen suffered.

Of the three children, only Rebecca still lived at home and witnessed firsthand her father's psychological deterioration. It seemed, as Penny put it, that "Owen just totally changed personalities." As time passed, Owen hardly spoke to or acknowledged Rebecca except when he was drunk. A star athlete and academic overachiever, she would beg her father to come to one of her basketball or hockey games, but to please come sober. Instead he would appear drunk, not only embarrassing Rebecca but making her feel unloved. Like so many children of alcoholics, she had hoped that if given the choice between drink and her, Owen would choose her. Still, she never stopped hoping against hope that one day her father would love her as much as she loved him.

One day during her senior year Rebecca drove the family car off an unfamiliar road. She claimed she had blacked out. Fortunately, she was driving so slowly that she was not hurt. It seemed to have been an accident, but Penny had her doubts. She suspected that Rebecca might have tried to harm herself, but she wasn't really sure.

Life continued as it was. Owen's life had spun so far out of control that Penny obtained a legal protection of abuse order against him. On three separate occasions Penny tried to leave her husband, but he always wooed her back by promising to change. At one point he entered a rehabilitation facility, but his success was shortlived. And when Rebecca happily told her parents that she'd earned a four-year scholarship to a prestigious university, Owen ignored her. Crushed, Rebecca left home for college in the fall of 1989.

Eventually Owen became abusive toward Penny and their children. Penny had no choice but to leave him and file for divorce. She moved from Oregon to Arizona and began a new life. Owen, meanwhile, became even more depressed. Yet to the community he remained an upstanding citizen. Penny recounted several occasions when the police caught him driving drunk and simply let him go. That's how well he kept up his act of being a happy, well-adjusted family man.

It seemed this was another of her father's traits that Rebecca inherited as well. To those who knew her, she seemed an outgoing, happy, popular young woman. Yet only three weeks after starting her freshman year of college, Rebecca took two bottles of an over-the-counter sleeping pill in an attempt to end her life. Penny flew to be at Rebecca's side in the hospital.

Once Rebecca recovered, she went home with her mother. There she began receiving therapy on an outpatient basis, and within several months she announced she was ready to go back to school. That Christmas Rebecca returned to her hometown, determined to be reunited with her father, but he rebuffed her overtures, and she was devastated. By then he had begun abusing cocaine in addition to alcohol; his businesses and finances were in ruins. Unbeknown to his daughter, Owen had come to the attention of law enforcement authorities, who were closing in on him for alleged illegal business activities.

The last time Penny spoke to her husband in early 1990, he begged her forgiveness. The next month she traveled back north, where she and Owen were to meet and finalize their divorce. Shortly after Penny arrived at the county courthouse, she was told to phone her attorney.

"Penny, I have some bad news for you," he said. "Owen's shot himself. He's dead."

"I screamed and dropped the phone," Penny recalled. "He'd always said if it got bad enough, he was going to kill himself. He'd always said he was going to live life to the fullest, that he was going to leave no stone unturned. 'It's all or nothing,' Owen always said."

Owen ended his life by placing a rifle barrel under his chin and pulling the trigger. "Rebecca, her brother, and her sister insisted on seeing their father, because we really didn't believe he was dead," Penny said. "We went to the funeral home. The undertaker had wrapped Owen's head in gauze. It was a nightmare, especially for Rebecca. She went up to the casket and was there for half an hour. I had to drag her away. It was terrible, and I don't think she ever recovered from it."

Outwardly, however, Rebecca seemed to be coping. She returned to school but quit going for counseling, saying she'd "had enough of it." Later she dropped out of school as well, and with her sister moved to Arizona to be near her mother. After a few more months she felt strong enough to move back to her hometown. Perhaps being around her old friends would help, Penny reasoned. Sometimes Rebecca would talk to Penny about what was troubling her, but other times she would simply clam up. Still, Rebecca assured her mother that if she ever got depressed, she would call her.

"I was thinking everything was fine. Rebecca was living with our relatives; she'd enrolled in school." She had also met a young man, Peter, whose father was also an abusive alcoholic. She felt that he truly understood her. One day she made a special request of him: "I want you to show me how to shoot a gun because my daddy hunted. I want to learn, too." Surprisingly, Peter thought nothing of it when Rebecca added, "But I don't want you to tell anybody else. This is our secret."

One evening in February Penny came home to find a message from her son on her phone machine. When she reached Andrew he said, "Mom, we've lost Rebecca. She shot and killed herself!"

On the flight back north, Penny thought about her daughter. "There was an irony to it," she said. "Because there were people who were afraid Owen was going to kill someone or hit someone with his car. So when Owen died, a lot of people said, 'Thank God he didn't take anyone with him.' But what he did was, he took my daughter."

It was soon clear that Rebecca's suicide was not the result of a momentary loss of control; it had been carefully planned. She had given friends and relatives different versions of where she planned to be that Saturday morning. In fact, she had saved a key to the house she had grown up in, which was now empty and for sale. Sometime early that Saturday morning, she parked her car in the garage and entered the damp, chilly house. She went into a closet located beneath a staircase, closed the door behind her, then shot herself once in the head with the .22 caliber handgun she had used for target practice just days before. It was after dark that evening when friends found her body.

Penny delivered the eulogy at Rebecca's funeral, which was held in the same church as her father's just over a year before. In it she not only paid tribute to her daughter but shared a profound understanding of the forces that led up to that day:

"It was easy to love Rebecca. She appeared self-confident, loving, caring, positive, determined, dedicated, focused, and successful. And so she was. She succeeded in everything except dealing with the loss of her father. . . . And to her, failure was unacceptable.

"We will never fully recover our balance in life until we let go of our emotional attachment to that which we have lost. Rebecca's loss was overwhelming. Her father's illness was devastating. It affected all of us deeply. It was beyond her, and why wouldn't it be? It's tough being a teenager today under normal circumstances. She was frightened and afraid to share her true feelings about her father. Reb couldn't tell us because she didn't want anyone to think she was anything less that the successful student, athlete, friend, sister, daughter she was."

Four months after Rebecca's death, Penny found a manila envelope marked, "To my mother, Penny," among some of her notebooks. Inside was a copy of Owen's eulogy, a family picture, and Rebecca's suicide note:

> Mom,
> I am leaving this note for you because you and I experienced a lot together, and I don't want you to take the blame for any of this. Since Dad died, I have not felt like myself at all. I've been going through the motions of life and have tried to appear like I was a normal and happy person on the outside. But on the inside, I have been an emotional wreck, and thoughts of death and my father have never really left my mind. I thought coming back home would help me feel closer to my father in some way. But reality is that he is gone and nothing can ever bring him back. I feel so alone without him, and a big chunk of my heart was ripped out when he took his own life. So for me, there is only one solution: to follow my father to his grave and to die the exact way that he did. The pain is too overwhelming for me to keep on living.
> Please remember me as the happy-go-lucky kid that I was before things got to be so messed up. Think of me in my dad's arms (in heaven or wherever we both are) and know that I am happy because I will finally have the love he could never give me while he was alive.
> I love you with all of my heart and hope that someday you will understand all of this and will be able to find happiness again.
> Your daughter forever,
> Rebecca

George's reading for Penny is among his most extraordinary, for in it he accurately discerned the complexities of both Rebecca and her father and their relationship here on earth. This reading serves not only as a caveat against suicide, but a promise of hope for all, no matter what they endured in this world.

"There seems to be a male presence around you. A female, too."

"Yes," Penny acknowledged.

"The young one is related somehow."

"Yes."

"The male close to you passes young by today's standards?"

"Yes."

"Somebody pushes me that they're the father. Is your dad passed?"

"Yes."

"He passed on a while ago."

"Yes."

"Because, I mean, even if it was thirty years, he's still the male close to you by blood who's passed on."

"Yes."

"Does he pass young by today's standards?"

"No. He was eighty-three," she replied.

"Wow!" George exclaimed. "He comes in [with a] very young [feeling]. Was he young at heart?"

"Yes."

"Someone keeps talking about your husband. Are you married? Did your husband pass?"

"Yes."

"Someone keeps coming around you saying, 'husband, husband.' Obviously, he passes young by today's standards. You certainly don't look old."

"Yes."

"Did his dad pass? That's the other male that's around who kept pushing father. Because his father's with him."

"Yes."

"*Your* father, also. He's passed."

"Yes."

"Also a strong motherly presence. Did your mother pass?"

"Yes."

"And his mom, too?"

"Yes."

"You have children."

"Yes."

"Because your husband keeps talking about family. He says *children*, so I take it there's more than one."

"Yes."

"He says, 'Please tell them you've heard from me.' He passes tragically?"

"Yes."

"Age as well as circumstances."

"Yes."

"It's beyond his control? It's not that he has to apologize, [since] there's nothing he can do about this. 'It went too far.' Does that make sense?"

"Yes."

"That's why he's saying he can't do anything about it. It goes too far. Are you afraid you let him down? He keeps saying, 'You never let me down.' "

"It does make sense," Penny said.

"Your husband had kind of a rough life here."

"Yes."

"This is nothing against you or your family. He wants me to explain that clearly before I say what I'm going to say. Your husband says he was not a happy man here."

"That's true."

"But that's not your fault, nor your children's fault. It's his own fault. He's not complaining. He's telling me he just was not a happy man here. His greatest struggle is with himself. His greatest enemy is himself. He's his own worst critic."

Penny nodded.

"Did he break away from you?"

"Yes."

"Because he apologizes for breaking away. Divorce or separation. I don't know what he means. He was there but not there. That's how he's putting it. He just never could seem to find himself [when he was here on earth]. But, he says, in the hereafter he has finally found himself. He understands [now]. That's why he's happy and at peace. On the other hand, he also wants to play Devil's advocate, so to speak. He says he could have found himself on earth if he had given himself the chance. It's as if his motto is, All or nothing. It's not that he was a failure here. It's just that it had to be all or nothing."

"Yes."

"He has trouble with drink."

"Yes."

"Because he's apologizing for drinking. He has an addiction. Drinking, drugs, or both."

"Yes."

"He's apologizing to you for that. Because I feel I'm talking to a man who had a nervous breakdown and didn't even know it. It's as if his whole system just goes to pieces. If there's illness involved in his passing—which I'm not sure there is yet—it's more emotional than anything else."

"Yes."

"He says his emotional illness contributes to his passing. In what way, I don't know. But that's how he explains it."

Penny only nodded her acknowledgment to each of George's statements.

"You have dreamed about him? He says he's come to you in dreams. There's a young female passed over, also?"

"Yes."

"Actually, you and she were very close. She's coming very close to you."

"Yes."

"She passes tragically?"

"Yes."

"He's tried to reach out. You have prayed for him, and he definitely thanks you and asks that the prayers please continue. He is all right. I see [as a psychic symbol] Virginia Slims all around him. It's a symbol that he's come a long way [on the other side]."

"Okay."

"It's also beyond *her* control? Now, has your husband passed before her?"

"Yes."

"Are they father and daughter?"

"Yes."

"He claims he's there for her when she comes over. He said it was his daughter, and they've come a long way over there. So apparently they had a lack of communication here. He gives me the impression they've settled their differences over there. I wouldn't say it was a total horror story, but there were some rocky roads [here]."

"Yes."

"Because your husband also apologizes that at times he was like a little boy trapped in a man's body."

"Yes."

"And that's why he's coming through like a little son. Mentally, emotionally, he's a boy, a teenager. Even your daughter refers to him as a son. I think what she's trying to do is refer to him in a way that I can understand I'm dealing with somebody who's like a big kid."

"Yes."

"Your daughter knows she's going to pass?"

"Yes."

"She says she's not shocked by death. Does she pass very quickly?"

"Yes."

"That must be what it is. She shows me a vision of Saint Joseph, which is a symbol of a happy death. In spite of the circumstances, she passes peacefully. But she says that it happens very quickly. She obviously doesn't suffer prior to her passing."

"Good."

"Now, this could be symbolic. She's showing me an accident. Does she pass accidentally or does she pass very suddenly as [one would] in an accident?"

"Yes, it was sudden," Penny replied.

"Does she pass from any health problem?"

"No."

"Then her passing has to be classified as accidental. She's showing me a car accident, not that she passes that way."

George's confusion in interpreting the messages is understandable. Remember that in September 1988 Rebecca was in an automobile accident after she blacked out and drove off the road. At the time Penny thought that Rebecca subconsciously wanted to die.

"She's injured internally?"

"Yes."

"Is she also trapped? Could she have felt trapped emotionally?"

"Yes."

"Because I feel I can't get away from some situation. I feel a sense of being trapped. For whatever reason, she does apologize to you for this tragedy. But it is beyond her control. Was there any injury to her head? Something's funny in my head."

"Yes."

"There are injuries internally, too."

"Yes."

"Again, I'm feeling that she's losing air."

"Yes."

"She's lost oxygen to the heart and the brain. Again, she's showing me a symbol of a vehicle. Although she's not in any type of vehicle accident."

Here, again, George's confusion may have been related to Rebecca's prior automobile accident. He continued, "Does she fall or collapse?"

"Yes," Penny replied. "It's possible."

"I'm trying to figure out why I feel like I'm going down. Something shocks her system internally. [There are] injuries."

"Yes."

"You and your daughter were very close."

"Yes."

"You're definitely good friends as well as mother and daughter. And that hasn't changed."

Penny nodded.

"You lost a pet?"

"Yes."

"One she was close with. Is there a dog passed on? She talks about a dog being there with her."

"Yes."

"So it must be one that she felt close with. A family pet."

"Yes."

"Regarding her death, is she in the wrong place at the wrong time? For her, maybe?"

"I don't know."

"I don't understand how she means it. I don't understand what she's trying to tell me. Does anything enter her body? It feels like something's going on that doesn't belong."

"That's right."

"It definitely would cause upset internally."

"Yes."

"She may not mean this literally, but now she talks about a weapon. There's a weapon involved?"

"Yes."

"Oh, okay. It is in the literal sense. There's a blast?"

"Yes."

"It sounds like gunshots. I hear the sound of a blast to the side of me," George said, pointing to the left side of his head.

"My daughter was left-handed," Penny said.

"She is shot."

"Yes."

"She takes her own life."

"Yes."

"Because she's talking as if she was hemming and haw-ing about it. Now I understand why she's telling me it was beyond her control emotionally. She can't turn back. She admits now that she does a thorough job. She shoots herself in the head."

"Yes."

"Was she on anything at the time?"

"No."

"Then she's not in the right frame of mind at the time. She is very depressed, because I feel like my emotions are down, like I've had a nervous breakdown. I just feel a col-lapse in my system."

Penny nodded.

"I wanted to make sure she hadn't been drinking or doing something that might feel that way. It's a natural response. One thing about her, she's down to earth.''

"Yes."

"She does say this wasn't the right thing to do. She says, 'I know it's a little too late, but you have to start somewhere.' One thing about her, though, when she does put her mind to do something, she gets the job done. Because I will say that since she's gone over there [to the other side], she's kind of snapped into things. She realizes this wasn't the right thing to do, but it's too late now. She can't turn back the clock. She did have a lot of her father in her, though.''

"Yes."

"She admits that even though she and her father didn't get along, ironically, they are very much alike. She's got his stubbornness. She's got his drive."

"Yes."

"But she also oppresses herself. She's her own [worst] critic. She doesn't like to be argued with.''

"Yes."

"Your daughter admits she basically had a life of emotional ups and downs. Because she admits that like her dad she's not a happy person [on earth]. Again, that's no one's fault. Not yours or anyone else's. She had her good days and bad days, like anyone would. But she always seemed confused, she says. Maybe not openly but within herself. Her struggles are with herself and with your husband.''

"Yes."

"Did she keep a journal or something like it? Do you have it?"

"Yes."

"She's talking about writing a journal. Did she write anything personal in it? She talks about writing a lot of anxieties and feelings in it.''

"Yes."

"But she was going through a really bad time most of her life, within herself. Not that she's trying to paint a picture that her life was a total disaster here, but it was a very big struggle in her eyes.''

"Yes."

"Unfortunately, this time it goes too far. That's why I feel like I'm depleted emotionally."

"Yes."

"Again, like your husband, she had a nervous breakdown and didn't know it. Her whole system breaks down."

"Yes."

"But the first step to progressing in the hereafter is to recognize that she should not have taken her life. This was not the right thing to do. As much as there was a lot of struggle in her life and a lot of challenge, she knows she could have overcome it if she had just given herself more of an opportunity. But it seems at the end everything is just going downhill. It's like the straw that breaks the camel's back. She gives me the feeling that she'd been through things like this before."

"Yes. My daughter had tried suicide before."

"She says that like the phoenix, she'd always rise again and overcome, but this time she felt battered down. She gets easily frustrated with herself because now she realizes from the hereafter that she could have overcome [problems] this time. She's kind of angry at herself for not giving herself the chance. She says she, like your husband, is responsible for her own actions. She also wants you to know that you did not fail her in any way. She knows that at times you're kind of mad at her for doing this."

Penny nodded again.

"She says, 'Please don't be mad at me. It's bad enough being mad at myself.' "

"Okay."

"This wasn't the right thing to do, she says. Not only for herself but also for what was left behind. Because she knows you have to live in the shadow or aftereffects of [what she's done]. She says, 'I've moved on. I can say that I didn't do the right thing. I have to make up for it. But you have to live with the memory of it.' She says she certainly didn't mean to cause you this anxiety. She says it would be so much simpler if once you're dead, you're dead. But it doesn't work that way. You see and feel what's going on here [on earth], and you realize what mistakes have been made.''

''I learned later, that the night my daughter died, she was talking about her father and said that once you're dead, you're dead,'' Penny explained.

''Have you dreamt about her, also?''

''Yes.''

''Because she says she's tried to reach out to let you at least know that she's all right. Did you go through a period when you were kind of disappointed in her?''

''Yes.''

''She says she knows you're disappointed in her. You might still be going through it. She says your disappointment, anger, is justified. That's all right, she says. That's part of the process. You also have anxiety about why she didn't turn to you if she needed somebody to talk to.

''She knows that she's let you down and she's sorry about that. She not only let herself down but she let you down. You certainly would have been there for her if she needed any type of help.''

''Yes.''

''She's honest and straightforward. She says you've had a hard life to begin with. You were married and things didn't work out the way you might have liked. You've had a hard life, and [your daughter's suicide] puts the icing on the cake. She's really sorry about that. She certainly didn't want to bring that on you.

''Were you thinking of changing residence? Because your daughter says you'll probably change residences. Which might be for the better. I see the birth of a child in front of you.''

''My first grandchild was born last month.''

''The birth of a child in front of you also symbolizes a whole new beginning. It means going in a new direction, starting anew. At this time, it might be a better thing to do.

''Your daughter is inclined to be very moody.''

''Yes.''

''She's not a drinker, but she's got your husband's moodiness. She realizes now she might as well have been drinking. It's the same thing. It's as if she's addicted to her moods. There's tension [within her]. She realizes that she's her own worst enemy. That's why your husband had to come to her in the hereafter. Not only to settle their differences but also because they were very much on the same wavelength emotionally. Your husband had been through it, so he knew how to help your daughter. Did your husband kill himself?''

''Yes.''

''He wanted to die. It's like he just gave up. He didn't want to be bothered, like he drank himself to death, as they say. He says he killed himself.''

''He did.''

''Because he keeps saying, 'I killed myself, also.' There was that moment of uncertainty, because he drinks. He literally kills himself. But he kills himself *before* that, emotionally. That's what he means. He's probably giving me both feelings. He's saying to me that he was dead way before he killed himself. He's progressed over there [the other side] to a degree. That's why he had to come to your daughter's help. That's why he crossed her over when she passed on. Does he pass first?''

''Yes.''

''He says he comes to her when she passes on because he, like her, committed suicide. Your daughter definitely has a lot of him in her. Emotionally, they're almost identical. She took his passing pretty badly.''

''Yes.''

''It definitely rattles her cage. It was the straw that breaks the camel's back, again, when her father took his own life.''

''Yes.''

''They were close, but they weren't that close. They had this taffy-pull type relationship: I can't live with you; I can't live without you.''

''Yes.''

''So in a way, she probably got very mad at him and at life. She's a very delicate person, emotionally and mentally. So she's an easy target for mood swings.''

''Yes.''

"Do you take the name Charles or Charlie?"

"Yes."

"Passed on."

"Yes."

"Would your husband know him? Because they keep telling me that Charlie is there with them [on the other side]."

"Okay."

"They keep saying, 'Charlie is here with us.' Would he know your daughter? It's almost like he's an uncle figure to her. She keeps referring to him as Uncle Charlie."

"Yes. He's a favorite uncle on my side of the family."

"The name Jennifer, Jen? It sounds like she's saying Jen or Jean."

"Yes. Another school friend."

"Do you take the name Betty or Elizabeth?"

"Elizabeth."

"Passed on."

"Yes."

"That's my mistake. I heard Elizabeth, and I made it Betty. Then somebody told me to go back and say Elizabeth. She's saying hello to you. Wait a minute. I have this feeling about your daughter. Is it her?"

"Yes."

"It is. Okay. It sounds like her voice. It feels like she's near you. Her name is Elizabeth?"

"That's one of her names."

"Is that her middle name?"

"Yes."

"Why doesn't she give me her first name? I don't like middle names. But it's definitely her."

After a pause, George asked, "Do you take the name Michelle? A friend of hers."

"Yes."

"She's calling out to her friend."

"Okay."

"Now I know why your husband said before that you didn't fail him. It's because he also took his life. Your daughter became traumatized by her father's death. She's traumatized almost to the point of obsession. I keep [psychically] seeing scenes from an opera in which they dramatize suicide. It's from the opera *Tosca*. It's my symbol that your daughter is almost like the character in that opera. She's very tortured emotionally.''

''Yes.''

''She wanted to know why she was going through such struggles. She just wanted to be happy in life, but, like Tosca, she commits suicide in the end. But now she just wants you to know that she's all right. She's coming along. She still has her days trying to deal with herself, but she's learning how to understand herself. I'm sure you had your moments with her [when she was] here. Now that she is in the hereafter, there's nothing you can do about it. All you can do is pray for her. You can't keep tabs on her to make sure she's all right. She and your husband have made progress with each other [in the next stage]. She says it's up to her to find herself. But there are people helping her [on the other side]. It's like in *The Wizard of Oz* where, at the end, Dorothy says she had to discover [things] for herself. Others can't do it for you. The scarecrow couldn't think for Dorothy. The lion couldn't be brave for her. Dorothy had to find it out for herself.''

''Okay.''

''Now, this has nothing to do with organized religion, but she asks that you pray to the Scared Heart of Jesus on her behalf or that you light a candle for her and consecrate her soul. If you have, please do it again.''

''I did light a candle in a Catholic church on the first anniversary of her death.''

''Oh, good. Because I keep seeing [the Sacred Heart of Jesus] over your head, and she's pointing to my statue of the Sacred Heart. It's my symbol for people who take their own lives. Always pray to the Sacred Heart because that has helped her to progress in the hereafter. She progresses on her own by understanding herself. That's the key. Just don't feel that you let her down in any way. It may be a hard thing for you to accept, but she confesses she let herself down. It's similar to somebody trying to admit they're an alcoholic. Sometimes when someone takes their own life, it isn't too easy for them [to admit it]."

"Yes."

"Do you take the name Connie or Ronnie? Bonnie?"

"Yes."

"Someone close. Anybody your daughter would have known?"

"Yes."

"It's Bonnie. Were they close?"

"Yes."

"Because it sounds like she's calling out to Ronnie. Then she said, 'No, it's Bonnie.' She says tell Bonnie you've heard from her and ask her to pray for your daughter."

"Okay. Bonnie was in my home when my daughter was found. She's a good family friend."

"Your daughter says that she's working on the other side in what we on earth would think of as a home for animals. It's a way for her to love and trust again."

Penny nodded.

"Your husband says the actual transition [to the other side] was peaceful. He says he was just so unhappy here that anything would have been better. As far as he's concerned, when he took his own life, things couldn't be any worse than they already were. He doesn't go over in the right frame of mind. He says he's dead *before* he dies."

"That makes sense."

"Your daughter had one hell of a temper. She could definitely let go. She's like her dad. But now she's taking steps to learn how to control herself. There were times when she just wanted to be left alone. Even on the other side."

"Yes."

"Even on the other side she kind of still feels like she wants to be left alone. That's why she was sent to a special therapeutic home in the hereafter where there are animals around her. She can feel safe again and do things at her own pace and in her own time. She says, 'I know I won't be here forever.' She says where she's at now is another step toward finding herself. . . . Does the name Lily or Lillian mean anything?''

"Yes. That's my maternal grandmother."

"Your daughter said that before, but I didn't pay any attention to it. She'd said, 'Lillian has come to help me, also.' Even though they didn't know each other here. People [on the other side] help her. They chip in. But it's up to her to do it herself. She wants to do it. But she wants you to know that she's not in a fog or lost in gloom. She says her most difficult struggle is with herself. She knows now that if she'd taken on the challenge [on earth] she could have succeeded. She could have overcome her struggle if she had given herself more time. And you're frustrated with her because you also know she could have done it if she'd just given herself a chance. You know she was capable of achieving when she was positive and put her mind to it.''

"Yes."

"Do you take the name Cathy or Cathryn? It's around your daughter.''

"I don't know."

"All right. I'll leave it go. They make friends over there and bring them along [in readings]. Also . . . it sounds like Nina.''

"Yes. A cousin who's living."

"There's a lot of tragedy around you. The sad part about it is that you have to live in its shadow. But hang in there. Continue to pray, as you have been doing. Particularly [continue to pray] to the Sacred Heart of Jesus.''

"Okay."

"I think with this they're going to close. They're telling me to let go. Your daughter wants to go back and rest. She asks that you continue to pray for her. She's all right. She's getting there. She has let go of the anger at herself for doing it [committing suicide]. And *you* have to let go of the anger at her for doing it. Realize that you did not let her down. *She* made the choice. It was the wrong choice. Your daughter says, 'Until we meet again.' She signs off.''

• • •

After the reading Penny said, "I'm angry that Owen was there to cross Rebecca over. At first I was angry that they were together, because I always wanted to protect my daughter. But she killed herself for her father, and I understand now that she has to work that out for her father, *with* her father.

"In the reading Rebecca knew I was mad at her, and she wanted me to forgive her. She shouldn't have done it! She could have worked it out here. She could have. She had all kinds of help. So many people loved her. But how many kids at nineteen could live with the torture she did, especially the last five years of her life?"

Penny has put together the pieces of her life. "To tell you the truth, there have been days when I've told my psychiatrist that if somebody opened a door and said I could go to heaven, I would race right through it. But I know from George's reading that suicide is not the answer. If I don't work it out here, I'm going to have to work it out there."

7

The Murdered

As we have seen already, a parent whose child has died usually suffers a long, enduring grief. Every family's story is unique; their loss personal, and impossible to compare. While the death of anyone we know and love is hard to accept, the one aspect all children's deaths share is that they seem to violate a basic law of nature. There is nothing normal, right, or fair about any child's death. When such a death does occur, parents and other survivors often find themselves feeling vulnerable and insecure. They may think, If this can happen, what can I depend on?

These normal grief reactions are multiplied many times over when a child is murdered. Parents and other bereaved ones may torment themselves imagining the child's last moments. Whether the killer was someone known to the victim or the act was random, the child's death brings into sharp focus the breakdown of modern society. Further exacerbating grieving parents' distress, the circumstances of death makes it a public death, the concern of the media and the police. The family must then face additional burdens, as their child's death becomes grist for newspaper and television news reports and a puzzle to be solved by local law enforcement. If the child's killer is arrested and tried, families find themselves reliving the incident again as the case wends its way through the judicial system. If the killer is convicted, his annual appearances before a parole board may mark another "anniversary," as the victim's survivors often do all they can to ensure that he serves his full sentence. While increasing numbers of parents strive to see that the criminal justice system works for, not against, them, they frequently feel victimized by it, their grief never finding resolution.

The most overwhelming product of a child's murder is the sense that the world is simply out of control. Shocked survivors wonder, What kind of society do we live in? The answer is one in which there exists more than one handgun for every man, woman, and child; one in which approximately 7,725 children under the age of twenty-four are murdered every year. About 2,200 of these are under eighteen.

For these and other reasons, parents whose children are murdered have an especially difficult time. After their daughter Lisa was murdered, Charlotte and Robert Hullinger found that existing avenues of support did not address their unique needs. Mrs. Hullinger was inspired to establish Parents of Murdered Children and Other Survivors of Violence in 1978. The group's membership is not limited solely to parents, and it has grown to over 38,000, a sad testament to the growing problem of violence.

Not surprisingly, George's work is well known among members of Parents of Murdered Children, and he has done many readings for them. At one time or another, virtually every parent must confront his or her own deep, frightening feelings of hatred for their child's killer. Some cope with it, but many others speak of feeling compelled to seek revenge. The one issue that arises in most readings is that of forgiveness. "Children who come through in readings who have been murdered often say that there is no place over there for that kind of hatred," George explained. "They also say that once they cross over, they cannot understand anyone here feeling that kind of hatred at all. That's why they forgive, and they ask their parents and others to forgive. That's not to say they think it's easy for us to do; they know it isn't. But they also realize that forgiving is the greater thing to do.''

Often the only person who can convince someone obsessed with vengeance to let go is the victim. But in this, as in nearly everything else, death doesn't confer upon human beings the power to work miracles. Sometimes, as in the case that follows, the advice is heard and understood, yet the parent is not fully swayed.

Juan, seventeen, was the youngest of Emilio and Irma's four children.* He lived with them and a sister in their comfortable suburban home. "He was always a respectful son to his mother and me," Emilio recalled. "He was never a troublemaker. He would never start a fight, but he would never walk away from one, either."

One summer evening Juan was hanging out with several friends when he witnessed an altercation between a buddy and another young man. He intervened, hoping to settle the dispute peacefully. Instead the boy swung at Juan wildly. Juan punched him in the stomach, then turned to walk away. His assailant took out a knife and stabbed him three times. Juan died three hours later.

"I was too angry to think about anything but killing the boy who killed my son," Emilio said. "I was really actively planning to kill him. We know it wasn't premeditated, but my son was an innocent victim. He wasn't armed. He just tried to protect his friend.

"A week after Juan died," Emilio continued, "my wife went to Parents of Murdered Children. I think that has been good for her in combination with her strong religious faith. She is very serene, considering. For me, though, there has been nothing but the anger and wanting revenge.

"When my wife told me about George Anderson, I admit I wanted to go, but for different reasons than my wife. For

---

*At the request of the subject, all names, and other biographical details and facts pertaining to their case have been altered to protect their identities. Everything else in this story, however, is true.

her it was reassurance of what she already believed in and accepted: the afterlife. For me, one reason I wanted to go to George was to ask my son how he felt about me killing his murderer.''

About midway through the reading, in which Juan first explained to George who he was and how he had died, George turned to Emilio and said, "He says his relationship with you was special."

"Yes."

"He says you and he were 'pals and best friends.' Those are the words he uses."

"Yes."

"Your son says he doesn't want to show any preference between you both. He loves you both. But he is concerned about you. He says it was you who was hit the hardest by his passing."

"Yes," Emilio admitted.

"But he says he's not dead. You must not think that. He is alive, and he's close to you. He's closer than you can imagine. He knows you feel guilty that you weren't there to protect him."

"Yes," Emilio answered, his voice breaking.

"But he was an adult and had to fend for himself."

"Right."

Several minutes later George said, "Your son holds no grudge. He says what happened, happened. 'There's nothing I can do about it now,' he says. But he looks at you. He knows you're very bitter and angry."

"Yes," Emilio declared.

"He says you want to kill the guy who killed your son!"

"Yes!"

"Your son says, 'What good will that do? It won't bring me back.' He says to please let go of all the negative thoughts. 'Two wrongs don't make a right, and it will only make matters worse,' he says to tell you."

"I don't know," Emilio replied.

"Well, your son says let it go."

Emilio did not respond.

"Now, this other person who did this," George resumed, "who stabbed your son, he's been arrested."

"Yes."

"He's a young male, also. I feel like he's around the same age as your son."

"Yes. Just a little older."

"But the police have him."

"Yes."

"That's what your son says. He says you'll only make it worse if you take things into your own hands."

"Will I?" Emilio asked.

"It's as if that's all you have on your mind."

"Yes, pretty much."

"Your son knows how angry and bitter you are. He does not want you to go on being so unhappy. Do you go to a support group or a bereavement group? Or for therapy?"

"I do," Irma offered.

"Your son recommends that you go to group therapy with your wife," George told Emilio.

"Okay," he replied.

Moments later George told Emilio that he heard Juan saying, "Dad, don't be stubborn for once. Killing the guy will give you no satisfaction. It won't bring me back. It will only make matters worse, and you'll have to pay for it."

"He keeps saying that," George added. But Emilio would not even acknowledge those words.

"He keeps saying that you need to let go of the anger and forgive the person who killed him," George continued.

"I don't know," Emilio said.

"He knows how hard that is. But as he said before, he doesn't hold a grudge, and he wants you to do the same. Please let go of the anger and negativity. He says he had to learn to go on [in the hereafter]. And you need to do the same here. You can't bring him back, unfortunately. Just know he's alive and well. Know that he's not alone. . . . 'Don't do it, Dad.' He can't say it enough times."

Emilio was silent.

"Do you take the name Mick or Mickey?"

"No."

"Maybe Nick. Mick or *Nick*?"

"Yes," Emilio said.

"It's Nick," George said. "Is he the one who stabbed your son?"

"Yes!" Emilio exclaimed.

"That's what your son keeps saying."

"Yes."

"But he was arrested, and he'll be punished for what he did. What goes around comes around. The guy who killed your son will pay for it. Your son emphasizes that."

At the end, Juan closed by saying through George, "Don't kill the guy! Let it go, for me. Know that I'm close."

After the reading Emilio said, "Going to George helped. It doesn't bring back my son, but it was a comfort. He definitely gave me something to think about. It was clear from the reading that Juan doesn't want me to kill the guy. So what should I do? I'm still so angry, and I want revenge. But I don't want to disappoint my son.

"I just take it one day at a time. This destroyed my life. But I'm thinking about my son's advice. Have I changed my mind? I don't know yet."

The majority of murdered youngsters are young men. Vastly overrepresented within that group are young men of color who live in urban areas. Statistically, roughly 50 percent more black males between the ages of fifteen and twenty-four are victims of homicide than white males in the same age group. Overall, 93 percent of black murder victims die at the hands of other blacks. Nowhere is this tragedy more frequently played out than in the inner city, where, as in the case of Tyrone Nelson, there is no safe haven from crime.

Tyrone grew up in a black neighborhood that had been overtaken by drugs and crime.* His mother, Joyce, worked

---

*At the request of the subject, this name has been altered. Everything else in this story, however, is true.

hard to give her son and his ten-year-old sister, Valerie, the best life possible. She taught them both to always "play by the rules," she said, and to "avoid trouble." Clearly Tyrone followed his mother's advice. He did well in school, then graduated and took a full-time position in a local restaurant. He looked forward to being promoted into management and perhaps going to college. He hoped to marry his high-school sweetheart, Barbara, and one day move to the suburbs, away from the grinding poverty and violence. All in all, Joyce felt she had done a fine job of raising her son. Unlike many of his peers, Tyrone was hardworking, conscientious, respectful; he had goals and was determined to fulfill them.

Nevertheless Joyce often felt uneasy. She knew that Tyrone was streetwise and savvy. He knew all the neighborhood troublemakers; he knew who was into drugs, who carried a gun. He realized that one way to avoid trouble was to look tough, so he worked at body building. Tyrone sensed danger and made it a point to avert his eyes from those who would read his glance as a challenge.

Every afternoon he boarded a city bus and rode several stops to work, where he put in an afternoon and an evening shift. One Friday night in late July, however, he got off work early. At around eight he arrived home, quickly showered, and changed for his date with Barbara, who lived just a few blocks away in a brownstone.

"Tyrone's going to see his lady," Valerie teased her older brother.

"Quiet!" he replied as he laughed and playfully placed a hand on her head. "Bye, Ma!" he called, heading for the door.

"Be careful," Joyce said to him, as she always did.

"I will, Ma."

"And don't be too late!"

"I won't."

Tyrone took Barbara out to a movie, after which they stopped at a diner. At Barbara's house they spent about a half hour talking before he kissed her good night and left for the short walk home.

It was about half past midnight. On a darkened street, Tyrone was accosted by a group of young men. How many there were, who they were, is still unknown. What was said and why are also mysteries. What is known is that two shots shattered the night. Several people from nearby buildings reported hearing cries after the shots; two witnesses told police that they saw three men fleeing the scene, but there may have been more. In a neighborhood where gunshots are common, and criminals stalk their prey—and each other—no one was shocked or surprised.

The first shot hit Tyrone in the stomach. He was able to cry out for help and stagger several feet. Then his killer fired the second, lethal shot, which hit him in the head. He collapsed and soon died in a pool of blood on one of the dark, mean streets he dreamed of escaping.

Joyce was devastated by Tyrone's death, her immediate grief made all the more painful by the police department's apparent lack of interest in the crime. He was clearly not a victim of robbery; perhaps, the police concluded, it was just a case of mistaken identity. To the police and the local media, he was simply another statistic, another young black man caught in the web of violence. His story sounded so much like so many others, the local newspapers and television news granted it only the briefest mention.

"It was as if the police didn't want to be bothered," Joyce said bitterly. "When I'd call to ask them if they'd made any progress, they'd act annoyed. They said they'd call me if they came up with any suspects or a motive. But I never heard from them unless I called them. Sometimes they'd put me off by saying the detective on the case wasn't in. Mostly, though, it was 'There's nothing new about your son's case.'

"So I was trying to keep myself sane. To the police, I'm sure it was just another crime statistic, another black boy who was killed. But that was my son. He didn't deserve that way of dying. He was a good son. You know, I cry myself to sleep every night for him, until I can't cry anymore. It was hard enough to raise my children without a father.

"The other thing that bothers me is who killed him and why. Nobody saw the shooting. I don't know if they were strangers who mistook Tyrone for someone else or if they were people he knew or recognized. About the only thing the police would tell me is that they didn't rob him. So why did they kill him?"

Joyce and Valerie were heartened by the tremendous out-pouring of support they received at Tyrone's funeral. Joyce sought counseling and comfort from the minister of her Baptist church. A quiet, soft-spoken woman, she felt herself far too introverted to join a support group. At the same time, though, she found herself increasingly angry over her son's death. Between that and the stress of having to raise her daughter alone in the environment that had claimed her son, Joyce was beside herself, unable to accept that all she had done to instill the best values, to teach him to watch out for himself had proved to be in vain.

"I thought that by keeping him looking straight ahead, Tyrone could avoid the bad things and the bad people. I always told my son, stay away from trouble. But it found him anyway."

While George is the first to admit that neither he nor the spirits have all the answers, people still come to him hoping that he might be able to divulge some answer, end some mystery. As we saw before in Emilio and Irma's reading, it is possible for a victim to identify his killer. However, in that case, Juan knew Nick before he killed him. This case was entirely different. Joyce sought to learn from George something that might lead to her son's murderers. However, the fact that Tyrone did not offer this information in the reading gives credence to the police's conclusion that he probably did not know the men who killed him.

"He says he's family by blood," George began.

"Yes."

"He passes on as a young adult."

"Yes."

"There's talk of a motherly presence. Has your mother passed?"

"No."

"Your grandmother, then."

"My grandmothers have passed," Joyce confirmed.

"You were close with a grandmother," said George.

"Yes."

"Because he keeps talking about a motherly presence with him, and I feel it's probably a grandmother. Even if you didn't know her—or he didn't know her."

"Right."

"This young male who passes draws close to you and says he's the son. He's your son," George said.

"Yes."

"He sees what you've been through since this tragedy occurred. He says, 'I'm sorry this happened,' but it was beyond his control. Unfortunately, you are living in the shadow of what has happened. He's very close with you, not only as family but also as friends. He draws close to you."

"Yes," she acknowledged.

"He had his ups and downs with you. He apologizes if he was—I'm using his words—'a chop breaker.' But you always loved each other. That was always understood. You had that kind of 'I can't live with you, I can't live without you' relationship. Your son had a rough life here."

"Yes," she agreed.

"Did he make it more difficult for himself?"

"Sometimes."

"He feels he had a rough life here," George said. "But it's not your fault. He realized that he's responsible for his own actions. His life was tough here, but his heart is in the right place. He's a typical young person."

"Right."

"He thanks you for your prayers. He says he receives your prayers, and they help him a great deal. Please don't stop."

"Okay."

"He knows you want to know that he's all right. He is telling you that he *is* all right now. He's at peace and all right. He knows how much you miss him. You'd rather have him here than where he is, but that cannot be. He's not overly religious, but he is spiritual, in his own way. Again, he does ask for prayers."

"Right."

"This could be symbolic," George said. "Is his passing accidental, or it comes upon him very suddenly, *like* an accident?"

"I believe that it happened suddenly," Joyce answered.

"He says his passing is very quick. He claims he doesn't suffer prior to his passing. In spite of what it looked like," George added.

"All right."

"Your son says he's dead before there is any experience of suffering. So he says to be at peace. 'I didn't suffer.' Because he says you've been tortured with the thought that he had suffered; that he'd been in agony. He says no, he was out of the body before he experienced any agony."

"All right," she said, seeming relieved.

"There is something about his head," George went on. "He keeps hitting me on the head! Was he injured there?"

"Yes."

"He obviously passes on from an injury to the head. There's a shedding of blood, internally."

"There was blood *from* the head," his mother clarified.

"There's bleeding both internally and externally."

"Right."

"He's a very bright young man," George observed.

"Yes."

"He does come through very bright. He's smart, but he could be naive."

"Yes," she agreed.

"He's not as street-smart as he'd like us to think he is. And that's what got him into that mess. He can be too trusting. He trusted the wrong people at the wrong time."

"Yes, that's right."

"You might have questioned his choice of heroes at one time. But he's not a bad person by any means. He's just an innocent around the wrong kind of people. P. T. Barnum once said there's a sucker born every minute. Not to be disrespectful, but your son tends to be taken in. Was he left [to die] when this tragedy happened? Everybody left him and ran away.''

"Yes.''

"You always worried about him,'' said George. "And you still do. He says, 'You don't have to worry about me anymore. I'm all right. No harm can come to me anymore.' There are people in the family who have passed on that are with him. He said, 'Dad is with me.' Is that your father?''

"My stepfather.''

"He passes on before your boy. And he met your son and crossed him over. Your stepdad is your father; that's the way he feels. He loves you like his own daughter. He says don't worry about your boy. He was there to meet him and take him into the light, even though he came over a little rambunctious! But that's normal for your son. Your stepdad says, 'As long as your son is with me, you know he is in good hands.' ''

"Yes.''

"You have had a very tough life, too,'' said George. "Your son apologizes, because your life hasn't been easy. And you didn't want your children to have to go through that, also.''

"Yes.''

"And this is just the straw that breaks the camel's back. Your son says that since this tragedy happened, you just want to die. Your son also says, 'You can't.' You have to hang in there, for your sake as well as for your family's sake. If God came to you tonight and said you were going to die, you couldn't care less. But you have to go on, as difficult as it is, because someday you'll see your son again. If you can just have the assurance that he's with your stepfather and that he's all right, that doesn't take away the pain, but it makes it a little easier.''

The boy's mother nodded.

"Is there a weapon used in your son's passing?'' George asked.

"Yes.''

"Because I hear a gun going off [psychically]. He must

have been shot in the head. I feel like somebody points a gun at me and is shooting me in the head! Your son claims he was murdered.''

"Yes."

"The person did not deliberately mean to murder him," George explained. "Your son was in the wrong place at the wrong time. He says that he forgives. He's not holding on to any hatred, because there is no place for that in the hereafter.''

"Okay."

"Your son was inclined to be on the go a lot—kind of fast-living. Rushing . . . He says you have another child."

"Yes."

"But he was the one that was a big worry," George said. "He was your cross to carry."

"Yes."

"There was some kind of argument. Was he involved in some kind of illegal activity?" George asked. "Or these other people were?"

"Yes," said his mother, "the others were, I think."

"Because there were some kinds of illegal goings-on, even though your son is innocent. He's not involved. I don't feel that he's going out causing trouble. These other people are. Somebody bullies him—and pulls the trigger on him. Do they know who shot your son?" George asked.

"I'm not sure," she replied.

"There seem to be two or three people around him when this occurred. They just left him. They just shot him and left him! He dies instantly. Yes," George repeated, "he dies instantly. Was he in a rough neighborhood?"

"Yes."

"You and I wouldn't want to take a stroll through there.''

"No," Joyce answered. "I wouldn't."

"It's like they were part of a gang, and they're in their territory. Your son is there, naively. One of them pulls the trigger on him. They don't like him; they don't even know why.''

Joyce said nothing.

"Your birthday just passed," said George. "Your son extended you white roses, and he wishes you a happy birthday."

"Oh, Christ!" she blurted.

"Because you just barely made it over the holidays . . . Your mother is still living."

"Yes."

"Your son sends his love to her, and he thanks her for her prayers. She's been praying for him constantly. She is a very devoted woman."

"Yes, she is."

"He says he's your only son."

"Yes," she said sadly. "He's my only son."

"You have another child, a daughter. He is calling out to his sister. They got along well. He's older than she is?"

"Yes."

"He says he's around his sister like a guardian angel."

"Okay."

"They were becoming friends. Your son had his moments, but he was starting to mellow. He was becoming more mature."

"Yes."

"And you and he were getting closer," said George.

"Yes."

"He calls to his father."

"We're divorced," Joyce explained.

"Your son's actually sensitive," George observed. "He tries to hide it. His sensitivity makes him a little defensive."

"Oh, yes," she agreed.

"His sister's kind of outraged by his death. She's been very upset by it."

"Yes."

"He singularizes his sister, because it's bad enough to be a mother who loses her son. But the siblings react [with hurt and anger], also. He calls out, 'Please tell my sister you've heard from me. Tell her that I'm with her.' He doesn't want his sister to be outraged, because to hold on to that negativity, that bitterness and outrage, is only going to make her life unhappy. So he wants her to go on because he *is* around her. They will be together one day.

"Your daughter might have dreamed about him. Your son says he has come in dreams," George said.

"That's right," she acknowledged.

"He seems like the type of guy you don't argue with," George remarked, then asked, "Is there a Bob, or Robert?"

"Yes."

"Passed on."

"Yes.

"That's my cousin," she explained.

"He passed over young, also."

"Yes."

"He's in his thirties or forties."

"Yes."

"He passes before your son. He was also there to welcome him into the light."

"Oh, good," said Joyce, sounding pleased.

"You are perfectly justified in being outraged at your son being murdered, but your son says to try to let go of the anger and bitterness, because it will only eat you alive. And, unfortunately, it is not going to change what has happened. He's trying to look at it as a matter of fact. But at the same time, he's being sympathetic.

"Do you belong to a support group?" George asked.

"No."

"He suggests it. Only because you should talk to somebody else who knows exactly what you're going through."

"Like therapy?"

"It would be other parents who really understand what you're going through," George explained.

"Right."

"You can be stubborn. Now you know where he got it from."

Joyce smiled.

"He calls out to 'Michael,' " George said. Joyce took the name. "Is that his father?"

"Yes. My ex-husband."

"Your son says they had their ups and downs. But it's

still his father. . . . Your son also says to tell you he is in a totally nonthreatening environment. You were worried about that.''

"Yes," she admitted.

"You need not worry. He says his aunt and your grand-mother are with him. They passed before your son, and both welcomed him into the light. He knew this aunt, and they always liked each other. They always got along well.''

"Yes."

"This aunt is your sister, and your best friend."

"Yes."

"Your sister says when she passed that your heart was really broken.''

"Yes."

"She's sending you her love and tells you she will look after your son. He's in good hands.''

"Good."

"Your son is called by a nickname," George said.

"Not by me; by his friends," Joyce explained.

"Your son says you feel guilty about enjoying your life because he is not here. A few times you felt like taking your own life. He and your sister both say do not do that. It's wrong. Your daughter needs you. You have a purpose here you must fulfill. Your sister is watching over you like a guardian angel. She says, 'Tell Momma you've heard from me. I don't care if she believes it or not. Tell her to continue to pray for me. Tell Momma I'm with Jesus.'

"Your mother has had a rough life, also," George continued. "She certainly knows what you're going through; she's been through it, also. Your sister says again, 'Please tell Momma you've heard from me. I'm happy and at peace. I'm crazy about your son and so happy he's here with me.' She says, 'Your loss is my gain, and we have some great times over here. And no harm can ever come to either one of us again, in any way,'" George said.

"Good."

"Your sister passed from health trouble."

"Yes."

"You helped take care of her; you and your mother. She

thanks you both and blesses both of you for caring for her prior to her passing. You were better than a nurse.'' That comment brought a smile to Joyce's face.

George continued, ''Your sister fades off into a coma toward the end. She shows me a picture of Saint Joseph, symbol of a happy death. She says you and your mom felt bad because you didn't get to say goodbye to her. She says she doesn't want to say goodbye because she is still with you.''

''Yes.''

''Your sister is a live wire!'' George remarked. ''All I feel are smiles. She's a happy person. Great with jokes. She's a very positive person.''

''Yes.''

''Your sister had trouble in her lungs and heart. And that weakened her organs.''

''Yes.''

''She felt bad for your mother. So your sister suffered in silence. She says to tell Momma, 'When she gets here with me, she'll get the vacation she never got on earth. Tell her not to be afraid to pass on. Keep telling her she's a good mother, and she's always done good by us.' When the time comes, your sister will welcome your mother into the light. There is nothing to fear except fear itself.

''Your mother did all the raising of her children. She's the heart of your home.''

''Yes,'' Joyce answered.

''Did your mother have a miscarriage? Did you lose a brother?''

''Yes!''

''He's with your sister,'' George said.

''Okay.''

''Your son shows me you walking down a path. It's a symbol of you continuing your life. Your son is of two minds. He wants to fit in, and yet he doesn't want to. He says his name is short. He's showing me vowels. He keeps circling the vowel *y*.''

''Yes, there is a *y* in his name,'' Joyce said.

''There are two vowels in his name. The name has six letters.''

"You're right."

"The other vowel is *e*."

"Yes."

"The name starts with a *T*?"

"Yes."

"He shows me that the name starts with *T* and ends with *e*."

"Yes."

"Tyrone," George stated.

"Yes!"

"But there's a nickname."

"Yes," said Joyce. "Some people called him Ty."

"There's an outpouring at his funeral."

"Yes."

"It's a ridiculous shooting. But many people loved him."

"Yes."

"He's athletic."

"Yes."

"Now he's telling me to call him Ty," George explained.

"Yes. He preferred to be called that."

"He gives you white roses. He says you're leaving flowers at his grave."

"Yes."

"He is going back, and your grandparents, your sister, cousins, stepdad—they all embrace you with love. Your son calls out to his dad and to your mom and his sister. He says to go on with your life 'until we meet again.' He's at the finish line. He is okay and will be waiting for you. He says, 'Mom, you did a very good job by me. But sometimes I didn't do a good job by myself.' "

George went on, "He's talking again about what happened. He says the people who shot and killed him did *not* know him."

"Police thought my son was [a victim of] mistaken identity," Joyce explained.

"He didn't hang out with a bad crowd," George said.

"No. He tried to avoid that."

"But he was naive. He thought no one would hurt him. He thought he could avoid troublemakers even though he's in a tough neighborhood. But he couldn't. He was trying to find his way in life. But then he's in the wrong place at the wrong time," George concluded.

Joyce left the reading happy having heard from Tyrone. Still, she did not receive the answers she wanted regarding her son's killers. Between the evidence and the reading, it's safe to assume that Tyrone did not know his killers and that his family may never know why he died. At least Joyce could take comfort in knowing that somewhere her only son was still alive.

Twenty-five-year-old Thomas Reilly also dreamed of a better life and was willing to work hard to achieve it. Unlike Tyrone Nelson, however, he lived in a world far removed from the daily crime and tension of the inner city: suburban Long Island.

The only child of his mother Meg's previous marriage, Thomas was living with her and his stepfather Edward Holland in October 1991. But he was about to start his own diesel-truck servicing business and buy his own home. He and Ed were very close, and that afternoon the three had attended a charity softball game in a local park. The night before Meg and Ed had gone shopping for Thomas's birthday, just two weeks away.

That night T.R., as Thomas's friends and family called him, said good night to his mother. "I'll be hanging out with friends. Then later we'll go down to the pub and meet some of the guys and go to Vinnie's* for some pizza. I'll see you tomorrow."

Later that evening, around eleven-thirty, Meg and Ed were awakened by the phone. When Meg put the receiver to her ear she heard a frantic voice blurting out, "T.R. had

---

*At the request of the subject, this name has been altered. Everything else in this story, however, is true.

an accident! They took him to the county hospital!''

Meg hung up and shouted to Ed, ''Get dressed! Get the car out of the garage! T.R.'s at the hospital! He's had an accident!''

Before leaving, however, Meg phoned Nassau County Medical Center and asked to speak to someone in the emergency room. ''Can you tell me what happened to Thomas Reilly?'' she asked.

In a flat, cold monotone, a doctor said, ''We lost him. We couldn't save him. Your son's dead. He died of two gunshot wounds to the chest.''

''No, you don't understand,'' Meg replied, not comprehending the doctor's words. ''I'm looking for Thomas Reilly. He was in an accident.''

''No, you heard me,'' the doctor answered. ''He's dead. He was shot twice in the chest.''

Meg simply couldn't accept what she was hearing. ''No one would hurt T.R. Everybody knew him! He grew up in the neighborhood,'' she told the doctor. Then it dawned on her and she screamed hysterically into the phone, ''Not T.R.! Not T.R.!''

Ed took the receiver and listened as he was told to go to the local police precinct. The details recounted here came from eyewitnesses via police reports and local news coverage. As of this writing, the man accused of shooting Thomas Reilly is awaiting trial. At the police station, Meg and Ed were informed that someone had shot up the bar and killed their son. Tom was sitting in the bar, which he often frequented with friends, when two or three patrons began arguing. What happened next wasn't clear, but the dispute escalated when one of the men took out a handgun and opened fire, wounding two other patrons. Upon hearing the gunshots, everyone in the bar ducked for cover.

The gunman fled the bar with Thomas Reilly in pursuit. They ran into a parking lot, where police believe the gunman turned suddenly and shot Tom in the chest, mortally wounding him. Tom was lying moaning on the pavement, blood pooling around him, when the gunman allegedly ran back, stood over his victim and shot him in the chest a second time as horrified witnesses looked on.

This time several other patrons chased the suspect, who was caught about fifteen minutes later. In the meantime, police arrived, and an ambulance rushed T.R. to the hospital. He was pronounced dead about an hour later. The gunman's other two victims were treated for their wounds and later released.

Everyone in the bar was at a loss to explain why Thomas pursued the gunman. He did not know him and by all accounts was not involved in the argument. He had not been drinking, either. It just didn't make sense.

But those who knew T.R. well were not surprised at all. "He's a tough kid, but he had a heart of gold," Ed commented later. "I just wish he'd have had more sense than to go after a guy with a gun. But who knows. How can you second-guess him?"

Meg was devastated by her son's senseless killing. Her doctor prescribed tranquilizers to help her through the funeral. Hundreds of friends, family members, and colleagues attended Tom's wake and funeral. In the days and weeks that followed, Meg found herself unable to function, alternately crying out that her son was dead, then minutes later talking out loud to him as if he could hear her. Every day she would look at one of his photographs and shout, "T.R., why did you have to run out of the bar? Why'd you have to get killed for that?"

Within days of the funeral Meg attended a meeting of Parents of Murdered Children. There she learned of George's work. She was also attending therapy and depending heavily on the strength of her husband. Still, it wasn't until after her reading with George that she could feel at peace about her son, although, as she said later, "I can never forgive."

George's reading for Meg and Ed is an interesting example of how the spirits use a range of seemingly meaningless details that have great significance for their survivors. Thomas's concern for his loved ones and his determination to ensure that they knew they were hearing from him is clear here.

• • •

"Are you husband and wife?" George asked.

"Yes," Ed and Meg answered.

"A male comes between you. You've got to be connected somehow. Otherwise he'd go to the side of one of you. There's also another male passed over. The male who comes between you claims he passed young. Right?"

"Yes."

"Does he pass as a young adult?" George asked.

"Yes," answered Meg.

"He's related by blood. That's true. He comes to both of you. He knows you both."

"Yes."

"He says he's the son passed on. Is he your son?" George asked Meg.

"My son," she acknowledged.

"I was just going to say . . . Are you the stepfather?" he asked Ed. "He certainly looks upon you as a father, even though biologically you're not. Emotionally you are. You obviously pray for him, because he thanks you for praying for him in your own way. He asks that it please continue." A few moments later George said, "Your son passes tragically."

"Yes."

"He apologizes. Not that he has to. But it's beyond his control. His hands are tied. Not literally. Simply, 'It's out of my control.' His passing is accidental?" George asked.

"Yes," she acknowledged.

"He's telling me he does not pass on from a health problem. He's showing me a vehicle-type accident to symbolize he passes on—as we'd understand it—accidentally, and not from a health problem."

"More or less," Ed replied.

"He passes quickly, though," George said.

"Yes," Meg answered.

"He's injured internally," George said.

"Yes," she confirmed.

"Something is wrong in here," George commented, pointing to his chest. "He loses air."

"Yes."

"Among other things, I feel like I can't breathe that well. There's an injury to the chest area. The injury is more internal than external? I mean, it could show externally, but it's worse inside," George said.

"Yes," Ed said.

"He might mean this symbolically: A weapon is involved."

"Yes," Meg answered.

"A gun or a knife."

"Yes."

"He's shot," George said.

"Yes."

"Because I hear [psychically] gunshots. I'm listening to what he's telling me. I heard gunshots go off, and he says, 'I'm shot in the chest.' "

"Yes."

"He's murdered," George said.

"Yes."

"Because he's telling me . . . Can I say it's accidentally, though?"

"Yes."

"That's what he means. That's why I'm hemming and hawing over the words. He's telling me he's murdered but it's not the way you think it is. I saw 'REDRUM' written in front of me, and he said he's murdered, but he's at the wrong place at the wrong time."

"Exactly."

"In other words, whoever murders him doesn't stalk him."

"Right."

"There's more than one person involved in your son's murder."

"He was the only one killed," Meg replied.

"No, no," said George. "I mean, was there more than one involved in his murder? Was there someone else? I feel like there was a second person."

"There were more people shot," Ed explained.

"Oh, okay. Maybe that's what he means, because he's

telling me there's more than one, and I didn't understand what he meant. Did somebody go off the deep end?''

"Yes," Meg said.

"It looks like somebody just lost his mind. Your son forgives who shot him. It's an accidental murder. The person goes off. They're out of their mind. Your son was in the wrong place at the wrong time. This obviously happens in public.''

"Yes."

"Was the person [who shot your son] almost like a sniper?''

"Yes," she replied, "just about."

"It feels like he's just picking off people randomly!" exclaimed George. "He has nothing against your son.''

"He didn't know him.''

"This person's got some ax to grind with society and starts killing people. Again, your son says he was murdered. Obviously there was a total state of fear and panic when this happened. Was your son in a crowd?''

"Yes."

"He says you're uncertain if he suffered prior to his passing. Because the gunshots are going off, and people are panicking and scurrying. Your son's hit. He's lying there. He's killed instantly. He says he does not suffer prior to his passing. Was this out in the street?'' asked George. "I feel like I'm in a mall or a street, and all of sudden somebody just started shooting.''

"Yes," Ed said.

"Scary. But it also troubles you, because you didn't have a chance to say goodbye to him. You weren't there with him when he passes on. It's as if you feel he died alone. He says he didn't die alone. Souls from the hereafter, like your parents, grandparents, and other people came to him, to comfort him and to bring him into the hereafter.

"I don't mean to sound graphic. But your son says he literally doesn't know what hits him. But, again, he says he forgives. He seems like a down-to-earth guy. He says, 'If I hold on to it, it's not going to bring me back.' Nothing can change what has happened. He says he's moved on, and he's safe and at peace in the hereafter. He says that no matter what, no harm can ever come to him again. He says, 'Mom, I'm all right, I'm all right!'

"You've memorialized him? He talks about a memorial. He's pretty pushy! So he must know what he's talking about. I'll have to let it go until it's explained. I'm not understanding what it is. You and he were very close, though," George said to Ed.

"Yes."

"I don't know the kind of relationship he had with his natural father, but it certainly seems like you and he had a nice relationship. He thanks you for being good to him prior to his passing. He was just starting to come into his own."

"Yes," said Meg.

"Because it seems that he was growing up for real. He knew his direction. He was stable," George said.

"Yes."

"He might have gone through his teens like everybody else. But he seems to have been a little on the rebellious side. He knows he was a pain in the you-know-what, and he apologizes for that. But, as he says, his growing up and his change of life from adolescence to adulthood might have been just a little more difficult emotionally than it would have been for somebody else. His was just a little more difficult. He was quick-tempered. He admits he was very defensive. He was very sensitive. But, unfortunately, his sensitivity made him extremely defensive at times. So, again, he apologizes for that.

"As his mother and stepfather, you certainly had your moments with him. There's not only the senselessness of his death, but also the fact that he was starting to finally grow into a young man. This is also what troubles you. He says his life has not been snuffed out. It is still going on. It's just that it's going on in the hereafter. As I said, this is a senseless murder. He says there is nothing we can do to change what has happened.

"You have your good days and your bad days. Definitely there are more bad days. You're ready to rip your hair out. Know that he's all right. He didn't suffer. He knows you love him. Be at peace as much as you can for the holiday season. This has nothing to do with Christianity, but I see Jesus appearing behind you, saying, 'Peace be with you.' They're both trying to put you at peace. Your son says to stop putting yourselves in these terrible nightmares. What's happened, happened. And someday, he says, 'We'll all be together again.' It's as if he went to a foreign country to pursue a career. And you know he's there, but because of airfare and time . . . ''

The couple nodded that they understood.

After several moments George told Meg and Ed, ''You're always going to experience this grief, and that's okay. You're allowed to have this grief. He just doesn't want it to destroy you. Especially with the holidays coming up. You *dread* this time of year, from Thanksgiving on. He says, 'This is when I'm closest to you.' But you're so caught up in your grief that you don't see the forest for the trees. He says to sit in your own home quietly and allow yourself to feel him. This emptiness that hits home is ten times worse, and unfortunately, unless somebody has gone through what you're going through, they don't know what you're experiencing. So your son says, 'Believe and know that I'm with you.'

''Also, there's some synchronicity. . . . A song comes on the radio that connects you. You get a signal to let you know he's near. You talk aloud to him as if he's there. Then other times you think he's dead. 'So why are you talking to me?' he asks. 'I'm *not* dead. I'm still there.'

''He has kind of a rough life. Not that he's complaining. He's just stating the facts. He admits he was his own worst enemy. He could create his own rough life.

''He was kind of angry at his natural father,'' said George. ''He had hostility toward him. Justified hostility. He might have resented you at times. He apologizes to you, that it was just kid stuff. He doesn't want you to think that he meant to hurt you. It's just that sometimes he was so angry, he didn't know where to direct his anger. So he made you feel inadequate, that you were to blame, that you weren't a good enough mother. He says, 'I'm sorry I did these things to you. I didn't mean to hurt anyone.'

"It's just that he was hurting, and that's how he reacted. He says that's not the right thing to do. He's very bright, and he learns quickly. Because he learns very quickly over there, even in the short time he's been there."

"Did you also lose a pet?" George asked.

"Oh, my God, yes!" Meg exclaimed.

"There's a dog there with your son."

She laughed.

"Did the dog pass before him?"

"Yes."

"He says he has to give credit where it's due. He says the dog was the first to reach him in the hereafter." Meg smiled. "He loved the animal," George added.

"Yes."

"And the animal loved him."

"Yes."

"He says when the dog passed on, he was heartbroken."

"He was."

"He was devastated. That was his baby, his little buddy," George explained.

"Yes."

"Your son goes in a sleep state. He passes over in his sleep, as we'd understand it. Then he's in the tunnel, and he says the dog runs to him and nudges him. The dog woke him up. Then he says that he realized it was his dog! He wondered where he was going. That's when the dog took him into the light. So he says that he and his dog are back together again. So really, the dog is the first living thing that welcomed him into the hereafter.

"It's funny," said George, "your son was trusting; yet not trusting. He would have trusted his dog before a human any day. But in any case, he says that's when he knew he was in a safe place. Because he knew the dog wouldn't take him anyplace that wasn't safe."

Meg began to cry.

"Do you take the name Mike, or Michael?" George asked.

"Yes," she said.

"Passed on. Because he keeps saying, 'I met Michael.' Is he a father figure? An uncle or grandfather."

"It's *my* brother," Ed interjected.

"Oh, I understand. That's my mistake. Your son said he was like a father figure. But obviously he's like an uncle to your stepson. Your brother passes young as well. He wants you to know he always loved you. It wasn't expressed. You and he seem to be opposite. He seems to have a good life in the fast lane. But he's all right and at peace. And he asks that you pray for him."

"Okay," Ed replied.

"Did you lose another child?"

"No."

"Did you ever miscarry? Somebody in your family lose a daughter?"

"My sister did," Meg said.

"Oh, okay. There's someone around," George said.

"Your son started talking about the sister passed over, and it was around you. I thought he meant that you lost a sister or that you had a miscarriage. She was a youth?"

"No."

"Oh, she was grown up. But a young woman."

"She was middle-aged."

"She's young by today's standards, in any case," George explained.

"Right."

"Did she pass after your boy? No—I'm sorry. I'm incorrect. She says she was there to help him into the light, also. She was close to you."

"Yes," Meg acknowledged.

"Do you take the name Bill, or William?"

"Yes."

"Passed over."

"Yes."

"He's with your son."

"Okay."

"He's a father figure. He is your son's grandfather. William. And Margaret. Your son's with them," George said. "The name . . . Grace?"

"Yes."

"Passed over."

"Yes."

"She's a mother figure."

"Yes."

"It's your mom," George said. "She spoke Italian."

"Yes."

"She says she met your son in the hereafter. She comes across as a very nice lady."

"Yes."

"Without telling me, your son has a common first name."

"Yes."

"But I can shorten it."

"Oh, yes."

"He keeps telling me you used the shortened form of his name."

"Yes."

After a few minutes of trying to determine the meaning of the psychic symbols being communicated to him, George said, "Do you take the name 'Tom'?"

"Yes."

"Is that your son?"

"Yes."

"Saint Anthony is off to your side," said George. "He's dressed in black, which is a sign of an unusual passing. You'll hear news of a passing, but you're not shocked by it. Nor are you greatly affected by it. It could be somebody who's very elderly and could go at any time. It's not your immediate family or anyone who will affect you drastically."

"Okay."

"Do you take the name Pasquale, or Pat? Is he a father figure?"

"Yes."

"Like an uncle," said George.

"Yes," Ed answered.

"Also, is there a 'Thomas' passed over, besides your boy?"

"Yes. His grandfather. His natural father's dad," Meg replied.

"Your mother-in-law has passed on, also."

"Yes."

"Because your son claims his other grandparents are with him."

"Yes."

"And whether or not there was a lack of communication between him and his dad, they are still his grandparents. He says they are there, also."

"Okay."

"He's very independent," George remarked. "Your son almost prefers to do things on his own. Because he doesn't want any of the relatives over there to take this personally, but he says he lives by himself over there. He says only the dog is allowed!"

Meg laughed.

"I mean, your parents—grandparents—these other people are all there if he needs somebody. There's somebody there for him. But he's independent in the sense that he says, 'I've got my own place: me and the dog.' That's the way he wants it. He's not unsociable. He's friendly. He'll go out with people. But he likes his [time], being alone. He prefers to live on his own.

"He does have his friends over there; people he's met. But he's got his own place. I keep seeing a vision in my head. He keeps telling me to tell you how beautiful it is there, and it's always nice weather. It's a beautiful balance to society here. There's no hatred. No struggle. No negativity. Not like in this dimension.

"There can be other levels," George went on. "But you wouldn't put yourself there where he is if you're not a nice person. There's peace and tranquillity there. He wants you to know that. He knows you'd much rather have him here than where he is. But he wants to tell you that at least if he must be there, know that he's happy. That's the main thing. He's happy, and as long as he has the dog, he's fine.

"He definitely has a relationship with the dog. It's his best friend. He said when he followed the dog into the light

and he realized he'd died—as we understand it—he knew
he was going to a good place. But he does have a lot of
friends. There's a tremendous amount of people who know
him and remember him with love.

"Your son says he and his dog will be waiting for you
in the hereafter. But until that moment, he says, 'What you
can give me as a Christmas gift is peace in your heart.' Go
on with your life peacefully and productively as best you
can. It doesn't mean you don't love him. He just wants you
to be happy. As much as you want him to be happy where
he is. He says it works both ways," George said.

After the reading Meg said, "George helped me. I needed
to know that T.R. didn't suffer." She said she had no doubt
that she'd heard from Thomas. One such example occurred
when Thomas said through George, "The weather's nice."

"When T.R. was about twenty-four, he withdrew his
money from the bank and went to the Bahamas," Meg
recalled. "The first night when T.R. didn't come home, I
thought he stayed with a friend. But the second night I
became worried. So I called his boss, who told me T.R.
had gone to the Bahamas. What? I couldn't believe it. Well,
on his way home, T.R. called me from Miami and asked
us to pick him up at the airport.

"I told him no," she continued. "I said, 'Whoever took
you there can bring you home!' Then I asked him if he was
out of his mind. Just taking off like that and telling no one.
All he could say was, 'Well, the weather was nice.'"

Meg felt that the reading helped her deal with her grief.
"My therapist saw a marked improvement in me. She was
surprised. She asked, 'What happened? Why do you seem
happier?' I explained to her about George, and she was
amazed.

"I'm less angry at Thomas now than I was before the
reading. Hearing him explain that he was in the wrong
place at the wrong time the night he was killed has helped
me.

"When the man who's accused of killing T.R. goes to

trial, Parents of Murdered Children is going to help me with the criminal justice system. I deal with my anger now by hoping that justice will be done.

"I'll always miss T.R., and I can't forgive the man who killed him. But my goal is to heal."

Cindy Beaudoin, seventeen, was bright-eyed, intelligent, vivacious—everything a parent could want. A cheerleader with an interest in architecture, a beautiful, slender woman with a tomboy streak, Cindy was full of surprises. Yet her father, Paul, was not really surprised when she happily announced on February 28, 1989, that she had joined the Connecticut National Guard. He recalled her as a little girl, playing army with his canteen and helmet.

Although Cindy's patriotism and sense of duty were unquestionable, she, like millions of other young people, joined the National Guard not only to serve her country but to take advantage of its tuition program. After serving six years as "a weekend warrior," Cindy's college tuition would be paid in full. In the fall of 1990 Cindy was a freshman at the University of Connecticut, living at home with her parents Paul and Phyllis and a younger teenage sister, Stephanie. Although Cindy knew all about military service—Paul Beaudoin had served in Vietnam and was a lifelong reservist himself—she never imagined that she would find herself near the front lines of a war half a world away as part of Operation Desert Storm. On February 28, 1991—exactly two years to the day after she'd joined the Guard and mere hours after President George Bush announced the cease-fire—medic Cindy Beaudoin would become the only woman reservist to die in that war.

Her death was further distinguished by a swirl of controversy: The army contends that Cindy was not killed in action but died as the result of wounds "self-inflicted by souvenir bomblets," a noncombat status that precludes her from receiving even the most routine military honors.

In his extensive investigative report for the *Hartford Courant*, newspaperman Bob Sudyk sought to discover what really happened that day, as members of the 142nd

Medical Company of the Connecticut National Guard traveled in a thirty-vehicle convoy across the Kuwaiti Desert. Virtually every aspect of the unit's involvement in the war, from its fitness for duty to the army's training procedures, is open to question. At the heart of the controversy regarding Cindy is a simple, small but deadly device, the American-made M-42 cluster bomblet.

Resembling a tiny canister, the antipersonnel bomblet is just three inches long and about half that in diameter, and weighs barely half a pound. According to Sudyk, ''The M-42 is designed to burn through tanks and explode shrapnel. . . . Upon impact, the bomblet is capable of burning through 2.75 inches of armor plate.

''This . . . submunition is packed inside the shells fired by a howitzer or multiple-rocket launching system. The shells explode in the air, expelling hundreds of bomblets that can blanket an area covering two football fields. Nylon ribbons arm the bomblets as they fall, unthreading the firing pins.''

Only one officer of Cindy's 140-member unit had prior combat experience. Despite that and the fact that hundreds of thousands of pieces of unexploded munitions were scattered all over the ground in Iraq and Kuwait, the army did not see the need to warn about their dangers. The army's position was simply to alert soldiers not to pick up anything they could not identify. It has been estimated that roughly 120 of the 403 Desert Storm casualties, or nearly 30 percent, were the result of exposure to American-deployed munitions.

The army maintains that Cindy caused her own death by picking up and having somewhere on her person an M-42 bomblet. While that is certainly within the realm of possibility—witnesses reported seeing her, as well as several superior officers, handling the bomblets they discovered in the sand—eyewitness accounts of that fateful day challenge the army's conclusions.

February 28 was a clear, quiet day. The convoy traveled across a seemingly peaceful expanse of empty desert. To either side of them the little white ribboned bomblets pep-

pered the sand. A bit farther away lay the bodies of dead
Iraqi soldiers, some burned, some in pieces. After hearing
news of the cease-fire, several British medics who were
traveling with the convoy asked to stop and bury Iraqi dead,
something called for in their army code. Despite their running low on food, water, and supplies, the soldiers were
overjoyed that the war was over, and several stepped out
into the sand to collect souvenirs, including the deadly
unexploded cylinders.

When several asked a superior officer what the items
were and if they were safe, he erroneously told them that
they were spent shells or parts of parachute gear. Several
soldiers remained suspicious, and just before Cindy boarded
the British army ambulance in which she was to ride, a
British soldier ordered her to get rid of a bomblet she'd
picked up. Presumably she obeyed.

The convoy continued through the dunes, pocked by dec-
imated Iraqi Republican Guard bunkers, charred enemy
tanks, and corpses. Sometime that afternoon they came
upon six Iraqi soldiers waving white flags in surrender.
While these prisoners were being searched, Cindy hopped
out of her vehicle, the fifth from the front, to walk around.
Several soldiers report seeing a stray dog approach them.
It refused food, then cocked its head and ran away, as if
answering its master. Cindy was climbing back into her
ambulance when a loud explosion came from the end of
the line. Heeding shouts of "Sniper!" Cindy leapt from her
vehicle and, clutching her M-16 rifle, hugged the ground.
Just minutes later, as several eyewitnesses would tell dis-
believing military investigators, a white stream of smoke
headed straight for Cindy, then another explosion sounded.
Two soldiers claimed they saw at least one Iraqi soldier
moving toward them. The army later discounted their tes-
timony.

Cindy lay in the sand, her right leg obliterated, her ab-
domen blown open. A British medic ran to her and admin-
istered a powerful dose of opium. The ambulance Cindy
was placed in raced to the front of the convoy, where they
awaited a medical helicopter to rescue her. They would wait

three hours, during which time Cindy was comforted by friends and her little white teddy bear Binkie, a Christmas gift from her sister. Although everyone reassured her that she would not die, Cindy's life slowly ebbed away. By the time the chopper landed—its first attempt at an earlier location was thwarted by heavy ground fire—Cindy had grown quiet and pale. She died on the helicopter without Binkie, who was retrieved from the ground and given to Cindy's friend in the unit, Jean Kazlauskas. Jean, along with two other soldiers, was severely wounded five days later when an M-42 bomblet hidden by a fellow guardsman exploded in her tent.

Back at home, in Plainfield, Connecticut, the Beaudoins were getting ready for church when the phone rang. It was March 3, three days after the cease-fire. A friend of Paul's told him he'd heard a rumor that something had happened to Cindy. Paul told him he was wrong. But just as he was hanging up the phone, a neighbor's car screeched into their driveway. Cheryl Hurley ran into the Beaudoins' kitchen, trembling. The priest, she said, was telling everyone to pray for them. "Is Cindy okay?" she asked.

"Nothing's wrong," Paul replied. But he began to feel uneasy. He phoned a colonel he knew, but was told by his wife that he was not home. Just then a knock came at the door. Paul answered. The guardsman, whom Paul knew personally, began, "Paul Beaudoin, it is my regretful duty to inform you on behalf of the President of the United States and the Governor of Connecticut . . ." Accompanying the soldier was the colonel Paul had just tried to reach.

Initially the Beaudoins were told that Cindy stepped on a land mine and died in combat. But after investigating the tent explosions, the army retracted her killed-in-combat status. While the family was permitted to keep the Purple Heart she'd been awarded posthumously—in error, the military now maintained—it would not be included in her record.

Over the coming days and months the Beaudoins' misery over Cindy's death would be further compounded by a se-

ries of mistakes and oversights. They were appalled to learn
that other people had known of their daughter's death before they were officially informed, upset that her body was
misplaced for several days during transit back to the States,
and shocked when they finally learned of her desire to be
cremated—after she had been buried.

A medical expert quoted in Bob Sudyk's story contends
that the injuries suffered by Dr. Mark Connelly, who died
in the first convoy explosion, "were not consistent with the
many bomblet victims he'd treated." As a result of his in-
depth investigation and the opinions of experts and eyewitnesses, Sudyk concluded, "There's no evidence that
shrapnel from a bomblet killed Cindy." This, combined
with the army's decision not to autopsy either Cindy or
Connelly, the eyewitness reports, and other forensic evidence suggest very strongly that Cindy did not die from a
self-inflicted accident.

"The army wants us to believe it was friendly fire [which
would include the M-42], not Iraqi fire," Phyllis said. "I
think maybe the U.S. Army doesn't want bad public rela-
tions about the fact that there were young men and women
in that convoy who shouldn't have been on the front lines.
They were not trained for what they faced, and they had
limited fire power to defend themselves."

The Beaudoins are committed to fighting until they learn
the truth of Cindy's death and her honor is restored. They
are considering suing the army; all they want is a written
apology. They would also like to see a Congressional probe
into the incident and the army's behavior in its wake.

"We have to defend Cindy," Paul said. "She's not here
to defend herself. The army took away her Purple Heart. I
wish the army would stop looking for someone to blame.
Now we've channeled our grief into fighting the army."

Understandably, the incident is particularly painful for
Paul. Cindy's last Christmas home, he gave her the wooden
rosary beads that had protected him in Vietnam and *his*
father during World War II. "She was proud to serve her
country," Phyllis said. "She went there to do what she was
told to do—as a soldier."

• • •

"Is there a female close to you passed over?" George asked the couple.

"Yes," they both acknowledged.

"They are two females and a male, too."

"Yes."

"There's a young female."

"Yes," Phyllis answered.

"She's the first one to come through. She stands between the two of you. She has her arms around the two of you. I take it you're linked somehow; you're husband and wife," George said.

"Yes," Paul replied.

"Because she keeps telling me there's a link between the two of you. She's talking about a daughter. Is she your daughter?"

"Yes," she said.

"Okay. That's what I'm looking for. She keeps saying, 'I'm the daughter.' You're her parents. There's also another female. She's talking about 'grandmother.' Did one of you lose a mother?"

"Yes," Phyllis answered.

"Because she's saying your mom is with her."

"Okay."

"Your father has passed," George said to Paul.

"Yes."

"She says your father is with her. Your daughter passed young by today's standards?"

"Yes," Phyllis replied.

"She's saying she's a young female; beyond the age of ten," George said.

"Yes."

"Because she's an adolescent all grown up. Your mother has passed, also," George said to Paul.

"Yes."

"Because she keeps talking about another grandmother with her as well."

"Yes."

"There's another [group] of people behind them. Your

grandparents are back there,'' George said to the couple.

"Yes," they answered in unison.

"Did you miscarry?"

"No," Phyllis replied.

"Did somebody else in the family lose a child?"

"Yes."

"Your daughter talks about another child being with her."

"Yes," Phyllis acknowledged.

"There are a son and a daughter."

"Yes."

"There are two other souls with her. They'd be cousins."

"Yes."

"Because she keeps telling me there are other passings of children in the family. Was the loss of [another daughter in the family] a miscarriage?"

"Yes, I believe so," she answered.

"But the son was born."

"Yes."

"Your daughter is very easygoing," George said.

"Yes."

"Also very tranquil."

"Yes."

"She was just talking to me, and I felt very peaceful. She has the maturity to explain everything to me. She's telling me to keep my mind clear and not to become impatient. She definitely comes close to the both of you. It's like she's standing in front of me, telling me, 'Now listen carefully.' She's inclined to be on the stubborn side," George said.

"Oh, yes," Paul agreed.

"There's a streak of rebelliousness in her. Her passing might have come at a time of stubborn rebelliousness, as she called it. She knows that you love her, and the feeling is mutual. But she tells me it wasn't a fairy-tale existence. I mean, you were having your ups and downs. Again, I get that streak in me that I want to get hostile or rebellious. She tells me she feels she could have been even closer to you; not that you and she weren't close when she was growing up. She says she knows that as adults you understand. Because it's true that she could be very quick-tempered. Like Dr. Jekyll and Mr. Hyde. At times she could be very easygoing; on the other hand, very stubborn, adamant, and strong-willed. A very sensitive young woman," said George.

"Yes," Phyllis answered.

"Very sensitive. It actually makes her defensive. Her sensitivity can be a little overpowering at times. It makes her inclined to be defensive. She passes tragically."

"Yes," Paul replied.

"Your daughter says it was beyond her control. Is that true?"

"Yes."

"She apologizes for it, because she's telling you she is sorry. Not so much that she has to [apologize]. But more because of what you're going through. Both of you."

"Okay," Paul said, choking back tears.

"This could be symbolic," said George, "so please just say yes or no. She shows me an accident. She doesn't pass from a health problem."

"No, not a health problem."

"Even if she doesn't pass in an accident literally, she's cluing me to get away from health. She is injured."

"Yes."

"Because she's talking about injuries. Does anything affect her chest area? Internally?"

"Yes."

"I feel like I can't breathe," said George. "Something must have cut off her air. Once she tells me what it is, I'll understand why I'm getting that feeling. There's also injury to her head," George explained.

"Yes," Paul answered.

"I feel like I'm not getting enough oxygen to the brain. She does pass very quickly, though. She claims she does. Because she tells me there is no suffering prior to her passing."

"Okay," Phyllis said, crying.

"Even if she's not dead but she's unconscious, she's not aware of any suffering," George assured them. "In spite of the circumstances, she says she passes very quickly. Were you afraid your daughter was mad at you?"

"I was," Paul admitted.

"She keeps saying, 'I'm not mad at you, I'm not mad at you.' Again, I can feel her between the two of you. I don't see her clearly, but I know she's there. Was there a bad exchange of words prior to her passing?"

"No," he answered.

"Was there tension in the home? Your daughter is talking about typical growing up. She's saying there is tension. It's not that you're at each other with machetes. It's just that there's a lack of communication between parents and child. It's not overwhelming, it's typical. She just wants to let you know that she's maturing, and she is *not* mad at you. . . . You obviously have been praying for her," George said.

"Yes," he replied.

"She keeps thanking you for prayers—in your own way—and she asks that it please continue. Not that anyone is overly religious, but she knows the value of it. I don't know if I have the right word," said George. "Did she have trouble inwardly with her passing?"

"I don't know," Cindy's mother said.

"Something is not right *in* me," George explained.

"Yes," said Paul.

"It's more internal."

"Yes," Phyllis agreed.

"I feel [the injury] is not showing. I would see it internally. Something is wrong with her heart and her head. I keep getting the feeling that I'm losing air. Was there also a fall?"

"Yes, just prior to it," Paul said.

"Because she talks about falling. But it's not as if she falls from the Eiffel Tower or something."

"Yes."

"Was she uncoordinated?" George asked.

"We don't know," Phyllis answered.

"Probably from the fall. I feel like I'm dizzy," George explained, describing the sympathetic sensation.

"I would say right after this," Paul offered.

"She talks about people around her."

"Yes."

"She's in a crowd when [her passing occurs]."

"Yes."

"Because there are a lot of people around. Is there a weapon involved? She's showing me a weapon. That can also be a symbol."

"Yes."

"Were there any exchange of words prior to her passing?" asked George.

"Yes," said Phyllis.

"She gets herself into some kind of altercation."

"Yes," Paul confirmed.

"There seems to be some kind of exchange of words or hostility. I feel like I'm in an intense situation prior to her passing. Was she 'technically' murdered?"

"Yes," he acknowledged.

"She says she was murdered, but it wasn't deliberate."

"Yes."

"That why she's saying it was an accident. She's murdered, but it's not by Joe Blow stalking her, she's telling me. It's not premeditated. I'm at the wrong place at the wrong time. It's an accidental type of murder."

"Right."

"Also [something] affects the back and the front of the chest, as well as the torso," said George. "Something is not right. I keep getting that lack of oxygen. She's shot or stabbed." After a moment's silence, George said, "Wait. Is there a blasting sound?"

"Yes," the couple answered together.

"That's what I need to know. Thank you. I'm hearing a blasting sound. I want to say gun—and I don't want to say gun. That's why I'm saying gunshot with hesitation. There's definitely some kind of blasting sound. Would it have cut her?" George asked.

"Yes," he acknowledged.

"That's why I feel like I'm knifed. That's why I said shot *and* knife. Because there was this blasting sound, and I felt a cut. Something cuts her."

"Right."

"It's a careless type of murder. I use that word loosely, if you understand what I mean. It's a careless, accidental murder. That's what your daughter calls it. She doesn't blame anyone. It's really not intentional or somebody's fault. 'I'm at the wrong place at the wrong time,' she says. Do you understand why there's a blasting sound?"

"Yes."

"It sounds like a very loud gunshot. It has an explosive sound. Something explodes."

"Yes."

"I keep hearing this 'boom,' " George went on. "It looks like she's being pushed. But she's not being pushed by a person. It could be the impact of the explosion. I felt like I was being thrown or pushed by it. That's why I could be getting the loss of air. It looks to me like you get the [heck] scared out of you. There's the sound, plus the cutting feeling. It's not a knife, but something is cutting into me. There's pressure from the impact of the blast. Was there a shattering? Or was there damage to a building?" George asked.

"Yes."

"Or around [a building]."

"Yes."

"I'm very positive that this impact was very destructive," said George. "It possibly shatters a window. But your daughter also claims that she did not suffer prior to her passing."

"Okay."

"Those cousins [I mentioned earlier in the reading], they passed on before your daughter."

"Yes."

"Because she claims the cousins were there for her when she passed on. Probably because they got along. She says you didn't have a chance to say goodbye to her. She says don't feel that way. 'I don't want to say goodbye to you, because I'm still here with you. I'm not going to say good-bye.' She knows you would much rather have her here physically than spiritually. Unfortunately, for the time being, it has to be that she's here spiritually. She says loved ones—grandparents and others—were there for her. A lot of people were there for her. They want to assure you that she did not pass alone,'' George emphasized.

''Okay.''

''Were there any vehicles around her?''

''Yes.''

''Was *she* in a vehicle?''

''Yes.''

''Because I keep feeling I'm in a vehicle. She's telling me to say *vehicles*. Do you know why?''

''Yes.''

''A vehicle explodes!''

''Yes,'' said her father.

''That's probably why I feel I'm enclosed in a small area when something shatters. She's enclosed in the vehicle,'' George said.

''Yes, just prior,'' replied Paul. You will note, however, that Cindy died inside a vehicle, the helicopter. It's possible that she was trying to make that point here. She will also bring it up later in the reading.

''She's been in an enclosed vehicle. Then she's on a wheeled vehicle . . . that's open when she passes on.''

''Yes.''

''This vehicle makes noise. It has almost a motorcycle sound.''

''Yes.''

''And while she's with this vehicle, an explosion happens. It blasts them out. She's in the enclosed vehicle when this explosion takes place.''

''We're not sure about that,'' he explained.

''Was there another explosion?'' George asked.

''Right,'' Phyllis acknowledged.

''It feels like I'm in a battle, and there are a number of explosions going off around me. It's like somebody's dropping bombs. Boom. Boom. Boom. She's in an open area.''

"Yes. In the truck," she answered.

"Was there shrapnel—or what I think is shrapnel?" asked George. "Something cuts, like shrapnel or explosive materials. Is she away from home when this occurs? Far away."

"Yes," Paul acknowledged.

"She's far, far away, she says. She's actually *in* a battle."

"Yes."

"Was she in the military?"

"Yes."

"I felt I saw a woman appear, and she saluted me," said George. "She looked like she was dressed in a uniform. My chauvinism took over. I said, 'How can you be in the military? You're a woman.' And she gave me this nasty look. So, in other words, your daughter was killed in action," George concluded.

"Yes."

"That's why she's telling me she's murdered, but not the way I would think. Now I understand. She's a victim of circumstances. She's a victim of war. Yes, there is a murder, but not in the typical way we understand murder. It happened recently," George said.

"Yes," her father acknowledged.

"I'm trying to think what war happened recently. . . . "

"The Persian Gulf War," Phyllis blurted.

"That's why she is pointing to the yellow bows in the window!" exclaimed George. "I've left the yellow bows up since then for parents who've lost children," he went on to say. "I have so many people coming here who've had a loss in wars.

"Now I understand why she was in a large, open space. That would be the desert. Was she in a plane or a helicopter when she passed over, or before that?" he asked.

"Just prior to passing away, she was in a helicopter," Paul answered.

"That's the enclosed vehicle. Then she's in a more open vehicle that's on the ground. Was the helicopter hit?"

"No."

"The helicopter had landed, and she is out of it," George said.

"Yes."

"She's telling me she passed on after that."

"After the helicopter."

"Right. Is there friendly fire?" George asked.

"We don't know. That's what we're trying to find out," he replied.

"Were the Iraqis actually attacking?" George asked.

"We don't know," both parents answered.

"Well, it's almost like I feel both: It's as if they're under attack and fired upon. It also could be the Iraqis firing in the wrong direction. That's what I don't understand. She tells me they are under fire, but there seems to be confusion [as to where it's coming from]. Was she around a truck [at the time]?"

"Yes," he said.

"Is she with military personnel [connected with a] hospital?"

"Yes."

"Because I saw her in a nurse's uniform. That's what threw me. She's a military personnel, but she's military health personnel."

"Yes, that's right," acknowledged Cindy's mother.

"That's why I saw the two uniforms. That's why she changes uniforms. She shows me the red cross on a truck. But she said, 'I don't literally mean that.' She means she's a medic. I couldn't think of the word quickly enough. Had she been in an ambulance, or just been around them?" George asked. "Again, there are other vehicles that I see. Was she outside when she was killed?"

"Yes," he answered.

"She keeps telling me she's out there. All around her a battle's going on. But she's trying to help the wounded or help outside when they are hit by bombs or missiles."

The couple nodded but said nothing.

George continued. "Was she technically in Kuwait?"

"Yes," Paul said.

"She's very down-to-earth."

"Yes."

"She says the details of her death are driving you crazy. But she says, 'It's not going to bring me back, even if you know the details. It's not going to turn the clock back.' So for your own sake, she's pressing you to try to be at peace, knowing that she is all right. Does the name Marie mean anything at all?"

"It's her middle name," Phyllis replied.

"I heard her say . . . something Marie. It was her voice. Don't tell me her first name. If you hear me talking out loud [to her], don't pay any attention. Just don't answer."

"Okay."

"There are five letters in her name. There's an *e* sound."

"Yes."

"She's playing 'spiritual Scrabble.' She tells me there are five letters [in her first name], but she doesn't tell me what it is. It's a common name. I've heard it many times before, she says."

The mother and father nodded and smiled slightly. For the next few minutes George struggled to psychically hear the message, hoping it would include the spirit of the young woman telling him her name.

"She keeps showing *n*. Is there an *n* in her name?"

"Yes. It's practically in the middle," Phyllis told him.

"There's an *i* in her name."

"Yes."

"Is 'i' the second letter?"

"Yes."

"She's showing me *Linda*—but that's not it. Now she's telling me to call her Cindy," George stated.

"Yes. Cindy. That's her name," Phyllis confirmed.

"So it's Cindy Marie."

"Yes."

"She's a very ambitious young woman. Was she in the reserves?"

"Yes."

"She seems to know what she's doing. She's very sharp. There's a little confusion here and there. But she says if I take my time, I'll be able to understand everything she says to me."

"Okay."

"Did you also lose a pet?" George asked.

"Yes," the father answered.

"Dog or a cat?"

"Cat."

"Because she's telling me the pet is there with her, but it passed before her."

"Just *after* her," Paul corrected.

"Oh," said George. "She claims she meets the pet over there very soon or around [the time of] her death. It seems that it has to be put to sleep, and she woke it up over there."

"It was in a coma. And then it was put to sleep."

"And she woke it up. It's there with her. I'm sure just like one of the family. She just wants to let you know the pet is there with her, also," George said.

"Right."

"Was she married? Or was she seeing someone at the time?"

"Yes. She was seeing someone."

"She's trying to call to somebody that there was a romantic involvement with. I'll just leave it with you."

"Okay."

"Your birthday is coming up, or just passed? Or an anniversary? She gives the two of you white roses, and she congratulates you. She's saying it's more an anniversary. She extends the roses to both of you," George said.

"Yes, okay," the couple answered.

"She says there was a lot of tension and yelling with that battle. It looks like somebody pushed her. Now that I know she was in a battle, an explosion could have pushed her, and she could have been hit with some shrapnel. That's why I feel the cutting feeling. But I'm not being knifed. Then there's a blast. She said guns were involved. Not with her death, but guns were obviously being shot. The government did not give you any answers."

"Right," Paul acknowledged.

"Because, she says, the government does not know. It's as if there's too much confusion going on in battle."

The couple listened attentively.

"Did you memorialize her?" George asked.

"What do you mean?" Paul asked.

"I can see a picture of her. A memorial."

"Yes."

"Do you know what she means?" George asked.

"Yes," said Phyllis.

"Do you have a picture of her in your home? I'm sure you do."

"Yes."

"With a candle near it."

"Yes!"

"But the memorialization is something more. It's a [result of] this war."

"Yes."

"She's thanking you for a memorial. I see a framed picture. She's a sweetheart—but a tough cookie," said George.

"Yes, she is," Phyllis concurred.

"Because that's how she comes across. To know her is to love her. She's a very good person. Very down-to-earth. She's a sweet person, but don't mess with her."

"Yes."

"She's a tough nut to crack. The main thing is that she wants you both to know that she is all right. You've dreamed about her."

"Yes," said the mother.

"She says she's come to you in dreams," George said.

"Yes."

"She wants to let you know she is here and is all right. She would make friends and have a job in ten minutes, no matter where she went."

"Yes."

"She's just that type of person. If she was sent to outer Mongolia, she would have found a way to fit in. She wasn't that shocked by death. It all happened very suddenly. She doesn't suffer. But she knew she could see action over there. She would have preferred to come home, naturally, and so would you. But she says she knew there was that risk that she could be going over into a war. Anything is possible. . . . I'm sure you're not thrilled, but you are *very* angry over her death?"

"Yes!" Paul answered emphatically.

"Definitely!" Phyllis added.

"She knows in your heart you don't feel like someone during World War II [whose lost loved one was treated as a hero]. It's not that you want it, but there isn't the honor that goes with dying for your country. She knows both of you are kind of ticked off over this. It's a senseless death. She's caught. She's a humanitarian, and she's caught up in the peril of what's going on.

"But she asks the two of you not to be so teed off about it. Try to put it behind you, because she doesn't want you to be angry. This makes you miserable. Unfortunately, it's not going to bring her back. Someday you will see her again. Especially around this time of year—the holidays coming—it gets very hard. She's not here. The anniversary of her passing; then, too. A part of you feels, from your upbringing, that it is kind of honorable when someone passed on fighting for their country. Yet you'd rather have your daughter back. She says it's okay to feel like that. It's like the movie *For the Boys,* with Bette Midler: Her son gets killed in the war. There's that scene where she says to her husband, 'Honor my country.' She spits, 'I want my son back!' Your daughter was giving me the same feeling; showing me that scene.

"You feel that way, but you don't *want* to feel that way. You're kind of caught in a taffy pull between the two extremes of feelings. Your daughter says it's okay. You're allowed to feel that, 'I want my daughter back, and her death was in vain.' ''

"Right."

"You wouldn't push her around, but she is basically a peaceful person. She says it's rather sad that in 1992 people in this world still don't all get along. Your daughter says that over there [on the other side], there is no sense of struggle or harm, unless you choose to put yourself out of harmony. Then you have no place over there," George said.

He continued. "She says that you were always praying for her protection, and you kind of feel let down."

"Right."

"She says that unfortunately it was an accident. [Again] she was in the wrong place at the wrong time."

The couple nodded.

"Does the name Katherine mean anything at all?" George asked.

"Yes," said Paul.

"Passed on?"

"No," Phyllis answered.

"Your daughter knows her."

"Yes."

"She's asking how Katherine is. So I take it that everything is all right with her. There must have been a lot of people who prayed for your daughter."

"Yes," Phyllis acknowledged, "there are so many people."

"You are Catholics," George said.

"Yes."

"She's thanking everyone for all the prayers and memorials. She's more delighted for the support her family has been shown.

"Was she in the army?" George asked.

"Yes," she said.

"The Army Reserves."

"Yes."

"She didn't sound very happy when I said 'Army Reserves.' She kind of looked at me; I see her switching uniforms. She salutes you, and she goes into a nurse's or medics-like uniform," George explained.

"Also, her life was coming into focus. Don't feel she's been cut down in her prime, because her life will continue to go on in the hereafter. She still continues her medical-like work over there—but spiritually, since it's not in the physical sense. So she says she is still going on with her work in the hereafter.

"The [pet] cat is with her, and she's there with family. Again, she's a very adaptable girl. It's funny—she doesn't cry over spilled milk. She's kind of trapped, and there's nothing she can do about it. [Her attitude is] 'I've got to move on.' She's very confident, adaptable, and she's going on with her life. But, on the other hand, she doesn't want either of you or the family to think that just because she's moving on with her life that she doesn't know what you're going through.

"As for your daughter, she's gone through the experience of walking from one door to the next—to the hereafter. For her, it's over with. But you're in the shadow [of her passing], and she knows how much you love her, and how much you grieve over this. She says, 'Please just think that someday you will see me again. We will be together.' . . . She says her grandmothers were there when she came over, so she didn't die alone. Again, what makes it worse was that she was so far away from home."

The couple nodded.

George continued. "Were you saying the rosary for her?"

"Yes," Phyllis replied.

"Because she shows me white rosary beads, and she thanks you for it. And she asks that it please continue. She wants you to know that you're not wasting your time. You both have devotion to the Blessed Mother. And remember, *she* lost a son, too. So basically, they know how you feel," George said.

"Your daughter was really anxious to be discerned, to tell you and your family that she's all right. Spiritually, she's herself again. She's back to her old self; the person that you knew. Maybe not as stubborn! She's learning to be more flexible. She's learning because she's working with young people in the hereafter. She works in what [we would think of as] a hospital. But over there it's a *spiritual* establishment.

"When you think of the loss—of the tragedy—think of

what you heard her say today," George said.

"Okay."

"Is there a Paul?"

"I'm Paul."

"I heard 'Paul.' It could be your daughter calling out to you. But it also seems like it's somebody else who'd passed over [calling out]," George explained. "Did others get killed in the battle with your daughter?"

"Yes," he said.

"Did she make the choice to go? She says, 'I can't blame anybody but myself. This is what I wanted to do,' " George said.

"Yes."

"Do you belong to a support group?" he asked.

"We've been thinking about it," Phyllis answered.

"The only reason why she suggests it is because you need to be with someone who knows exactly how you feel; not to hear other people's horror stories. Because there are a lot of emotions that are being held in. And you don't know how to express it. She says up ahead you may want to consider a support group."

"Okay."

"It's not that anything is wrong with you. But you can get a lot of the anxiety and bitterness out. She extends pink roses to you as a spiritual blessing, and this is also done in love. If anything, know that she is all right. Again, it's like getting a long-distance call from your daughter in another country. She says tell the family that you've heard from her and know that she's all right and at peace. Until we meet again. She sends her love. And they're going back now," George said, concluding the reading.

As of this writing, the army still has not reversed its position on who is to blame for Cindy Beaudoin's death. In March 1992 she along with ten other members of the 142nd Medical Company were titled for wrongful possession of battlefield souvenirs.

8

"Don't Worry, I'm Not Alone"

═══════════

After a child has passed from this existence to the next, even survivors who have a strong faith in an afterlife worry that the child may be alone. This concern is particularly acute in mothers and fathers. Much of a parent's anguish in grief results from the sudden feeling of impotence, of being unable to do anything for their lost child.

Bereavement counselor Mary O'Shaughnessy described the reaction that she often sees in fathers of children who died young: "They feel that the children are out there looking for them to protect them, somehow. And the fathers can't get to them. That's a major frustration."

As we saw in the earlier reading for Travis Elwell's family, the need to ensure a child's safety—wherever he is—can be overwhelming. Travis's friend's father committed suicide to be with his son; Rebecca, the young woman whose suicide followed her father's, also sought to be with her deceased loved one again.

While a reading with George can provide loved ones with the comfort of knowing that the deceased child is at peace, some still worry that they are lonely on the other side. But as George has described in countless readings, there is a sense of community on the other side that bridges from this world to the next and back again. Culturally we are conditioned to think of death as a lonely experience. For those who are deeply religious, there is the concept of being completely alone in one's moment of judgment. For others, the loneliness is believed to derive from the deceased's lack of contact with us. But, again, as George has shown, that is not what it's like at all.

What follow are five cases, each completely different from the others but in two respects. First, all the deceased passed as children. Second, and most important, they come through in their readings to illuminate and explain why no one we love is ever alone on the other side.

The family of someone who dies from a painful disease or disability is often understandably concerned with whether the physical suffering endured here continues on the other side. Since, as George explained, the suffering is physical, it dies with the physical body. There are illnesses and physical problems that entail a kind of suffering and pain that goes beyond the physical. AIDS is clearly one of those diseases. Today, over a decade since this killer became a household word, AIDS remains misunderstood and feared. The result is that sometimes even good people succumb to ignorance and fear, shunning AIDS sufferers at the time they most need support and compassion.

Stan and his wife, June, were the parents of two children, Allison, born in 1972, and her little brother Richie, who arrived three years later.* Their home, in the Southwest, was a sprawling ranch-style within driving distance of camping and fishing grounds and a beautiful mountain range. Richie lived for the outdoors and had many friends. He was your typical happy little boy.

One rainy Saturday when Richie was eight years old, he and a group of classmates were being driven to a local theater to see a movie. Suddenly the driver, one of the other

---

*At the request of the subjects, names and other biographical details and facts pertaining to their case have been altered to protect their identities. Everything else in this story, however, is true.

boys' father, swerved to miss an oncoming car. The car skidded across the highway then crashed into a utility pole. Miraculously no one was killed, but the driver, his son, and Richie were critically injured.

For several excruciating days Richie lay in the intensive care unit in critical condition. Due to massive internal and external injuries, he underwent emergency surgery and received blood transfusions. Within a month, however, he began to recuperate. He still bore some bruises and remained bandaged where he had received the worst injuries, in his chest and head, but the doctors assured Stan and June that Richie's injuries and his broken arm would heal without any permanent damage.

Stan and June, sensitive to Richie's emotional well-being, made a point of explaining to him that the trauma he'd experienced was simply an accident, "something that happens when we don't expect it to, something that is no one's fault." A few months later, his arm still in a cast, Richie was begging his parents to let him play softball, go camping, ride his bike, even climb mountains. When his parents told him that the doctor wanted him to wait until he got a little bit better, Richie would jump in frustration and ask, "Why not? I feel better now!" From all indications, Richie was well on his way to putting the accident behind him.

Stan, June, Allison, and Richie felt their lives return to normal. All seemed well until April 1984, the unseasonably chilly and damp spring following the car crash. Richie developed a cold and flulike symptoms that he just didn't seem able to shake. June surmised the bad weather was to blame, along with the fact that many of Richie's schoolmates were coming to class ill. When his fever and fatigue persisted despite a course of antibiotics, June began to worry. Finally, when he began to wake up each morning with his pajamas soaked in perspiration, she became alarmed, certain that he had contracted pneumonia. An X ray confirmed her diagnosis.

Richie began taking even stronger antibiotics, but June and Stan saw no improvement. He still seemed exhausted and, if anything, worse than before. He also looked thinner. Richie's doctor admitted him to the hospital for a round of diagnostic tests. Several days later he called Stan and June into his office to tell them what he had found. Little Richie had AIDS.

AIDS, acquired immune deficiency syndrome, is an as yet incurable disease that cripples and eventually decimates the human immune system. The human immunodeficiency virus, which is believed to cause AIDS, is transmitted a number of ways, all involving direct contact or exchange of virus-bearing body fluids. These include sexual contact, contaminated needles and surgical equipment, and blood-product transfusions.

Today the U.S. blood supply is automatically screened for the HIV virus, among other pathogens. However, because the test used identifies not the HIV virus itself but the body's antibodies to it, it is possible that blood from someone who was HIV-positive but donated before his body had produced antibodies to the virus might slip through. Experts claim the chances of that happening are quite small. But at the time of Richie's accident, the HIV screening was not yet in place, and he, along with many others, contracted the HIV virus through contaminated blood products. Today there are an estimated four thousand children under the age of thirteen who have AIDS; most contracted it from their mothers at birth or through breast-feeding.

"Our lives turned upside down," June recalled. "It seemed inconceivable," Stan added. "If you can imagine being hit by a lightning bolt. That's what we felt like. Remember, this was 1984. There was even less knowledge then about how AIDS was transmitted. People thought you could catch AIDS from casual contact, that it was easily contagious. Of course, it isn't. So in addition to fighting for Richie's life, we felt we had to fight ignorance and fear wherever we turned."

"We just didn't bring it up in public to others," June said. "There was really very little in the media about AIDS that helped us at the time he got sick. There were so many misconceptions.''

''We had our share of problems sending him to school,'' Stan said. ''We live in what I like to think of as a fairly enlightened community, but the fear and the stigma about AIDS were just unbelievable! It was like we were under some kind of emotional siege.''

''I remember once when someone in the neighborhood, who knew Richie was sick, asked how he was. My whole body tightened,'' June said, recalling the moment. ''If anyone asked for details, we'd say Richie had leukemia. But the thing was not to discuss it at all with anyone else, if possible. We had no idea how long he'd live.

''Then we had to explain to him what he had. How do you tell a nine-year-old that he has AIDS? The answer is, with great difficulty,'' she continued. ''He was a bright little boy. We told him that he'd gotten sick from the blood he received after the car accident. A lot of people don't understand it, though, so don't talk about it to anyone else, so we don't frighten them. Was that the best thing to tell him? Who knows.''

''Unfortunately,'' Stan said, ''that was reality in 1984.''

''So we taught him to do what he had to do to deal with it. And we explained to our daughter as well. So she'd be as ready as possible for any questions or hostility,'' June said.

''I think the worst was when Richie asked us, 'Am I going to get better?' '' Stan recalled sadly. ''We told him there are always new medicines being made to make you feel better. I mean, what else could we say? We told him not to worry about that. The doctors would do the work.''

Richie returned to school. ''I wouldn't say he was warmly welcomed,'' June said. ''But it wasn't with the hostility we'd heard from stories about kids with AIDS in some other parts of the country, where parents and children were forced out of the community.

''Richie was really more isolated from his peers than he'd ever been. That was hard on him. And some parents and other adults, they avoided us like the plague.

"Our other frustration was having no one to really talk to about it. Back in 1984 and 1985, people who didn't know any better were calling it 'the gay disease.' Of course, it wasn't. But we always feared anti-gay bigotry and remarks would be directed at Richie. I think I would have cracked if that had happened."

Richie's family was fairly successful at keeping his true diagnosis a secret. They took care of him at home and reminded him to be careful when he was out playing. "We didn't want him to feel like an invalid. We wanted him to be able to do things normally for as long as he could," June said. "But, remember, we couldn't be public about him being sick. We were coping with a whole range of things: the medical [aspect], the costs, the stigma, the psychological part. But you face all these battles. The most important one was to keep Richie alive and well as long as possible. You feel like you're fighting not just the disease—which is terrible enough—but also neighbors, school, relatives, hospitals, doctors.

"I know there were some people in town saying that their kids could catch AIDS from being in the same room with Richie! I think there were a few people who would have branded an *A* on his forehead. I'll never forget that."

"Thank God we never got threatening letters or obscene phone calls," Stan added. "I heard that happened elsewhere."

Despite a couple of setbacks, Richie's health remained fairly stable over the next few years. By 1989, when Richie was fourteen, his condition began to deteriorate. The HIV virus attacks the immune cells, which gradually, then sharply, decrease in number. As the number of active immune cells drop, the incidence and severity of infection increases until the body is left entirely defenseless. That September Richie was admitted to the hospital complaining of fatigue, myriad respiratory problems, and fevers. The following January his parents were at his bedside when he died.

"We knew he was going to die," June said. "But Richie's death was still a shock. I guess you're never prepared, even when you know it's going to happen. Richie was so brave. He never let anything get him down, even though he had no more close friends. The other kids stayed away.

"One thing that makes this so different," she continued, "is that you know your child is going to die. I mean, we all leave this earth eventually, but you can't look at a child with AIDS and think about a future. He's never going to be an adult, or go to college, or have kids of his own."

Stan's and June's feelings of isolation and betrayal did not die with Richie. "People offered us their condolences. Where were they when we could have used support and friendship? I wanted to scream, 'You're too late!' Why did everyone shun us and Richie like we were lepers? I think that, and then I also wonder if maybe we could have educated others about being the parents of a child with AIDS I don't know."

"We're really not religious, so that, frankly, was not something we could turn to in coping with our grief," Stan said. "I guess you'd call us nominal Protestants, but we don't attend church on a regular basis. Before Richie died, we gave no thought to an afterlife, one way or the other."

"But now it's different," June said. "I mean, my son is here and then he's not here. So where is he now? I needed to know. What purpose is there in a child suffering like this? Why did this happen?"

"Some of the religious attitudes toward AIDS honestly disturbed me," her husband offered. "I mean, is there a different heaven for gay people with AIDS or for people who get it from drugs or sex, and then a different one for kids who get AIDS from bad blood or some 'accepted' way? Does God divide them up in heaven? I can't accept that!"

One day June was browsing in a bookstore when she came across a book about George Anderson. After reading it, she and Stan decided to travel several thousand miles to see him. The idea that Richie's life on the other side might be as lonely and isolating as it had been here gnawed at them. Were things different for him there? Was he happy?

Was he being ostracized because he had died of AIDS? Or was he welcomed there and loved? Richie's parents had to know.

"A male passed," George said to the couple.

"Yes," June and Stan replied.

"He's a young male."

"Yes," they answered.

"He's family to you—by blood."

"Yes."

"There's an older male, too, who's passed."

"Yes."

"He points to you," George said, indicating Stan.

"Yes," he replied.

"It's your dad who passed."

"Yes."

"Your grandparents passed."

"Mine have," he said.

"Three of them have passed," June added. "I have a grandmother who's still alive."

"Okay. The young male says, 'I'm the son.' It's your son."

"Yes."

"He knew he'd pass?"

"I think so," Stan said.

"Because he says he's not shocked by death."

"Oh!" June exclaimed.

"He passed in his sleep. He goes off into a coma," George said.

"Yes."

"He says he has a happy, peaceful death. He says it's like he went from one room to another. Then, he says, he was instantly free from pain and suffering once he was out of the physical body."

Richie's parents nodded.

"He thanks you for being good to him prior to his passing," George continued.

"Yes," both answered.

"Your son says you were always there for him."

"Yes, I tried. *We* tried," June said. "I hope so."

"He has health trouble. That's what he passes from."

"Yes."

"It comes upon him suddenly."

"You could say that," Stan answered.

"He's very courageous here. He tries to hang in," George said.

"Yes."

"You were with him at the end."

"Yes."

"He keeps thanking you for that. He knows you were there—even if you didn't think he knew."

"Good. I'm glad," June said.

"Was he very energetic? I feel like there's a lot of energy. It seems like he was on the go—always doing things—or wanting to. He's very active."

"Yes," Stan said.

"He says he has a rough time prior to his passing. . . . He goes through suffering here."

"Yes."

"But he's not in any pain or suffering now. He emphasizes that. He doesn't want you to worry about that. 'Don't worry, I'm content and at peace,' he says."

"Good," June replied.

"He's back to his old self. . . . There's no more suffering, he says again. But he sees you grieving for him. He sees your pain now. He wants to see you happy. It seems like he was happy when he was here."

"Yes."

"Your father passes before your son," George said to Stan.

"Yes," he replied.

"Because he says your dad was one of the first to welcome him into the light. . . . Also your grandparents were there for him," George remarked to June.

"They didn't know him. The three of them passed before my son was born," she replied.

"Oh, that wouldn't matter. They know him now."

"Right."

"Now, I know you acknowledged that your son passed from a health problem, but why does he also say his passing was accidental?"

"No."

"He says, 'health' and then he says, 'accident.' He shows the symbol for an accident."

"No."

"Then why does he show me a vehicle accident?" asked George.

"Oh, yes! Yes! I understand," June said.

"That's why he shows me a double symbol. First he said health. Then he said accident."

"Yes, that's right," Stan confirmed.

"How can it be both?" George wondered aloud.

"Should we tell you?"

"No. No. Let him do the work. They have to be the ones who tell me."

"Okay."

"Wait. Is there trouble with the blood?"

"Yes."

"Does he have trouble breathing? Because I [psychically] feel there's definitely something in the chest area."

"Yes."

"It feels like there's something there like congestion. I feel like I can't catch my breath," George explained.

"Yes," Stan answered.

"And did he get headaches? There's pressure on or in the brain."

"Yes."

"I see blood cells going crazy. It's in the blood."

"Yes."

"The illness affects him all over, like cancer."

"Yes."

"It's my symbol for leukemia or AIDS. But he says it's AIDS."

"Yes," June answered.

"He doesn't pass long ago."

"Right."

"Within the past couple of years."

"Yes."

"Because your son gives me the feeling he just got there. It's as if he's recently arrived in another country. And again, he says he's back to his old self."

June nodded and began crying. Stan reached out and took her hand.

"Do you take the name Alan?"

"No," June said.

"There's no Alan?"

"Not that I can think of," June answered as she regained her composure.

"Is there an Alice?"

"No."

"No Alan? No Alice?" George asked again.

"Oh, yes! I think I know what you mean," Stan said.

"Which one?"

"Could it be Allison?" he asked George.

"I'll accept that if he can tell me who it is."

"Okay."

"It's a young female. He calls to a sister. Is that her?"

"Yes."

"It's your daughter. His sister."

"Yes," June answered.

"She's living."

"Oh, yes."

"Counting him, you have three children?"

"No."

"Two, counting him?"

"Yes."

"Wait. Did you lose another child?"

"No."

"Did you ever miscarry?"

"Yes."

"Because your son says a young female is with him. A miscarriage. That's why I said three children. Your daughter here; your son and the young female with him. It would have been a girl if the cycle of birth had continued," George offered.

"I don't know," June replied.

"But they're together now."

"Your son is calling to Allison. 'Tell her you've heard from me.' She's older than he is."

"Yes."

"Because he keeps talking about his 'big sister.' Did he ever call her Allie, or something like that?"

"Yes. When he was little he couldn't say Allison. So he called her Allie," June explained.

"That's why I thought I heard 'Al' or 'Alan.' Then I thought he was saying 'Alice,' when it was 'Allie' or 'Allison.' "

"Right."

"They were close. Let me put it this way: They were getting closer as brother and sister."

"Yes."

"He wants her to know that he sends his love to her. Tell her he's all right. It seems she takes his passing badly, also."

"Yes," June replied.

"Your son says he's around her like a guardian angel. He jokes, 'Tell her you can't get rid of me that easily.' Did an accident have something to do with him getting AIDS?"

"Yes."

"That's what he means! He was too insistent. He keeps telling me there's a connection. The two—health and accident—are related."

"Yes."

"Was it a vehicle accident?"

"Yes."

"But that's not what kills him."

"No," Stan answered.

"He says the vehicle accident does not kill him. He survives that. I've got to figure this out. I wish he'd just tell me. Wait. Oh, that's what it is. He says he got AIDS as a result of the vehicle accident," George said.

"In a way."

"I'm [psychically] seeing a blood transfusion," George said.

"Yes."

"But there's an X over it. Was he given AIDS-contaminated blood?"

"Yes," June said, crying again.

"That's what he says. He's given 'bad blood.' As a result of the accident he gets a blood transfusion."

"Yes."

"Then as a result of that bad blood—as he calls it—he contracts the AIDS virus."

"Yes."

"So that's where the link is."

"Yes."

"He thanks you for being there for him. He admits he went through quite an ordeal. But you both made it much easier for him. You were always there to care for him. And he says you were understanding and patient. Without the both of you, it would have been much harder. Besides the illness, emotionally it would have been even rougher."

Both Stan and June were now crying.

"Was your son being ostracized or alienated by friends, especially toward the end?"

"Yes," June answered.

"Because he shows me hands pushing someone back to avoid someone. They don't want to be around him because he's got AIDS."

"Yes."

"He's a child when he gets AIDS?"

"Yes."

"Because I feel that he's treated that way in school. With friends his own age. Even adults kind of avoid him."

"Yes."

"People can be cruel," George remarked.

"Yes, we found that out," Stan said.

"True. But your son doesn't seem to carry a grudge. It's like he knows he has to move on [in the hereafter]. 'What's the point? I can't change anything now,' he says. 'Since I can't go backward, I've got to go forward.' He knows that attitudes in this dimension can be narrow-minded or clouded with ignorance, fear, and bigotry. But in the hereafter they don't judge that way. The fear and ignorance don't exist like they do here. So he says, 'Don't worry. I'm not being pushed away by anyone here.' In the hereafter he doesn't struggle with those attitudes from others.''

"George, can I ask you a question about that?" June inquired.

"Sure."

"Why is it that on the other side they seem more enlightened than we do on earth?"

"Well, fear, bigotry—those are negative feelings here on earth. Those are not emotions that are carried to the hereafter. Negativity, as we'd understand it here, is not recognized in the next stage. It's discouraged there."

"Thank you," June said.

"But, he says, what's important is that you were here for him. You never cast him aside. You were there with unconditional love. That's what he remembers and that's what mattered most to him. Your son says, 'Don't have any guilt. What happened was not your doing or your fault.'

"Are you planning more children in the future?" George asked.

"No," they answered.

"I saw Saint Philomena appear. It could be news of a future birth."

"Could it be someone else in the family?" June asked.

"Someone close to you? Sure," George replied.

"My sister is expecting. She's my younger sister," June explained.

"Okay. Because your son definitely gave me the feeling that there's a birth coming up, and it's around you. Do you take the name Al or Alan? I know I asked that before, but it comes back."

"No."

"Al? Albert? Alex?"

"Yes!" Stan exclaimed.

"It's Alex," George said.

"Right."

"He's with your son. He says he knows him. They're together. He's a father figure. Your dad?"

"That's my dad," Stan confirmed.

"Your son says it's his grandfather. He says, 'Grandpa is here with me.'"

"Right."

"Is there a Rose?"

"Yes."

"Passed on."

"Yes."

"She's an aunt?"

"Yes, a very close one," June answered.

"She's there with your son, too," George said.

"Okay."

"There's a Ted or Ed? I think it's Ted I'm hearing."

"Yes."

"Passed."

"Yes."

"He seems more of a friend."

"Yes," Stan said.

"He passes tragically. Suddenly."

"Yes."

"Not that long ago."

"Correct. Within the past year," Stan explained.

"He just wants to let you all know he's okay. He comes in like a good friend. A real pal."

"Yes, he was."

"Is there a Jack?"

"Yes. That's my brother."

"He's living?"

"Yes."

"But there's a distance between the two of you. Either physically or emotionally. I feel like he's away."

"Right."

"It's more of an emotional distancing."

"Yes."

"There's definitely a lack of communication between you two."

"Oh, yes."

"But your dad says, 'What else is new?' I'm not telling you anything you don't know."

"Right."

"Your son says there were some in the family who kept their distance when he became sick."

"Yes."

"It's as if you tried to keep your son's illness quiet. But someone in the family either knows or learns about it. Then some of the others act as if they could catch AIDS. So the fear and ignorance keep them away," George said.

"Yes."

"It's like these people create their own demons."

"Exactly," June responded.

"So, your son says, a lot of family and friends—or those you *thought* were friends—weren't there for you at the time."

"Right."

"But your son says it wasn't because they purposely wanted to be mean to him. It was more out of fear and ignorance, as he said before." George paused. "Do you take the name Ada or Ida?"

"Ida, yes," June answered.

"I feel like I go back a long time," George said.

"Yes, it's an aunt of mine who passed a long time ago."

"She's there, too. There's certainly no lack of loved ones with him. They definitely don't push him away, as some did here. So be happy for that."

"Okay."

"He's bright for his age. But he's a bundle of energy."

"Yes," June answered, smiling.

"He says we have a lot to learn on earth about how we treat each other."

"Yes!"

"But he also says don't dwell on the negativity of that. Be happy that he progresses [on the other side]. Even though you miss him here, and you'd much rather have him with you in the physical body. Since that can't be, you must go on here, just as he must there.

"He calls to his grandparents still on earth. There are three living."

"Yes," June replied.

"There's one he was closer with," George said.

"Yes, my mother," she said.

"She was there for him when he was ill, he says. She never turned her back."

"No, she didn't."

"He sends his love to her. 'Tell Grandma you've heard from me,' he says."

"Okay."

"Is there concern around her health?"

"Yes."

"Your dad, too."

"Yes," June said, beginning to cry again.

"Well, there's nothing I can tell you that you don't already know."

"Right."

"Is there an *R* in your son's [first] name?"

"Yes."

"I just [psychically] saw the letter *R* in front of me," George explained. "Is it Richard?"

"Yes!" Stan responded.

"Because I just saw [the character] from history—Richard the Lionhearted. Wasn't he the King of England around the time when Robin Hood was supposed to have lived? I think he's showing me a double symbol: that he went through [his illness] suffering in silence and was brave during the ordeal. And also as a symbol for his name."

"Yes, he was brave," June said.

"He's called by a nickname."

"Yes."

"It's a shortened version of his full name, Richard. He's called Rich?"

"Richie," Stan corrected.

"He says he comes to you in dreams."

"Yes, often," June answered.

"That helps you in your grief."

"Yes."

"That's how he can reach out when you're relaxed or in the altered state," George explained.

"Yes."

"But you have also been having anxiety-like dreams?"

"Yes."

"That wasn't your son. It was a manifestation of your own fears coming out in your sleep. Rich—Richie—says, 'Don't worry, people with AIDS aren't punished [in the hereafter]. They don't go to hell.' He says he's met others [who've passed] from AIDS. 'They got it all different ways,' he says. 'What's the difference now?' is their attitude. He says he's met other kids who've passed from AIDS, too. They don't ask, 'How did you get AIDS?' They don't care. It's not important how it happened. So in the next stage they don't do what we do here and discriminate. There's definitely no stigma about AIDS in the hereafter."

"That's good," June said.

"Have you memorialized him?"

"Yes," Stan replied.

"It's something in print. It's something that is written."

"Yes."

"There was a book and memorial about children with AIDS that his name was in," June offered.

"Now he's wrapping his sister in a blanket of pink roses. It's a greeting and a blessing. It's to thank her too for being good to him. Did he have the AIDS, or the HIV virus, for some length of time before he passed?"

"Yes."

"He says he was injured pretty seriously in the automobile accident."

"Yes."

"I [psychically] see medical tubes all over the place. Then he gets this bad blood, as he calls it. Then the AIDS shows up later on. He's sick for some time. He handles it bravely. He really hangs in there for as long as he can. He puts on a brave face. Then, finally, his lungs and breathing are affected. He goes into a sleep, like a coma. He keeps emphasizing that he's not suffering. He's fine and at peace.

"He definitely fought his illness," George continued as the couple wept. "But he admits he's glad the struggle over here is over. He didn't like the lingering. Did you lose a pet?"

"Yes. It was really his pet," June said.

"A dog."

"Yes."

"The dog was first to bark and welcome him. The dog woke him and then the others came to meet him and cross him over into the light. It's a big dog."

"Yes."

"Your son's a teenager."

"Yes."

"He shows me sixteen."

"Not quite."

"Would he be sixteen now?"

"Yes, just about."

"That's why he shows me sixteen. Obviously he's fifteen when he passes."

"Yes," Stan acknowledged.

"But he's younger than that when he becomes sick. He's less than ten."

"Yes. He was eight."

"He congratulates you on a new vehicle," George said to Stan.

Stan laughed softly. "Yes."

"Your son says, 'Way to go, Dad!' He says you needed it."

Stan just nodded and laughed.

"He wants you both to go on with your lives. He says since his passing, you've been in a standstill. It's a rut: work, sleep, eat. You've been unable to move beyond his passing."

"Yes."

"He keeps saying you must go on. You're not leaving him behind. He's still with you. He says you all could use a good vacation."

"Yes, I guess we could," Stan admitted.

"Well, go take it, he says. You need a rest. You're not responsible for his passing. He says you were good parents. He says, 'There are rumors about reincarnation here, and if they're true, I'll be back and pick you as my mom and dad again. But don't worry: I'm staying right here until you get here someday—so we can be together again.'"

Stan and June nodded, both wiping tears from their eyes.

"He says you keep asking why this happened. Like how could his passing have any meaning?"

"Yes," June said.

"Well, it's a question that can't be answered. There are reasons and lessons for everything. But we don't always know what they are. He says, 'Wouldn't you rather have had me for the time you did, than not at all?' "

"Of course!" June said.

"He says, 'My mission—my purpose on earth—was complete.' Did he play an instrument? I hear music."

"Well, he played a little guitar," June answered. "And he wanted to learn drums, but he was too sick by then," she added, her voice trailing off.

"He loved music," Stan said.

"Was he involved in sports? I see him in a uniform."

"Yes."

"Was he on a team, like in school?"

"No."

"He looks like [he's in] a baseball uniform. Little League?"

"Yes," Stan said.

"His room has everything in it. Posters, computer, audio, stereo. You've left it as it is."

"Yes," June said. "George, can I ask you one question?"

"Okay."

"What's my son doing now in the hereafter?"

"He says he works with other children and young people who cross over, similar to him. In other words, he works with children who've passed from AIDS. He helps them to adjust, to find themselves after they've made the transition."

"Thank you."

"Your son says you've been too lonely, too isolated. You haven't had real friends to talk to. And you've moved away from those you feel ignored or shunned you when he was ill."

"Yes."

"He says you need to talk. Are you going to a support group?"

"No."

"Thinking about it?"

"Not really."

"It's up to you, of course. But it wouldn't be a bad idea, he says."

"We've gone for some private therapy," June said.

"Well, he did emphasize group, to talk to others."

"Okay."

"Do you pray for him?"

"In our own way," Stan answered.

"That's the thing; you're spiritual, not religious."

"Right."

"He asks that you continue to pray for him in your own way. It's a help."

"Okay."

"He says stop being bitter. Let go of the bitterness. It's a negative emotion. He sees that you're depressed. It hurts him to see you living with the grief. . . . Stop torturing yourselves. There's nothing more you could do. You did everything parents could do. But you're going over and over in your minds, 'Why did this happen? How could this happen?' "

"Yes."

"He taught you about AIDS and love. By your example, you gave him love. Now, he says, you can teach others so the ignorance about AIDS can be erased. Someday the disease will be conquered or cured. But the discrimination and fear are enemies, too."

Stan and June nodded.

"Is there Michael, or Mike?"

"Yes."

"Living or passed?"

"Actually, both," Stan said.

"Because he says Mike is with him. He got in just under the wire! He comes in like an uncle," George said.

"Great-uncle, yes," Stan answered.

"And one is living, you said."

"Yes."

"Like a cousin or close friend."

"Yes, it's a cousin. They'd been friendly."

"He just says, 'Tell Mike you've heard from me.' "

"Okay."

"Is there any reason for concern around Mike?"

"I really don't know."

"Okay. I'll just let it go. Because he's withdrawing now. He and the others start to go back. Is your birthday coming up?" George asked June.

"Yes."

"Because he just handed you red roses. He says you like red roses best for your birthday."

"Yes, I love red roses," June answered, a smile on her lips.

"He keeps saying happy birthday."

"Yes. It's a few days from now. Next week," she explained.

"They're all withdrawing. They're going back now. He says, 'Remember what I've told you. Remember that we'll be together again. Tell my sister I love her.' Continue to pray. He's fine and at peace. He sends his love to all of you. And there he goes."

When a child dies, the dynamics of a family are changed forever. Bereavement experts often point out that survivors mourn not only the loss of that particular child but the myriad losses that follow: the funny way a little girl ate her spaghetti; how a teenage son sang his favorite rock song at the top of his lungs; the perfect bouquet of baby roses from a daughter on Mother's Day. The child who passed may have been the family clown, the one with a quip that took the edge off almost every family crisis. She may have been a conciliator, the peacemaker who brought everyone together. He may have been an only child, whose death suddenly makes his parents question whether they are still considered parents at all. No matter what role that child filled, death leaves a terrible void.

As George has learned from the other side, love transcends these two dimensions, as do our relationships. For the vast majority of bereaved parents who seek out George, their greatest tragedy is having lost a child. Rarely does he meet someone who has survived two children's passings.

In this extraordinary case, Bill and Mary Harrington lost five children (two to miscarriage) in twenty-five years. Their story demonstrates how attitudes toward the death of children have changed over the years and how despite at times of overwhelming grief, the bereaved can eventually endure and come to some acceptance. Especially important, however, it proves that families and family relationships continue on the other side, regardless of how well the children knew one another over here.

Baby Robert Harrington was born in September 1964, the fifth of Mary and Bill's children. They had recently moved from the New York City area to Sheboygan, Wisconsin, where Bill accepted a job as a chemist. The Harringtons were alone for Thanksgiving, miles from family and friends. New friends had invited them for the holiday dinner, and they returned home that night and got their children ready for bed.

Mary bathed, dressed, and nursed two-month-old Robert after the other four were put to bed. A little after midnight Mary took Robert upstairs to her and Bill's bedroom, where she put him down in his crib.

The next morning the kids were all home from school and anxious to watch television. The Harringtons had a rule that the children were not allowed in the recreation room, where the TV was, until Mom or Dad was up. Eight-year-old Billy, anxious to get going, ran into the room yelling, "Daddy! Daddy! It's seven forty-one, and you'd better get up and go to work!"

Bill sat up, casually glancing over at the crib. "Mary! Mary!" he screamed. "The baby!"

"What's wrong?" she cried, trying to wake up.

"That baby's not breathing!" Bill had barely finished the sentence before he had crossed the room, picked up Robert's lifeless body, and begun administering CPR. Mary grabbed a phone and screamed to the operator, "Help! My baby's not breathing!"

Within minutes the police and an ambulance had arrived, and Robert was rushed to a hospital, where he was pronounced dead on arrival. When Mary and Bill got to the hospital, they were met by a nun, who asked Mary if they wanted to see the baby one more time. They said yes.

The Harringtons said they will never forget seeing Robert lying on a table, still. It was a terrible yet precious moment, ruined by the nun's suddenly asking Mary in an accusing tone, "Didn't you know the baby was sick?"

"He wasn't sick!" Mary answered, shocked.

"Well, the baby had loose stool," the nun retorted self-righteously.

"I'm a nursing mother," Mary replied while thinking, *I am also the mother of four other children. I know if a baby is sick.* "A lot of nursing babies have loose stool."

The nun was not swayed. Mary and Bill turned to look again at their child, when the nun thrust a small plastic bag containing Robert's soiled diaper into Mary's hand.

This ugly incident angered and disturbed the Harringtons. Mary cried hysterically while she and Bill waited for their family physician to arrive. They learned that Robert had died of SIDS. The autopsy revealed that his adrenal system had collapsed and that kidney failure, blood poisoning, and finally heart failure followed. The doctor told the Harringtons that the baby must have had a fever, but Mary, who had worked as an infant and child care technician at a New York hospital, did not notice anything amiss. In the end, what did it matter? Robert was gone.

Bill and Mary felt more alone than ever. But as news of the baby's death spread through their new community, neighbors and friends came forward to offer sympathy and support.

Although Mary's doctor advised her not to have another baby right away, she became pregnant and suffered a miscarriage just three months after Robert's death. She had lost another baby to miscarriage in early 1963 following the birth of her daughter Judy. In 1966 the Harringtons became the parents of a fourth daughter, Christine, and two years later Timothy was born.

For Bill and Mary, life with their six children continued happily. But in the eighties tragedy struck twice. In 1982 twenty-five-year-old Billy died in a boating accident and was buried the Saturday before Palm Sunday. Then, only four years later, their daughter Judy died of asthma shortly after Christmas. Though she had suffered numerous attacks since the age of nine, Judy suffered a final, fatal attack and died at age twenty-four.

Mary took Judy's death especially hard. They were closer than mother and daughter, and had grown to be friends as well. When Billy died, Mary found herself depending more on Judy for support. Now she was gone.

Mary and Bill's marriage, which had endured earlier tragedies unscathed, began to unravel. Mary was prescribed tranquilizers to quell the unbearable pain. They barely had time to grieve when Billy passed on. Eventually Mary stopped taking tranquilizers and she and Bill both joined the Compassionate Friends. Mary also takes great comfort in prayer. With five of nine children now on the other side, Mary accepts one friend referring to her as "the sorrowful mother."

In this excerpt from their extraordinary and complex reading, Baby Robert comes through although, understandably, with less to say than Billy and Judy, who passed as young adults. Billy came through first, followed by Robert, then Judy. Interestingly, the two miscarried babies seem not to come through. Clearly, George was having trouble fathoming how one mother could have suffered so many losses, and, as we have seen in earlier readings, he is the first to admit that logical thinking sometimes hampers his ability to understand every psychic message he receives. It's possible that the miscarried children were there and present but that George did not discern them or could not distinguish them from the other children.

"Do you take the name Bob, Robert?" George asked Mary.
    "Yes."

"Passed on."

"Yes."

"Robert is there—"

"Yes."

"This Robert is another boy of yours. He passes on as an infant; a baby."

"Yes."

"Remember before [earlier in the reading] I kept saying you have four children [still living on earth]. Because he's talking about his brothers and sisters. He keeps telling me that he has brothers and sisters. Because he's calling out to his brothers and sisters," George explained.

"Yes," she acknowledged.

"Definitely less than two years old."

"Yes."

"Obviously you never got a chance to really know him. But from the other side he's gotten the chance to know you. He's very loving and protective around you. Everything I've said [thus far in the reading] makes sense, he tells me. Because now he would be grown up. But he states he's always been around you like a guardian angel.

"It was really your first heartache. Now your other son [Billy] who's passed on tells me why I kept getting mixed up; why I kept hearing [him] telling me [about] brothers and sisters. But he [Billy] says Bob—Robert—welcomed him into the light. Not only like his brother but also because he was always there for you as well.

"Again, be at peace about the loss. You've lost two boys. Wait. More? God! Because he talks about losing another child!" George exclaimed.

"Yes," Mary said.

"And I didn't believe him. Because, again, your son Robert is saying to be at peace about the loss of your children. You keep feeling like you struck out."

Mary began to cry.

"Because you've lost so many children. Your son talks, again, about another loss. Wait a minute. Did you lose a girl?"

"Yes."

"That's it, because he's talking about a sister. And I said, 'Wait a minute. Are you calling to a sister?' You also have a daughter living."

"Yes," Mary said, referring to Christine.

"Okay. That's what's confusing me. At the beginning of the reading, too, I heard somebody claim they were your son, and I heard somebody claim 'sister,' also. I kind of blocked it out."

Mary listened quietly.

"Was your daughter grown-up?"

"Yes."

"When your son started talking, he said a sister is with him, also. Did she also pass before him? Oh, wait. He's there first, because they're talking about the two of them together passed on. So apparently she goes after him. She's the more recent passing."

"Yes."

"She also passes tragically."

"Yes," Mary said, weeping.

"She says Robert crossed her over, also. Robert and your other son [Billy] were there, she says. Gee, I've got to listen so carefully. When I started tuning in on you, I heard somebody claim you lost a daughter and you lost a son. I clearly remember somebody saying, 'daughter,' but your son overpowered her. I figured I probably misunderstood something. You and she very close."

"Yes."

"Because you're not only mother and daughter, but you're the best of pals."

"Yes."

"Your daughter says that she kind of has a crazy sense of humor. Because she's busting my chops. She says, 'I've been here. I came into the room at the start [of the reading],' but I [George] kept mixing it up. She says her brother kept talking over her."

Mary nodded and smiled.

"She [Judy] says he was driving her crazy because she was afraid you were thinking she wasn't here. She says,

'I've been here since it [the reading] started.' She's kind of bawling me out!''

"She would."

"I heard somebody back there complaining they weren't getting their turn. She kept saying, 'Why don't you let me talk? Don't you know there are other people here? It's my turn, too, you know.' She passed tragically."

"Yes."

"Not that we're playing 'favorite child' here, but it seems the two boys' [deaths] were bad enough. But her passing—your daughter's passing—almost put you over the edge. I mean, you had been through it two times before, and now the daughter you had such a great friendship with as well as relationship . . . she says this is enough to drive you to drink."

Mary began to cry again.

"Again, this is not a feeling of favoritism. She knows your heart is most broken over her passing. Losing the boys was bad enough. But you really miss her. Because she was not only a daughter but, again, she was a tremendous support to you emotionally. So, again, it's like you lost your best friend. She says she was there for you when your son [Billy] passed on."

"Yes."

"You've done some heavy agonizing to yourself. Like, Did you do something to deserve this? Your daughter keeps saying that you did nothing wrong. You have *not* failed as a mother. You haven't done anything to deserve this type of suffering. So she says don't dwell on that negativity—like your son said before. Your daughter passes accidentally."

"No."

"Very suddenly, then."

"Yes."

"She has health trouble."

"Yes."

"She knew she was going to go. She basically figured that. She subconsciously knew she was going to pass on. But it happens very suddenly."

"Yes."

"There's a flock of people around you, and they're all talking at once! It's like being in a crowd, and everybody's like trying to get their two cents in, and I'm trying to figure it out. But your daughter says, again, don't feel you let her down. [She says,] 'How could you have known I was sick?' She keeps saying you're not infallible.

"So her death haunts you the most, because you feel you could have prevented it."

"Yes."

"That's why you're most brokenhearted over her passing. She says you could *not* have prevented it. She says it's hard to accept, but it was her time to let go. That's why she knew subconsciously that it was her time to pass. You've had dreams of her, also."

"Yes."

"She extends white lilies to you to let you know she's all right and at peace. She shows me a vision of Saint Joseph, which means a happy passing. You were not with her when she passed."

"Not at that moment."

"Because that drives you crazy. She keeps bringing that up. You feel you let her down. You were always there for each other, and then she passes so suddenly in a sleeplike state, and you feel you're not there for her. She lose her air all of a sudden?"

"Yes."

"I keep feeling I'm—it's almost like having a heart attack!"

"Yes."

"But it's from a lack of oxygen in the chest. She passes from a physical problem."

"Yes."

"It affects her heart. It's like she's having a heart attack. That's the best way I can describe what I'm feeling. But there's a closing-up of the lungs."

"Yes."

"She insists it's like going into a form of shock from [this condition]. It's almost like you were just starting to deal with your son, and then *this* happened and set you right back again.

"She's trying to reach out to you to put you at peace. You did *not* fail her. She's in the hospital on some sort of life support. She's hooked up to something, obviously."

"Yes."

"She knew she was going to pass on, and she says they wouldn't let you in there with her. They gave you a hard time about being there with her because she was in intensive care. She says if she could have had anything to say about it, she would have raised a ruckus in there. But the thing is, she says that she knows you were there in the heart. She knows you were there."

Through her tears Mary nodded that she understood.

"Wait. Does she have a family? She wasn't married."

"No."

"Oh, now I understand. She wasn't formally married, but she was emotionally. She talks about being involved. She's calling out to whomever she was engaged to."

"Yes."

"Your sons call out to their grandparents; the ones that are surviving."

"Yes. Okay."

"You went through a nightmare. Your daughters says you didn't have a chance to think. Then you went through a nightmare again. And again. You want to know, Is your daughter all right now that she's 'dead'? Where did she go? Is she at peace? Is she with her brothers?

"She says, 'Yes, I'm with my brothers. We're all together. And we *are* at peace.' She says don't be frustrated. Don't think she passed in agony, like she's unhappy. She says that she's all right. Do you take the name Bill, or William?"

"Yes."

"Passed on."

"Yes."

"Your daughter keeps saying, 'Bill is with me. William is here.' "

"Yes."

"That's your other son who's passed on."

"Yes."

"I think there are three [children passed] right now. Okay, Robert's here."

"Yes."

"Bill passes before your daughter, right?"

"Right."

"Bill is there. He welcomes your daughter into the light. He's there for her. He says that they're all together. Do you take the name Christine?"

"Yes. Living."

"Your daughter knows her."

"Yes."

"Your daughter's asking for Chrissy, or Christine. She says, 'Tell Chrissy, or Christine, you've heard from me.' They were good pals as well as sisters."

"Yes."

"She calls her Chrissy."

"Yes."

" 'Tell Chrissy you've heard from me.' It's funny, because I saw a personalized license plate not long ago. It was the name Chrissy. I kept seeing myself looking at that.

"Your daughter Chrissy is probably taking your other daughter's death as badly as you are. 'Tell her I'm all right. I'm around her like a guardian angel.' "

"Okay."

"Do you take the name Mary?"

"Yes."

"Your daughter knows her."

"No."

"Well, I guess she does now."

"Well, I'm Mary, and my mother was Mary. She did not know my mother."

"I guess she does now," explained George. "I heard your daughter call 'Mary.' And she calls a second time. She says, 'Mary is with me.' It would be your mother. She keeps saying, 'Mary is here,' and she says, 'I know her now.' So apparently she's met [Mary] in the hereafter. She knows that's her grandmother."

"Yes."

"You say the rosary for your daughter."

"Yes."

"Your daughter thanks you for it. Not that she's overly religious, but she knows the value of it, and she says, 'Please continue to pray on my behalf.' You've dreamt about her, also."

"Yes."

"She says she's tried to reach out to you to let you know everything is all right. There was a feeling when she came in that she was all worried about you. Now I feel more at peace, more in a state of tranquillity.

"There's a *u* in her name. That's the only vowel."

"Yes."

"[Her name] begins with a *j*. Is *u* the second letter?"

"Yes."

"There's *j, u.* I think [it sounds like] Julie. But it can't be Julie. Is that the same sound?"

"Yes."

"The last letter [of her name] is at the end of the alphabet."

"Yes."

"I don't believe I can't get it. Oh gee, it's—the name—Judy."

"Yes!"

"She's telling me her name [is] in the Bible. The Book of Judith. The nickname of Judith would be Judy. She was baptized Judy. And that's why she's telling me not to formalize the name."

"Yes."

"Her name is Judy Ann."

"Yes."

"Judy says you've had enough in life. And this one [her death] really topped it off. But she says, 'Just know that I'm okay and at peace, and you will see me again someday along with the boys [Bobby and Bill].' She says, 'We're here and you're there. And one day you'll have to come here.' She says, 'I'm back to life,' and she's moved on into the next life. So she says just hang in there with hope, knowing that you'll all be together again someday. Your two boys are going back along with Judy. 'We'll all be together again someday,' she says. She says to go in peace and know she's all right. She sends her love to you. And your sons send their love to you, Robert and Bill. Also your father-in-law and the other relatives.

"Robert and Bill and Judy are calling out to your family and your husband. 'We send our love, and just know we're okay and be at peace now about our passings.'"

As the Harringtons' deceased children made clear in the reading, a family life is a continuing, endless cycle of loss and renewal. In what some would consider an odd set of coincidences, the Harringtons' first grandchild, Sara, was born to their daughter Jean the day Robert's remains were reinterred in Pennsylvania, where the family moved. Five years later Jean's third child, a son, was born on September 26, 1988, which would have been Robert's twenty-fourth birthday.

For family members who have spent time together here on earth, no matter how short that time might be, it is not hard to imagine that their relationships survive death and that, as so many souls have assured George and their loved ones, they will again be reunited. The following case involves a family, which to outside appearances, would hardly seem a family at all. Because the woman who offered this transcript of her reading chose to remain anonymous, we have decided to tell the story through the reading alone.*

"There are two males [passed]. One's older. That's your father. But there's another. One who's younger."
    "Yes."
    "Did you lose a child?"
    "No."
    "Did you ever have a miscarriage?"

---

*At the request of the subject, some biographical details have been altered to protect her identity. Everything else in this story, however, is true.

"No."

"Because I feel like if the cycle of birth had continued it would have been a male—a boy."

"No. I never miscarried."

"You never had a miscarriage?"

"No," the woman insisted.

"I'm going to hold my ground. Did you lose a child?"

"No."

A few minutes later into the reading, after George had accurately discerned the woman's father, he asked again, "You sure you didn't lose a child?"

"No," she repeated.

"Well, you say no. They say . . . well, I'm just going to say what I hear [psychically]. You lost a child. Either through miscarriage or abortion."

The woman sat silently.

"You had an abortion," George said softly.

"Yes," she replied, beginning to cry.

"If the cycle of birth had continued, it would have been a boy."

Now the woman was openly sobbing. She covered her face with her hands.

"Your father says you're carrying the demon of guilt with you about it."

"Yes."

"They say [from the other side] you did not commit murder."

"What happened to the baby?" she asked.

"Well, the soul returns to the other side," George explained. "The cycle of birth was interrupted. The soul is disappointed, of course. But he understands why you did it. You couldn't handle the situation of having a child at the time it happened.

"He—the soul—is understanding. You should have no guilt. You have to let it go! Be at peace. Now remove the guilt and let it go. You felt like you killed him. But you had no choice. So let it go. Let go of the guilt. . . . Your dad says you're not alone. He's with you."

"Okay," she replied, nodding.

"There's another male who steps forward. A male close to you."

"Yes."

"He says he's your husband."

"Yes, my husband."

"He passes very young!"

"Yes, he'd just turned thirty [when he passed]."

"He passed tragically. Both age and circumstances."

"Yes."

"He says he came from a—he uses the expression—'screwed-up family.' He admits he was not an emotionally stable guy."

"That's right."

"But he says he loves you and knows you loved him."

"Yes."

"He passes in tragic circumstances. Your dad met him when he came over, so he wasn't alone."

"Oh, good."

"Boy, you never know. When you first walked in the room, I looked at you. And first I didn't even think you looked old enough to be married. You look very young, actually."

"I guess. I hear people say that all the time. I'm twenty-six."

"But your husband and your father say you've sure been through it all."

"It feels that way."

"Your husband's passing was sudden."

"Yes."

"He passes before you had the abortion."

"Yes."

"He passes not that long ago. Within the past couple of years."

"Yes. It will be two years."

"Because he says he was there already [on the other side] when the soul of the baby returned. And your father was there, too. Your dad met your husband and the baby. So they weren't alone."

"Okay." The woman nodded, but she was crying again.

"Your husband is apologizing to you. He says he wants to settle things. He wanted to get through."

"Yes. I've been dreaming about him in the past few nights."

"He passes suddenly."

"Yes."

"He feels trapped, he says."

"He probably felt that way."

"He knows he was pushy, demanding, and not in his right frame of mind."

"Yes."

"He falls or collapses."

"Yes."

"There were injuries internally."

"Yes."

"Was there bloodshed?"

"Yes."

"There's injury to his head and internally, also. And bloodshed."

"Yes."

"He apologizes to you."

"Yes. I understand."

"A weapon is involved." George paused. "He's more loosened up now to tell me. At the beginning I felt knotted up inside. He was very anxious. He was beating around the bush about the circumstances." George stopped again. "I hear gunshots."

"Yes."

"He shoots himself, he says. I see the Sacred Heart of Jesus appear. It's my symbol for suicide."

"Yes."

"He shoots himself in the head. That's what it feels like."

"Yes."

"Wait. Did he know you were pregnant when he took his own life?"

"I don't know. I don't think so."

"Because he says he didn't know it. But then after he shoots himself, that's when you had an abortion."

"Yes."

"Because he didn't know you were pregnant. It's like he takes his life. And then you find out you're going to have a baby. But then he sees your suffering because of the way he passes on. And that's what drives you to have an abortion. It's like you're overwhelmed. There's nowhere to turn."

"That's right," the young woman answered as she began crying again.

"You're suddenly alone. Your husband apologizes. He says he was too possessive. And he admits he could be hot-tempered. And then he's gone."

"Yes."

"He loves you. But although he can't change what's already happened, he knows he could be very difficult at times."

"Yes."

"Did he ever drink?"

"Yes."

"And then drugs."

"Yes."

"He admits he could be very uptight."

"Yes."

"When he said before he felt trapped, he meant emotionally trapped within himself. He's very low emotionally. Things are going very badly for him. Like he's worried about money. He feels like a failure. That's the straw that breaks the camel's back, so to speak. That snaps him."

"Yes."

"He just gives up."

"Yes. I guess so."

"Your husband talks about a lack of communication with *his* father."

"Yes. They didn't get along at all."

"Your husband says his father was there to meet him, so his father's passed on, also."

"Oh, yes."

"Well, now they say they've settled their differences. They both send their love to you.

"Who's Tara? Do you take that name, like in *Gone With the Wind*?"

"Yes. My daughter. My little girl."

"Because I heard [the song] 'Tara's Theme' from *Gone With the Wind* [psychically]. And then your husband says, 'Tara.' He says, 'Send my love to Tara.' "

"Yes. She's almost four."

"You have just the one daughter."

"Yes."

"Because I see a second child. You haven't remarried."

"No. No."

"Well, Saint Philomena appears over you. It's my symbol of motherhood. I'll leave it with you for the future. I see a second marriage. I'll leave it."

"I'm not planning it, but okay."

"Anyway, your dad and your husband say you're not alone. They're with you. They say you still speak to them like they're here."

"Yes. I do."

"Just know they're there. So talk to them. It's okay. They're there spiritually."

"Okay."

"Who's Mary? Because your father calls out to Mary."

"Yes. My mother."

"He sends his love to her. And he says, 'Stop smoking!' "

"Okay, I'll tell her."

"Do you take the name Pat?"

"Yes. My sister."

"Because your father calls to Pat. At first I didn't know if it was Pat, a male, but then he said, 'Patty.' "

"Yeah. Patty is my older sister."

"Your husband and your father say you have to go on with your life here. Even if you don't feel you're achieving anything, you are."

"It's hard, George!"

"Until it's your time to be reunited. And your husband says you've got a long way to go. He says calm down. You've been through a lot: his passing, the abortion, everything. So sometimes your temper gets to you.''

"Yes.''

"I see ice cubes. He puts ice cubes over you. It's a symbol to cool down. 'Cool your temper.' ''

"Okay.''

"Is there some reason why I'd hear a guitar playing?''

"Yeah.''

"Because that's what I'm hearing [psychically].''

"My husband used to play a guitar. When we first met, he played. He wanted to do it professionally, even. To be a musician.''

"Oh, well, then you know it's definitely him you're hearing from.''

"Yes.''

"He's definitely working his way out of his despair. But he's not suffering. He's frustrated at the mess he left you with. He doesn't want you to be angry with him.''

"He knows I'm not.''

"He calls to a brother.''

"Yes.''

"He was close to him.''

"Yes.''

"He took his passing badly.''

"Oh, yeah.''

"He—your husband—took his life at home.''

"Yes.''

"Someone found him.''

"Yes.''

"He says *you* found him.''

"Yes.''

"He apologizes for that.''

"Do you take the name Anthony? I [psychically] see Saint Anthony. I don't know if it's a symbol or a name.''

"It's him! My husband.''

"Because he says, 'This is Tony. This is Anthony.' He's called Tony for short.''

"Yes.''

For the next several minutes George gave names of friends, cousins, uncles, and aunts. The information was acknowledged as accurate, then George returned to Tony. "He realizes [suicide] wasn't the right thing to do, but he can't turn it back now."

"Yes, I know."

"He apologizes. He genuinely didn't mean for it to turn out this way. He didn't want to do this to himself—or you. He feels like he's responsible for you having the abortion, because if he didn't take his life, you wouldn't have [had an abortion]."

"That's right."

"But he does say again that he wants you to let go of the guilt. The soul understands what happened and why you did it."

"Okay."

"Know that he's not alone in the spiritual sense. He says he has no one to blame for his death but himself. You're not to blame. Never think that."

"Okay."

"There are people on the other side to help him—if you seek out that help. And he has. He says he's closer to you than you can imagine. Boy, once he gets going, he can talk! . . . But now he's going back. He's got work to do. Your dad, the others, they go back, too. Again, the soul [of the aborted baby] understands. Tony is around your daughter like a guardian angel.

"Now they all ask that you continue to pray for them. Your dad says, 'This is Pop going back!' 'This is Tony sending his love. Until we meet again.' And with that, they've gone back."

As this reading shows, to the spirits we continue to be related by love not only after death but perhaps before birth as well. As the soul of the baby whom this woman aborted attests, he is still alive; only his body died. Time and again George has received the same message from children lost to abortion.

Even when people are reasonably certain, from their faith and experience or after a reading, that there is an afterlife, that their loved ones are there, and that they still love us, it's not always easy to grasp what our loved ones' emotional lives are like there. As we have learned, they do continue to grow and progress on the other side. They learn how to deal with themselves and with others, to see what they may have done to make their lives or those of their friends and family better. We know that they are greeted and cared for by relatives and family friends, some known to them here on earth and others, not. Clearly the one binding principle on the other side is love, and it is not hard for most of us to understand those relationships flourishing.

But countless spirits have told George of relationships that are not continuations of those here but brand-new, formed on the other side. Very often these seem to parallel friendships their loved ones here begin after their deaths.

Brent Fitzgerald was just fourteen when he died of complications from a rare intestinal problem that doctors believed they had corrected permanently shortly after his birth. His death came as a terrible shock to his parents, Julie and Gary, and his older sister, Tracy. Although the family lived in New York, he was buried in the family cemetery in Illinois. Ironically, very shortly before Brent's death, Julie had taken him to that cemetery during a family vacation to show him the family graves and had taken a photograph of him there.

Julie said that she "basically hibernated" after her son's death. She and Gary went for private counseling, and then she joined the Compassionate Friends. In the following excerpts from Julie and Gary's reading with George, Brent revealed that he had befriended several children of parents Julie had come to know through the Compassionate Friends.

"Is there a John passed over? Your son knows him," George said.

"I think I know who it is," Julie replied.

"Did he pass before your son? Your son must have met him [on the other side]. He claims he knows John or Johnny. They're friends over there. Did John pass over young also?"

"Yes."

"Do you know his parents?"

"Yes."

"Because he's asking that you tell his parents you've heard from Johnny, if you think they can deal with it. He says he knows your son."

"Okay."

Later George asked, "John's family belongs to the Compassionate Friends?"

"Yes."

"Because he claims that you know his family through them. John says to tell his family you've heard from him."

Toward the end of the reading George asked Julie and Gary, "Do you know a Denis?"

"I'm not sure," Julie answered.

"Well, you belong to the Compassionate Friends," George said. "Maybe it's someone from there. Because he says, 'Denis is over here with me.' Your son says, 'I met Denis.' He said something about knowing the two O'Connor children, Denis and Peggy." George was referring to the children of Mrs. Elaine Stillwell, the Rockville Centre, New York, chapter leader of the group. Her children's story is recounted in *We Are Not Forgotten.*

Since Gary and Julie's reading Brent has come through in other readings George has done for bereaved parents from the same Compassionate Friends group. In each Brent sends his love to his parents and sister, naturally, but he also gives very specific messages containing details known only to Brent and his family.

In one instance Brent came through in a reading for another couple and said, "Give my regards to Danny." The couple relayed the message to Julie and Gary, not knowing that Danny is the name of Tracy's boyfriend. Another time Brent appeared during a reading for Mrs. Stillwell. "Please say hello to my mother," he said through George. "I know she's going through a very hard time." Also in that reading Brent alluded to having a brother. Until that time Mrs. Stillwell did not know that Brent considered his half-brother from Gary's previous marriage his brother. In these and several other detailed examples, Brent and other children on the other side have shown that they have become a community there, just as their bereaved parents have here.

But Brent has also made his presence known to his parents through direct communication, a topic that could fill a book by itself. "Ever since Brent died," Julie said, "he won't let me be pulled down. Sometimes I feel like I'm just being sucked down into a deep hole of depression. But then I'll get a sign that he's there.

"For example, on Brent's first birthday after he died, I was painting the upstairs attic room that was his, and I was really down. I opened a new, unopened can of spackle, and I couldn't believe what I saw! There was a little gummy bear stuck in the spackle. I just started to laugh, because it was his birthday. He was just telling me I'm not supposed to be so sad."

Julie finds these experiences reassuring. "I accept what George does," she said. "I don't think it's unusual or unnatural. I think it's natural. I think when you're more open to it, you can sense it. You can see it and process it. Whereas a lot of people might not even be receptive to it."

Gary's perspective is somewhat different. "About going to George, I was skeptical, but I kept an open mind. My experience with George reinforced my belief in an afterlife; it put things in perspective. I realize that I'll be joining Brent one of these days, so I'm not pining away out of lonesomeness, because I know it can be a heartbeat away, or a long time away. But it's academic, because forever is forever."

9

When I See You in Heaven

===

As in our two earlier books, we end *Our Children Forever* with excerpts from recent conversations between
Joel Martin and George Anderson, covering some of the
questions parents and other survivors of children commonly
ask.

> *I'm paraphrasing Elisabeth Kübler-Ross, the great
> expert on death and dying. From your readings, can
> you ascertain if there is something bereaved parents
> can learn from the death of a child? Something we
> can grow with, something we can use?*

Well, I think most bereaved parents would say that it is
a terrible struggle. I don't want to come across as if I'm
pontificating, because I certainly am not. But can we learn
endurance? Can we learn patience, with ourselves and with
others? Can we learn love? Can we turn that despair and
anxiety into a more positive channel, perhaps to help others
who have lost children? So there are things that we can
learn from the experience, when and if we choose to do so.

On the other hand, I must say that I do see those people
who stay inside their grief for the rest of their lives. They

never again experience joy; their lives seem to end with their child's death. Can I honestly say to them that it doesn't have to be that? I am not a bereaved parent; I really don't know. When I see those people, I think to myself, Can you really blame them? Perhaps this is a question only a bereaved parent could answer.

> *Do those on the other side ever say how they would like to see us handle their passings?*

They say, unanimously, that they wish we would try as best we can to realize that they have just moved on to the next stage of existence. They certainly don't want us to think that they don't understand our pain and grief, because they certainly do. They are often saddened to see how we suffer, and they do tell me of feeling frustrated because there's not very much they can do for us. Yet they do what they can; we're just not always aware of it.

> *Does the funeral service have any meaning to them over on the other side?*

I don't think that they think more of us or think that we love them more because of the kind of funeral or memorial we give them. Many of the young people and children who come through have commented on the tremendous outpouring of love and affection at their wakes and funerals. They will say something like, ''I'm happy for myself, but I'm more happy that my parents and family received that type of support from other people, that they know their child made such an impression on people for the short time [he or she] was here.''

They often remind me, too, that they have experienced death; they are now on the other side and have a much different perspective on it. For them, the death is over. They are moving on. They often say that the hard part is for their parents and other loved ones who are left, as they say, ''living in the aftershadow of death.''

*Even though they have left this existence and are well
and at peace on the other side, where we know friends
and relatives are caring for them, do they still need
us here? And if they do, what can we do for them?*

Even though we seem to be living in other dimensions,
that connection of love still binds us, and will forever. They
know that we need them, and they need us to realize that
they are still alive, that they are here with us, that they care
about us. As they have said to me so many times in readings, they do benefit from prayer, so that is one thing we
can do. But I think we should keep them alive in our hearts,
go on with our lives, and try to be as happy as we possibly
can. For example, after one child has died, to be sure not
to neglect the surviving children because of your grief.
They want us to be happy, they want us to know—and to
take comfort in believing—that we will all be together
again. They never, ever forget us, and I think they like to
know that we will never forget them.

It's pretty clear from those families for whom I've done
several readings over a period of years that the child who
has passed on is very much a part of their lives. David
Licata, the young boy who was killed by a hit-and-run
driver, and whose story opens *We Don't Die*, has come
through indicating that he is well aware of the problems
and developments in his family. He knew, for example, that
his grandfather had since developed cancer, and he reassured his parents through a reading that he would be there
to greet his grandfather when he crossed over. Clearly, they
play a role in our lives still.

Does a baby choose its parents?

It seems that is often the case. And that sounds great if,
say, the child is born into a loving, secure family. But it
makes you wonder what that means for the child who is
born unwanted, impoverished, or into violent or abusive
circumstances. I hesitate to venture into the area, because I
don't want to come off sounding like Shirley MacLaine. I

don't think that we have control over everything that happens. I don't think, for example, that people choose to have a terrible disease just so that they can learn a lesson from that experience. But there may be exceptions.

Some souls have told me that they chose a certain situation, or certain parents, because they wanted to learn a specific lesson to help in their soul progression. One of the problems with this concept is that, first of all, I really do not know the answer. And second, I'm not even so sure that what I do learn from my readings is the whole picture. For example, a parent who beats his child to death, the drug addict whose baby is born addicted—people like that—are not going to go out of their way to come to someone like me. Would those children come through and say that they chose that situation? Would they say that they made a mistake? Would they say that it's out of their control? I just don't know. I may never know.

But there is one area in which you have done many, many readings, and that is the case of children who are aborted. What do these children say to you?

Often the soul that would have entered the body right before birth—which is when they tell me that occurs—will come through. Interestingly, they come through to me especially if I'm doing a reading for someone who needs to hear from that child, particularly if there is a heavy sense of guilt attached to the abortion. The soul will put them at peace by saying, "I might not have liked the idea of you stopping the process, but I understand why you did."

I have had souls come through and say that they will come back again when it is a better time. Or that they left the body because they could see that there was a problem, physically. Personally, I am not pro-abortion, but I believe it is a personal decision. The children do come through and still consider themselves children of the mother who had the abortion. They will say that they understand the reason for the abortion, and they nearly always reassure their parents that they are at peace where they are. They never say that they were murdered.

I know that some people feel guilty even after the reading. But I say to them, be sure to understand why you feel that way. Who is telling you to feel that way? Then think about what the spirit of that child says to you about how he or she wants you to think about this experience. Of course, I can't interject my own personal feelings and opinions into these situations. But I've never had the soul that would have entered the body of an aborted fetus come through and say anything other than that they understood.

> *You say—and we say—time and again that being on the other side doesn't make you all-knowing. In other words, "dead" or "alive," we retain our humanity, with all its shortcomings and flaws. On the other hand, spirits do come through in your readings and they do mention, for example, choosing a particular family, knowing they were going to die, knowing that their time here on earth would be cut short. It's as if we know, but we don't know. What exactly do we know? Are there things about our lives that we can control but perhaps just are not aware of?*

It seems that we always hold the reins, whether we know it consciously or not. We choose which lessons we want our souls, or the essences of ourselves, to learn, to understand in order to grow. Other people around us also learn from our experiences, and vice versa. It's one hand shaking the other, so to speak. We are all participating in the drama.

But to answer another part of your question, sometimes we consciously know more than we would expect to know. We had one case, that of a teenage girl named Mindy Reitmeyer, who predicted her own death. She knew that she was going to die; she spoke to her friends and family about it. She even told everyone what kind of dress she wanted to be buried in. Now, many people would expect that she would die in some predictable, controllable way; for example, by suicide. Instead she died in a freak car accident. How do you explain that? I don't know.

Do children, particularly very young children, have a recollection of being on the other side?

Yes, I think maybe in the early stages. When my nephew's younger brother was born, he was just three. And he said to me, "I was in heaven before I came here, and George [the baby brother] and I made a deal that we would come, that we would be here together. And now, see, he's born!" I asked him what it had been like in heaven, and he replied, "Oh, when I was there, we would move around without having to worry about falling." I don't think this is something he picked up from television. He seemed very sure and not at all self-conscious about it. It wouldn't surprise me if it were true.

When a child dies, no matter what the age, it's very hard for us to understand why they were here for such a short amount of time. This can be said to be as true for the baby who dies shortly after birth as the child who dies at sixty.

I think that from a parent's point of view, any child who doesn't live longer than his parents had passed before his time. One problem is that we here on earth narrow and define things by our conceptions of time and space. As they tell us from the other side, these are artificial concepts; they don't exist there. Also, we tend to think that it is our right to live to be ninety-five years old and to die in our sleep. But, as we also know, that doesn't always happen that way. Perhaps your child learned her lesson or accomplished her mission in the time she was here. You may not think that she was here "long enough," but when it comes to any of our loved ones, no matter what their age, they are never here long enough for us. We are human; we will always want more. But we cannot have what we want all the time. Sometimes we just have to accept that a fifteen-year-old, a five-year-old, a five-day-old child did what they came here to do. Do we know what that was? Do we know why? Perhaps we will later.

From what they have told me, there are many possible explanations for why a soul would choose not to continue here. It's not a case of one size fits all. And I think that it's dangerous to take where one spirit says, "I chose to move on," and automatically think that means that all children who die young make that same choice. Perhaps there were other factors. It's hard to imagine what things are like on the other side, I know. But we always have to remember that we are as unique and complex there as we are here. Everyone's situations, reasons, and acts are different.

As children are growing up, is there any benefit to talking to them about death, whether they're ill or not?

Well, it's a fact of life, isn't it? When I see all the suffering people go through, it's very hard not to think that there's something wrong with how we look at death. In this society we either pretend that it doesn't exist, which makes it hard on survivors, or we make it all spooky and creepy. How many times have people asked me, "But isn't what you do scary?" They think it's like something from a horror movie. So between those two extreme reactions to death, there is really very little that people who are dying or who have a loved one who's passed can use to help them through their grief.

I'm not just saying this because it sounds good, or because virtually every spirit has told me this; it's a medical fact as well. Death itself is not painful. The circumstances that lead up to death may be, yes. But the actual transition we experience as we move from life here to life on the other side is actually a very pleasant experience. Perhaps if we could educate our children in such a way that we could diminish some of death's scarier connotations, we might make things easier for them when they do face death through life.

Finally, the goal of this book has been to help grieving parents. The bereavement expert Dr. Therese Rando writes that we have a special word for someone whose spouse has died—widow or widower—and a special word for someone whose parents have died—orphan. But we don't have a special word for parents who have lost their child. Any thoughts on that?

Maybe we should think of these parents the way their children who have crossed over do. They call them Mom and Dad.

A GLOSSARY OF PSYCHIC SYMBOLS

AIDS—the word appearing over a subject's head indicates either that the spirit passed from the disease or that the subject suffers from it.

an airplane—work-related (the subject or spirit works with airlines or travel) or future travel.

Angel of Death—a passing is imminent.

apples—ripe apples mean the subject is "ripe for a job change." When George sees an apple core, it signifies the core, or the heart, of a matter.

artist's easel—work or study of art.

automobile accident—can mean an automobile accident, any accidental passing, or a passing that was swift and unexpected, like an accident.

bells, ringing—someone on this side or the next is on the alert, usually waiting for someone to pass over.

black—when the subject appears to George to be surrounded by black, it means that someone close to him or her will pass on in the near future.

black spots—around an individual or around a particular area of the body usually indicate cancer, either in the past, present, or future.

blood—violence, a violent incident or death.

blood, seen bursting—a stroke or other vascular problem, such as an aneurysm.

blood cells—a disease related to the blood cells, such as leukemia or AIDS.

books, a hand writing—work, study, or strong interest related to writing; work around books, as in a library.

bread—abundance.

broken heart—romance gone bad, a broken love affair.

car wheel—auto accident or car trouble, either in the recent past or the foreseeable future.

cards—a large deck of playing cards indicates that the spirit of the reading had or the subject will be making a big deal in business.

classroom or school—the subject may be a student or is or will be learning something that will enhance their career.

clear water—usually in a glass or in a stream, a symbol of "clear going" in the future. A positive sign.

computers, electrical wiring, machinery—references to the careers of the subject or the spirit.

contracts—legal papers are being signed, either in the present or the future.

currency, piles of money—money coming to someone through an inheritance, job, or gift. May also mean that the subject or spirit works with or around money, as in a bank.

dog, or dog barking—indicates that the spirit was met and greeted on the other side by a deceased pet dog.

drink, on the rocks—indicates that the subject should exert caution in relationship ahead.

Empire State Building—New York City.

Felix the Cat—this cartoon character's appearance indicates that the subject will be hearing good news ahead.

a finger placed to closed lips—advises a subject to keep quiet about a situation.

glass of milk—relaxation is needed.

green fields—money or abundance.

gun—psychically seen weapons almost always indicate the means by which the communicating spirit was killed. Sometimes George will see a double-barreled gun, indicating that the person in question has been hit twice by tragedy.

hands tied—a spirit's way of communicating "There's nothing you can do about it."

hearts and roses—a love affair.

Sherlock Holmes—the subject or the spirit was involved with some kind of police or detective work, either in uniform or undercover.

horn of plenty—abundance ahead.

ice cubes—advises subject to "keep cool."

knife—see *gun*, above.

lemon—a large lemon on wheels suggests car trouble for the subject.

letters of the alphabet—a specific letter appearing psychically over the subject's head is a clue to a key word, such as the first letter of the spirit's name.

lightning bolt—something shocking and unexpected.

Lourdes water—sign of healing, related to the health condition of subject.

medals—symbolize "awards" or progress on the other side.

mercy killing—indicates the subject or spirit was involved in a mercy killing, often spelled out.

musical instruments—might indicate that the subject or spirit was a musician, disc jockey, songwriter, music teacher, or has a strong interest in music.

musical notes—may indicate someone being "in harmony." See also *musical instruments.*

New York Stock Exchange—someone works at or with the exchange, or is or will be involved with investments.

nose—a large nose means that someone else is butting into the subject's marriage with future marital upset as the result.

palm trees—travel or a move to a southerly, tropical location.

pentagram—a five-sided star indicates involvement with the satanic.

piano—someone plays either the piano or some other percussion instrument.

priests, nuns, other clergy—indicates that the subject or the spirit was or knew others in religious service.

question mark—indicates some mystery or question around a situation.

rainbow—optimism, a new beginning ahead.

REDRUM—the word *murder* spelled backward indicates that someone has been murdered.

red light—George takes this as a psychic symbol to stop psychic reading, that he is in danger of overexerting himself. This can also have a literal meaning, often indicating that an ignored red light or stop sign played a role in an auto accident.

rosary beads—generally means that the spirit, regardless of religion, is asking for prayers. When the subject or spirit is Catholic, it usually refers to the rosary of someone in particular, often identifiable, because George will be shown their color.

roses—white roses are a sign of congratulations or celebration from the other side. The roses may be offered by the spirit around the time of a celebration, anniversary, or birthday. Other times they are just presented as gestures of love or thanks.

Sacred Heart of Jesus—a symbol of Jesus' suffering on the cross, often indicates a spirit died by his own hand.

scales of justice—a legal situation in the subject's or the spirit's life.

Saint Anthony—if dressed in black, a symbol of death, loss, or tragedy.

Saint Joseph—the patron saint of fathers, carpenters, and death. His appearance symbolizes a peaceful death, one that occurs during sleep or unconsciousness.

Saint Peregrine Lazosi—patron saint of cancer victims. His appearance indicates that someone has or will die of cancer.

Saint Vincent de Paul—patron saint of charitable societies, his presence indicates that a person was giving while here on earth.

shamrocks—symbolize that the person in question is of Irish descent.

sinking ship—a situation "rocked your boat."

skull and crossbones—negativity, friction.

Smith Brothers—the famous trademark pair found on boxes of cough drops indicates a subject's or spirit's surname is Smith.

spider's web—being trapped.

spring cleaning—a spirit's way of saying, "Your life needs a complete overhaul."

star—creativity.

Star of David—the spirit or subject was of the Jewish faith.

stripes on shoulder—promotion, as in military service.

suitcases—future travel.

swastika—sometimes seen with the screaming face of Adolf Hitler, coils of barbed wire, concentration camp victims, and the Star of David superimposed over the image. This symbolizes that the spirit or subject were victims of the Nazis.

Switzerland—when George sees a map of this country, it means that the subject is being advised to stay neutral in a conflict.

towels, in knots—a short temper.

triangle—a love triangle, infidelity, adultery.

trumpets sounding—happy news.

turkey—psychic clue that an event occurred around Thanksgiving time.

uniforms—these symbols give clues as to the subject's or the spirit's occupation, and are distinguished by color. White for health and medical workers, blue for police, firemen, military, and so on.

washing machine—health difficulty related to kidney or adrenal malfunction.

wedding ring—a broken wedding ring indicates a marital breakup or discord in a romantic relationship.

windmill—someone has "been through the mill."

wolf—a sign of evil.

X—a large *X* shown over a scene, symbol, or word that George sees psychically means that it is incorrect, not what it seems to be, or that the subject is being advised not to take some action represented by that symbol. For example, an *X* over a vision of a wedding might mean that the spirit is suggesting his loved one reconsider an impending marriage.

yellow rings, murky—when these appear around a specific part of the human anatomy, they indicate illness or some malady affecting that area, in the future.

BIBLIOGRAPHY

We especially thank Elaine and Joe Stillwell for their help in preparing the Bereavement bibliography.

GENERAL

Bluebond-Langner, Myra. *The Private Worlds of Dying Children.* Princeton, N.J.: Princeton University Press, 1978.

Burns, Stanley B., M.D. *Sleeping Beauty: Memorial Photography in America.* Altadena, Calif.: Twelvetrees Press, 1990.

Cayce, Hugh Lynn, and Edgar Cayce. *God's Other Door and the Continuity of Life.* Virginia Beach, Va.: A.R.E. Press, 1958.

Chinmoy, Sri. *Death and Reincarnation.* Jamaica, N.Y.: Agni Press, 1974.

deMause, Lloyd, ed. *The History of Childhood: The Untold Story of Child Abuse.* New York: Peter Bedrick Books, 1988.

Ebon, Martin, ed. *Communicating with the Dead.* New York: New American Library, 1968.

———. *The Evidence for Life after Death.* New York: Signet/ New American Library, 1977.

Eliot, Alexander. *Abraham Lincoln: An Illustrated Biography.* London: Bison Books, 1985.

Ford, Arthur. *Unknown but Known.* New York: Harper &

Row, 1968.

Fuller, John G. *The Ghost of 29 Megacycles.* New York: Signet/New American Library, 1981.

Garrett, E. J. *Many Voices.* New York: G. P. Putnam's Sons, 1968.

Haberstein, Robert W., and William Lamers. *Funeral Customs the World Over.* Milwaukee: Bulfin Printers, Inc., the National Funeral Directors Association of the United States, 1960.

Hyde, Margaret Oldroyd, and Elizabeth Held Forsyth. *Suicide.* New York: Franklin Watts, 1991.

Jackson, Charles O., ed. *Passing: The Vision of Death in America.* Westport, Conn.: Greenwood Press, 1977.

Jacobson, Nils O., M.D. *Life without Death?* New York: Dell, 1973.

Kett, Joseph F. *Rites of Passage: Adolescence in America, 1790 to the Present.* New York: Basic Books, 1977.

Leavitt, Judith Walzer. *Brought to Bed: Childbearing in America, 1750 to 1950.* New York: Oxford University Press, 1986.

LeShan, Lawrence. *The Medium, the Mystic, and the Physicist.* New York: Viking, 1966.

McCaffery, John. *Tales of Padre Pio.* Garden City, N.Y.: Image Books, 1981.

McDannell, Colleen, and Bernhard Lang. *Heaven: A History.* New Haven and London: Yale University Press, 1988.

Martin, Joel, and Patricia Romanowski. *We Don't Die: George Anderson's Conversations with the Other Side.* New York: Putnam, 1988; Berkley, 1989.

——. *We Are Not Forgotten: George Anderson's Messages of Hope from the Other Side.* New York: Putnam, 1991; Berkley, 1992.

Meek, George W. *After We Die, What Then?* Franklin, N.C.: Metascience Corporation Publications Division, 1980.

Mitchell, Edgar, ed. *Psychic Exploration.* New York: G. P. Putnam's Sons, 1974.

Mohr, Sister Marie Helene. *Saint Philomena: Powerful with God.* Rockford, Ill.: Tan Books and Publishers, 1953.

Montgomery, Ruth. *Here and Hereafter.* New York: Coward-McCann, 1968.

——. *A Search for Truth.* New York: William Morrow, 1966.

——. *A World Beyond.* New York: Ballantine Books, 1972.

——. *The World Before.* New York: Coward, McCann, and Geoghegan, Inc., 1976.

Moody, Raymond A., Jr., M.D. *Life after Life.* Atlanta: Mockingbird Books, 1975.

——. *Reflections on Life after Life.* Atlanta: Mockingbird Books, 1977.

——. *The Light Beyond.* New York: Bantam Books, 1988.

——. *Coming Back.* New York: Bantam Books, 1990.

Morse, Melvin, M.D. *Closer to the Light.* New York: Villard Books, 1990.

——. *Transformed by the Light.* New York: Villard Books, 1992.

Neely, Mark E., Jr. *The Abraham Lincoln Encyclopedia.* New York: McGraw-Hill, 1982.

Osis, Karlis, Ph.D., and Erlendur Haraldsson, Ph.D. *At the Hour of Death.* New York: Avon Books, 1977.

Perry, Michael. *Psychic Studies: A Christian's View.* Wellingborough, Great Britain: The Aquarian Press, 1984.

Puckle, Bertram S. *Funeral Customs: Their Origin and Development.* London: T. Werner Laurie, Ltd., 1926.

Ring, Kenneth. *Life After Death: A Scientific Investigation of the Near-Death Experience.* New York: Coward, McCann & Geoghegan, 1980.

——. *Heading Toward Omega: In Search of the Meaning of the Near-Death Experience.* New York: William Morrow & Company, 1984.

Sanders, Charles W. *The School Reader: Third Book.* New York: Mark H. Newman & Co., 1846.

Sherman, Harold. *You Live after Death.* Greenwich, Conn.: Fawcett Gold Medal Books, 1972.

——. *The Dead Are Alive.* New York: Ballantine Books, 1981.

Spraggett, Allen. *The Case for Immortality.* New York: New American Library, 1974.

Spraggett, Allen, with William Rauscher. *Arthur Ford: The Man Who Talked with the Dead.* New York: New American Library, 1973.

Stearn, Jess. *Edgar Cayce—The Sleeping Prophet.* New York: Doubleday & Co., Inc., 1967.

Sugrue, Thomas. *There Is a River: The Story of Edgar Cayce.* New York: Holt, Rinehart and Winston, 1942.

Taylor, Ruth Mattson. *Witness from Beyond.* New York: Hawthorn, 1975.

Thomas, Benjamin. *Abraham Lincoln.* New York: Alfred A. Knopf, 1952.

Turner, Justin G., and Linda Levitt Turner. *Mary Todd Lincoln: Her Life and Letters.* New York: Alfred A. Knopf, 1972.

Wertz, Richard C., and Dorothy C. Wertz. *Lying-In: A History of Childbirth in America.* Expanded edition. New Haven and London: Yale University Press, 1989.

White, John. *A Practical Guide to Death and Dying.* Wheaton, Ill.: Quest Books, 1988.

Wilkerson, Ralph. *Beyond and Back: Those Who Died and Lived to Tell It.* Anaheim, Calif.: Melodyland Productions, 1977.

In addition, George Anderson and Joel Martin are the subjects of a chapter in Sharon Jarvis's *True Tales of the Unknown* (New York: Bantam Books, 1985) and *True Tales of the Unknown: The Uninvited* (New York: Bantam Books, 1989).

BEREAVEMENT

Bolton, Iris, and C. Mitchell. *My Son, My Son.* Atlanta: Bolton Press, 1983.

Borg, Susan, and Judith Lasker. *When Pregnancy Fails: Families Coping with Miscarriage, Ectopic Pregnancy, Stillbirth, and Infant Death.* New York: Bantam, 1989.

Bramblett, John. *When Goodbye Is Forever: Learning to Live Again after the Loss of a Child.* New York: Ballantine Books, 1991.

Cerza Kolf, June. *When Will I Stop Hurting: Dealing with a Recent Death.* Grand Rapids, Mich.: Baker Book House, 1987.

DeFrain, John, Linda Ernst, Deanne Jakub, and Jacque Taylor. *Sudden Infant Death: Enduring the Loss.* Lexington, Mass.: Lexington Books, 1991.

Friedman, Rochelle, and Bonnie Gradstein. *Surviving Pregnancy Loss. A Complete Sourcebook for Women and Their Families.* New York: Little, Brown, 1992.

Gunther, John. *Death Be Not Proud.* New York: Harper &

Row, 1949.

Knapp, Ronald J. *Beyond Endurance: When a Child Dies.* New York: Schocken Books, 1986.

Kübler-Ross, Elisabeth. *On Death and Dying.* New York: Macmillan, 1970.

——. *Questions and Answers on Death and Dying.* New York: Macmillan, 1974.

——. *Living with Death and Dying.* New York: Macmillan, 1982.

——. *On Children and Death.* New York: Macmillan, 1983.

——. ed. *Death: The Final Stage of Growth.* New York: Touchstone, 1986.

——. *Working It Through.* New York: Macmillan, 1987.

Kübler-Ross, Elisabeth, and Mal Warshaw. *To Live Until We Say Goodbye.* Englewood Cliffs, New Jersey: Prentice-Hall, 1978.

——. *AIDS: The Ultimate Challenge.* New York: Macmillan, 1987.

LeShan, Eda. *Learning to Say Goodbye (When a Parent Dies).* New York: Avon Books, 1976.

Limbo, Rana K., and Sara Rich Wheeler. *When a Baby Dies: A Handbook for Healing and Helping.* La Crosse, Wis.: Resolve Through Sharing, 1986.

Lukas, Christopher, and Henry M. Seiden. *Silent Grief: Living in the Wake of Suicide.* New York: Bantam Books, 1987.

Lukeman, Brenda. *Embarkations: A Guide to Dealing with Death and Parting.* Englewood Cliffs, N.J.: Prentice-Hall, 1982.

Panuthos, Claudia, and Catherine Romero. *Ended Beginnings: Healing Childbearing Losses.* New York: Warner Books, 1984.

Parrish-Harra, Carol. *The New Age Handbook on Death and Dying.* Santa Monica, Calif.: IBS Press, 1989.

Pizer, Hank, and Christine Palinski. *Coping with Miscarriage.* New York: NAL, 1986.

Quackenbush, Jamie, and Denise Graveline. *When Your Pet Dies.* New York: Pocket Books, 1988.

Rando, Therese A., Ph.D. *Parental Loss of a Child.* Champaign, Ill.: Research Press, 1986.

——. *Grieving: How to Go On Living When Someone You Love Dies.* Lexington, Mass.: Lexington Books, D. C. Heath

& Co., 1988.

Sanford, Doris. *It Must Hurt A Lot: A Child's Book About Death.* Portland, Ore.: Multnomah Press (date unavailable).

Sarnoff Schiff, Harriet. *The Bereaved Parent.* New York: Crown Publishers, 1977.

Schiff, Harriet. *The Bereaved Parent.* New York: Penguin, 1978.

Schoeneck, Therese S. *Hope for the Bereaved: Understanding, Coping, and Growing Through Grief.* Syracuse, N.Y.: Hope for Bereaved (date unavailable).

Scrivani, Mark. *Love Mark.* Syracuse, N.Y.: Hope for Bereaved (date unavailable).

Tatelbaum, Judy. *The Courage to Grieve.* New York: Harper & Row, 1980.

Tittensor, John. *Year One: A Lesson of Hope from Personal Tragedy.* New York: Penguin, 1984.

Worden, J. William. *Grief Counseling and Grief Therapy.* New York: Springer Publishing Co., 1991.

ABOUT THE AUTHORS

Joel Martin has been active in radio and television since the 1960s, as a producer, writer, talk-show host, and newscaster. For eight years he and George Anderson cohosted the top-rated *Psychic Channels* cable television series. A recognized authority on the paranormal, Martin is also an educator. Martin is the author, with Patricia Romanowski, of *We Don't Die: George Anderson's Conversations with the Other Side* (1988) and *We Are Not Forgotten: George Anderson's Messages of Hope from the Other Side* (1991).

In addition to the three books she coauthored with Joel Martin, **Patricia Romanowski** has cowritten eight other works of nonfiction, including three national bestsellers, among them *La Toya: Growing Up in the Jackson Family* (with La Toya Jackson) and *Dreamgirl: My Life as a Supreme* (with Mary Wilson). Her most recent projects include cowriting Annette Funicello's autobiography, *A Dream Is a Wish Your Heart Makes*, and coediting the first revised edition of *The Rolling Stone Encyclopedia of Rock & Roll*, which she originally coedited with Jon Pareles. She has edited dozens of books on music, popular culture, and contemporary issues and contributed to *The New York Times Book Review*.